Fiscal Democracy in America

"This is an excellent scholarly work on our deteriorating federal financial position and the need for a fiscal responsibility Constitutional amendment. Only a Constitutional amendment can force current and future Congresses to restore and sustain fiscal sanity. As the book notes, the federal government does not really have a budget since 74% of spending is mandatory and on auto-pilot."

—David M. Walker, *former U.S. Comptroller General*

"Kurt Couchman's book is an authoritative analysis of fiscal rules and budget processes in the U.S. Couchman brings a unique perspective to these issues as an advisor to several members of Congress. Many of the balanced budget rules introduced in Congress were deeply flawed, and he provides a careful analysis of these failed efforts. Much of the book is devoted to a principles-based fiscal rule, which is a refinement of the fiscal rules he helped several congressional champions develop. The proposed amendment incorporates provisions that have proven to be effective in other countries, such as the Swiss debt brake. This book will be a must read for legislators, policymakers, and citizens interested in reforming our fiscal rules and budget processes."

—Barry W. Poulson, *Emeritus Professor of Economics, University of Colorado*

"*Fiscal Democracy in America* is a timely and compelling blueprint for achieving the long-sought goal of a U.S. balanced budget amendment (BBA). Drawing from relevant experience in budget policy and legislative strategy, Couchman offers a practical approach to countering the tendency for democracies to accumulate deficits with robust institutional guardrails. This book not only explains why a BBA is necessary but also how to craft one that works. Essential reading for anyone who is serious about advancing a constitutional balanced budget amendment to secure America's fiscal future."

—Romina Boccia, *Director of Budget and Entitlement Policy, Cato Institute*

Kurt Couchman

Fiscal Democracy in America

How a Balanced Budget Amendment Can Restore Sound Governance

palgrave
macmillan

Kurt Couchman
Americans for Prosperity
Arlington, VA, USA

ISBN 978-3-031-91937-4 ISBN 978-3-031-91938-1 (eBook)
https://doi.org/10.1007/978-3-031-91938-1

This Palgrave Macmillan imprint is published by the registered company Springer Nature Switzerland AG
The registered company address is: Gewerbestrasse 11, 6330 Cham, Switzerland

To my parents Kevin and Nancy, who taught us the value of inspiration
and the need for perspiration to do something useful with it.
To my wife Elizabeth, for blessing me with so much love, support, wisdom,
and patience and for always believing in me.
And to our children, may they enjoy the bright future for which we strive.

Preface

These do not feel like America's best days.

Our society is still exceptionally innovative and productive. We enjoy freedom and prosperity that our ancestors could not have imagined. Equality under the law has advanced in leaps and bounds.

Yet something seems off. The American political system seems more focused on perpetuating conflict than seeking solutions to major problems.

While we squabble, the foundations of U.S. prosperity and self-governance erode: sustainable federal finances, the rule of law, and Congress as the primary maker of federal public policy. The integrity of the U.S. dollar faces external challenges from competing power centers abroad and from self-harm due to exploding debt burdens and other factors.

Vague laws have empowered the president and other executive branch officials to make decisions that properly belong to Congress. The law is no longer settled: it is whatever the executive branch can plausibly get away with claiming it means.

Fortunately, Congress has started the long process of reclaiming its proper powers with an assist from the Supreme Court. As a former congressional staffer with a constitutionalist outlook, I am deeply committed to re-empowering the people's representatives to do their job: deciding what the federal government will do, how, to what extent, and in the public interest.

The executive branch and legislative support agencies produce high-quality information and other resources, but they are not the focus here. No doubt they have room to improve, but getting our national legislature to use good information to make good decisions is the priority.

I have spent much of my two decades in the nation's capital city trying to figure out what is wrong with this place and how to get it working better. I have helped develop ideas into legislation and worked with diverse partners to refine them. Some have been adopted. Others are moving in that direction. Some got dropped.

The tough thing is that people often want "one cool trick." A silver bullet to slay the beasts of dysfunction and acrimony. That does not exist. There are literally dozens of institutional problems, most with one or more possible solutions, or at least ways to soften them.

Even *just* fixing the federal budget system has many pieces. Collectively, they would provide better information, capacity, and incentives for Congress to make thousands of substantive policy decisions each year.

One book cannot go through everything, and this one does not try to. It focuses on the best approach for a balanced budget amendment to the U.S. Constitution and a handful of the most important statutory complements. It is, by design, far from exhaustive, but it should be enough to highlight the interplay between policy, politics, and process in upgrading a complicated institutional matrix.

Ultimately, each proposal is meant to attract broad, bipartisan support by meeting people where they are. Whether I agree with them or not, I believe the vast majority of policymakers want to do the right thing as they see it. I have worked closely with Republicans, Democrats, independents, and others. Sometimes, I have persuaded others, and sometimes, they have persuaded me. That is how it should be.

But minds don't always need to be changed. Some coalitions have a common goal but for very different reasons. Others form by trading away what is less valuable to secure what is more valuable. That is not a compromise on principles, it is win-win negotiating.

Congress needs more space for deliberation and dealmaking. Today's deals too often add to the debt, undermine prosperity, weaken the rule of law, and make the future less bright, however. Further increases in the debt burden are becoming ever-more untenable, and a time of dramatic change is coming.

New institutions must simultaneously control the federal debt burden while helping members of Congress succeed as legislators who can get results. Having had the good fortune to take up this challenge, I see many reasons for hope and optimism about the future of America.

With better tools, Congress can deliver better outcomes while being a better place to serve. In doing so, our elected representatives can fix problems and ensure that America's best days are ahead of us.

Arlington, VA, USA Kurt Couchman

Acknowledgements Barry Poulson and John Merrifield initially encouraged me to embark on this project. After corresponding about their book *Can the Debt Growth Be Stopped?* they invited me in 2018 to contribute an essay on designing budget targets to an edited volume, *A Fiscal Cliff: New Perspectives on the Federal Debt Crisis*. On their recommendation, my essay "Effective Fiscal Rules Build on Consensus" teased the possibility of expanding that discussion to book length.

Romina Boccia, Barry Poulson, Robert Ordway, and Jeanne Couchman reviewed the manuscript and made many helpful comments and suggestions, as have several anonymous reviewers. Robert Ordway, Justin Amash, Will Adams, Dave Brat, Erin Siefring, Jodey Arrington, Mike Braun, Nathaniel Moran, Blake Moore, Adam Shifriss, David Barnes, and Will Burger have been among the most exceptional partners for developing and advancing the proposals highlighted here.

For guiding a first-time book author through the process, Christian Winting at Springer Nature/Palgrave Macmillan has been tremendous with initial conversations, selecting reviewers, advising on revisions, and otherwise taking this book to the next level. I am also indebted to Jill Balzano and Renisha Vencheslaus for keeping the project on track and adding professional shine.

Finally, my wife Elizabeth is my constant source of love, support, and so much more. From "tell me something fabulous" years ago, she has always pushed me to reach further.

Competing Interests The author has no conflicts of interest to declare that are relevant to the content of this book. The content is generally consistent with his employment at Americans for Prosperity, but the book is a personal project for which the author bears sole responsibility.

Contents

About the Author

Kurt Couchman is a senior fellow in fiscal policy at Americans for Prosperity. He develops, supports, and advises members of Congress and state legislators on innovative solutions to federal and state budgeting and governance challenges.

He previously served in government affairs roles at the Committee for a Responsible Federal Budget, Defense Priorities, the Cato Institute, Sunoco, Inc., and Air Products and Chemicals, Inc., and in the U.S. House of Representatives offices of Gil Gutknecht, Justin Amash, and Dave Brat.

Kurt is the author of "Effective Fiscal Rules Build on Consensus" in *A Fiscal Cliff: New Perspectives on the U.S. Federal Debt Crisis* (Cato, 2020), "Organizing Congress for Budget Reforms" in *Public Debt Sustainability: International Perspectives* (Lexington, 2022), and numerous white papers, blog posts, and essays, including the award-winning "Congress can rehabilitate the federal government with a comprehensive budget" for the America First Policy Institute's 2024 budget process reform contest.

He regularly comments on public policy topics through radio, podcast, and television appearances. His writing has appeared on *CNN.com*, *Fox News*, the *Wall Street Journal*, the *Ripon Forum*, *Tax Notes*, *Washington Examiner*, *Real Clear Policy*, *The Hill*, *The Federalist*, and numerous other publications.

Kurt has a master's degree in economics from George Mason University and a bachelor's degree in political science from Indiana University of Pennsylvania/Cook Honors College. He, his family, and their furry friends live in northern Virginia.

Abbreviations

ADA	Anti-deficiency Act
BBA	Balanced Budget Amendment to the U.S. Constitution
BCA	Budget Control Act of 2011
BCBBA	Business Cycle Balanced Budget Amendment
BEA	Budget Enforcement Act of 1990
CBA	Congressional Budget Act of 1974
CBO	U.S. Congressional Budget Office
CoS	Convention of States
CY	Calendar Year
FY	Fiscal Year
GAO	Government Accountability Office
H.J.Res.	House Joint Resolution
ICA	Impoundment Control Act of 1974
IMF	International Monetary Fund
JCT	U.S. Joint Committee on Taxation
OECD	Organisation for Economic Cooperation and Development
OMB	Office of Management and Budget in the Executive Office of the President
PBBA	Principles-based Balanced Budget Amendment
PGSA	Prevent Government Shutdowns Act
RBTA	Responsible Budget Targets Act
S.J.Res.	Senate Joint Resolution
SUBMIT IT Act	Send Us Budget Materials and International Tactics In Time Act
TRUST Act	Time to Rescue United States Trusts Act

List of Figures

List of Tables

CHAPTER 1

Introduction: The Growing Federal Debt Burden Reflects a Broken System

The federal government's budget dysfunction costs American citizens dearly. The costs will keep growing until Congress and presidents get their act together.

Budgeting is the hub of sound governing. Everything else revolves around it. Done well, a budget is the primary vessel for policymakers' choices about which activities are worth enacting, to what degree, compared to alternative uses, and within constitutional boundaries.

Effective budgeting also recognizes that means of financing—taxes, borrowing, and inflation—impose burdens on society beyond the revenue collected. Those budget tradeoffs, in turn, should inform the design of programs in legislation separate from budgeting to make best use of available resources.

A representative government should empower all legislators to participate in a healthy budget process. It is central to the U.S. system of policymaking. The Constitution clearly assigns legislative powers to Congress, including the powers to raise revenue and make appropriations.

Our representatives in Congress are our trusted custodians to promote the common good, wisely stewarding taxpayer resources to protect life, liberty, and the pursuit of happiness. Effective executive and judicial branches, including their checks and balances on each other and the legislature, make the overall system work. Yet we will focus on Congress here. It should be the strongest branch, but it is the weakest.

K. Couchman, *Fiscal Democracy in America*,
https://doi.org/10.1007/978-3-031-91938-1_1

Congressional budgeting is a mess, and our democracy suffers accordingly. Most members of Congress have little opportunity to see if colleagues agree with their ideas for advancing our interests even in the limited parts of the budget that Congress manages in any particular year.

Every dollar wasted is a dollar that cannot be spent on something more valuable. Some activities may be actively harmful, although legislators disagree on what areas those might be. Broken budgeting is chronically wasteful: continuing to allow money, personnel, and materials to flow into far-from-best uses means we miss out on some combination of better services and lower costs.

The breakdown in fiscal democracy has gone on for so long that chronic problems are becoming acute.

Americans have experienced unusually high inflation since 2021. It happened because Congress and presidents of both parties ran up the debt, especially during the COVID-19 pandemic. This forced the Federal Reserve—the Fed—to buy large quantities of federal debt, which monetized the debt and grew the money supply far faster than the real output of goods and services could grow. That gap between the money supply and output drove inflation, and a rapid boost in federal debt drove the money supply.

To combat inflation, the Federal Reserve's only practical option was to increase interest rates. Higher rates have made borrowing more expensive for governments and the private sector. The federal debt binge kept the Fed from reducing the money supply by selling off Treasuries. In a saturated market, who would buy them?

Federal debt is now high enough to impose debt drag on the U.S. economy. The debt slows U.S. economic growth, opportunity, innovation, and prosperity above about 80 percent of the economy. It is currently about 100 percent of GDP and growing. Economic growth slows more as debt grows higher because it diverts funds from investments and other current needs merely to service the past's accumulated borrowing. Uncertainty on how policymakers will ultimately resolve imbalances undermines investment too.

In addition to what we have lost from Congress misallocating resources, the debt burden has brought inflation, higher interest rates, and creeping stagnation that are putting the American Dream further out of reach.

Yet excessive government borrowing could do even more harm. At some point—and no one knows what might trigger it or when—buyers of federal debt might not bid for enough Treasury securities at prevailing interest rates. This could set of a negative spiral of ever-higher interest rates, rampant inflation, a debt crisis, and even default on federal debt, the supposedly risk-free foundation of global financial markets. The economic consequences would be dire: a nasty recession, financial sector turmoil possibly including a breakdown in the payment system, and big, sudden tax increases. Military crises from an American pullback of military power from much of the world and even threats to our constitutional order would be possible.

That fate is not guaranteed. We can still avoid the turmoil and damage. Budget expert and president of the Economic Policy Innovation Center Paul Winfree thinks we have about a decade until we pass the "event horizon" and debt crisis becomes inevitable.[1] The team behind the Debt Default Clock, which tracks factors that indicate an erosion of the federal government's soundness, expects "fiscal crisis and insolvency at some point in 2027 and ultimately default a short time later."[2]

That is why controlling the debt is back on the federal policy agenda. Annual federal government interest spending has quadrupled over the last decade. After a brief post-pandemic drop, deficits (annual borrowing) are rising with no end in sight. The federal debt burden approaches the highest level ever, threatening stagflation and a possibly catastrophic fiscal crisis.

Unfortunately, the congressional budget process is broken. Each budget cycle begins late, finishes late, and accomplishes little in the meantime. Congress is consumed with brinksmanship over routine government funding and raising the debt limit. Congress lacks the guidance of budget targets to support fiscal responsibility, and what little automatic enforcement exists does not work. Waste, fraud, and abuse are abundant, and members of Congress who point any of this out are often considered troublesome.

As a result, Congress is increasingly hungry for solutions. The coming opportunity to put the budget back on track will be greater than at any time in recent decades.

A Balanced Budget Amendment to the Constitution: A Solution and a Catalyst

America needs a well-written balanced budget provision in the United States Constitution. An adopted balanced budget amendment (BBA) would catalyze Congress to overhaul the federal budgeting laws to make reaching and staying in balance possible. Otherwise, the prospects seem dim for Congress to regain control over the budget.

A well-crafted BBA with solid implementing legislation is the best approach to fiscal rules. Regular people understand the wisdom of balanced budgets. It feels intuitive and right. Spend no more than you have. Both sides of the ledger should match.

The idea of a constitutional requirement for the federal budget to balance enjoys widespread support from the American people. A July 2023 poll found that 80 percent of voters support "a constitutional amendment that would require a balanced budget within 10 years." Support by party affiliation was 83 percent of Republicans, 79 percent of Democrats, and 76 percent of independents.[3]

True, economists tend to focus on the debt-to-GDP ratio to measure the burden of government debt, and some budget policy experts recommend related targets to Congress. But that approach requires too much explanation. Debt-to-GDP targets seem arbitrary, which could give policymakers more political wiggle room than is consistent with responsible budgeting.

Some say a balanced budget rule would be too blunt, but they are thinking of annual balance, which is indeed a bad idea. Besides, the budget balance in any given year matters much less than medium- and long-term trends in revenue and spending. A viable and thoughtful approach to balancing the budget requires some engineering to convert the popular balance principle into constitutional language and statutory law.

To be effective, a balance goal must be in the Constitution. Requiring balance through statute is unlikely to bind policymakers in the long run. Congress can change laws at any time, and it often does.

Congress routinely ignores toothless laws. Most members of Congress would be surprised to learn that an existing provision of law states that "Congress reaffirms its commitment that budget outlays of the United States Government for a fiscal year may be not more than the receipts of the Government for that year."[4]

Constitutional provisions, however, command great authority in our political conversations. We may have different ideas about what exactly they mean or how clear they are, but a provision in our foundational legal document enormously elevates the principle it propounds. Members of Congress cannot change constitutional provisions on their own and feel an obligation to respect them, if imperfectly.

Why a BBA Would Work

The U.S. federal government's fiscal future is troubled, but why do we need a balanced budget amendment in particular? After all, BBA skeptics point out that Congress could balance the budget at any time but chooses not to. In fact, Congress and multiple presidents reduced deficits without a BBA, leading to surpluses from 1998 through 2001.

A confluence of happy accidents (see Chapter 4) brought the Clinton-Gingrich balanced budgets; however, they are unlikely to be repeated. The biggest structural change has been that the large Baby Boomer generation has shifted from prime working age during those surplus years to retirement today, which means ever-more spending from pension and health programs. It is wonderful that people can live longer, healthier lives, yet associated imbalances in old-age programs represent much of the political and policy challenge for fiscal sustainability.[5]

In addition, Gene Steuerle's *Dead Men Ruling: How to Restore Fiscal Freedom and Rescue Our Future* explains that Congress has locked in deficit growth with automatic adjustments to spending and revenue policies.[6] Those adjustments and other factors have shifted fiscal policymaking from abundance to scarcity in recent decades. Congress needs tools that expand political cover to make tough-but-necessary changes that disappoint some but also protect and preserve the system's overall viability.

Moreover, cheaper travel and communications, especially from the Internet and social media, have constrained the negotiating space for legislators to make deals. A shift from a committee-led to a leadership-led model for Congress began before the Republican revolution propelled Newt Gingrich (R-GA) to House Speaker, but it has since accelerated and changed congressional dynamics as well.

Many Other Forces Operate on Congress

The application of the economic way of thinking to public officials—the Public Choice scholarship—helps us understand the need for rules like a BBA. Public choice starts with the basic premise that human nature is consistent: We all want more of the good things at the lowest costs, and we each assess benefits and costs differently. People's basic incentives do not fundamentally change when they enter public service. Understanding the behavior of politicians, bureaucrats, and others in the public sector requires a realistic assessment of their interests, usually some combination of personal and public interest motivations.

In addition, legislators, presidents, governors, and agency officials do not hear from a representative sample of the American people. They hear disproportionately—even overwhelmingly—from those with substantial stakes in particular decisions, for whom the benefits of organizing political activities exceed the costs.

This organizing includes pooling resources for political action committees to help finance candidates' campaigns, hosting members of Congress for site visits and townhall meetings, conducting regular fly-ins of people from legislators' states or districts to lobby for or against legislation—usually self-serving but wrapped up in a purportedly public interest rationale—and maintaining full-time lobbyists in Washington, D.C., to engage the legislative process and keep an eye on members of Congress.

Even the protocols for requesting meetings with policymakers are a kind of specialized knowledge that only opens the door to make the case. Most constituent emails and phone calls are organized by or reflect the activities of organized interests.

When legislators do what an interest group wants, they may get rewarded with campaign support, favorable coverage, endorsements, and more. When they do not, they may get low scores on organizations' scorecards, lose campaign support, or see interest groups throw their weight behind a challenger.

Most Americans are too busy living their lives to devote time and resources to all this. Typically, only those for whom the political process provides outsized benefits find political engagement worthwhile. These interest groups tend to get their way more than they should, and usually at the expense of the unorganized public. Special interest goodies provide large benefits to a relatively small group while imposing small costs on many others, but the differences in the value of organizing lead to what political economists call concentrated benefits and diffuse costs.

This special-interest-driven redistribution can happen in real time. For example, the U.S. sugar program is incredibly beneficial for those who grow and refine sugar cane and sugar beets. It raises annual per-person food costs only a little, but a little bit for 340 million people is a lot of money for the industry: $2.5 to $3.5 billion per year.[7] True, sugar-using sectors like bakers and confectioners oppose the sugar program. Their relative diffusion and ability to pass on higher costs to consumers, however, means they cannot match the militant vigor of the sugar cartel.

Redistribution also happens across time. The current constellation of interest groups and voters makes demands on a wide range of issues. Current supporters and opponents determine who gets to wield political power. A politician rationally, though often reluctantly, gives today's pressures more weight than future needs. If not, he or she is more likely to be on the outs, and someone less focused on the future is more likely to win the election. Shifting costs across time takes several forms, and one is running persistent deficits: borrowing more every year from future generations to finance current activities.

Running persistent deficits makes government activities seem cheaper, and when things are cheaper, people want more. This helps explain why the tax-cutting zeal from starve-the-beast enthusiasts has not controlled spending even as the distance to a balanced federal budget has grown and the fiscal responsibility credibility of its adherents has eroded.

Persistent, chronic deficits create a fiscal illusion that increases the overall demand for government services from the electorate.[8] Attempting to finance the full cost of current spending with current taxes would reduce public demand for the federal government to do everything for everyone all the time. A balanced budget rule would help policymakers and the public more accurately weigh the costs and benefits of spending and revenue decisions.

The incentives of the current budget system promote sprawl, excessive debt, and other dysfunction. Policymakers need rules to counter interest group pressures and reduce the temptation to steal—borrow—from the future. Incentives are not destiny, however. Most policymakers honestly do pursue what they consider to be the public interest as much as they can. Institutional changes shift individuals' cost–benefit calculations and the art of the possible. A small shift in incentives toward responsibility could have substantial effects over time. It is the power of compound interest.

Methodological individualism is at the heart of this conversation. Legislatures are, more in theory than in practice, bodies of equals that require organizing—perhaps even centralizing—forces to facilitate the emergence of agreement. Most institutions of society are more hierarchical and have someone in charge, but that model does not necessarily apply to a legislature. In considering the nature of outcomes, the forces operating on and the motivations of each participant matter. Trying to get Congress to act is like herding cats.

Finally, the rules of the policymaking game are the institutions that channel energy through the decision processes that lead to policy outcomes. The process shapes even the ideas that political actors can propose and adopt, and therefore, how, why, and what public policy emerges.

As the late Rep. John Dingell (D-MI) said, "I'll let you write the substance... you let me write the procedure, and I'll screw you every time."[9] Stated differently, better procedures can *empower* Congress to sort out disagreements more productively.

A Principles-Based BBA

This project began from a small part of a meeting I attended in 2010 at the Cato Institute, a nonpartisan public policy research organization with a libertarian orientation. As Cato's Senate-focused government affairs staffer, I sat in on a meeting between U.S. Senate candidate David Malpass and Cato senior fellow Bill Niskanen. When BBAs came up, Niskanen recommended something new, so I ran the numbers. Playing with variations turned into an early version of the Business Cycle BBA (BCBBA) that freshman Rep. Justin Amash (R-MI) introduced in 2011, brought 45 Republican and 14 Democratic cosponsors on board, and would champion for a decade.

That work ultimately led to another BBA, the "principles-based BBA" mentioned earlier. Introduced by freshman Rep. Dave Brat (R-VA) in 2015, it would let Congress fill in the details with implementing legislation through the regular process. It was bipartisan with 64 Republican cosponsors and one Democrat when it was first introduced. It fell short of its potential breadth of support—probably even more than the

BCBBA—mostly because the window of opportunity simply was not open.

America needs systemic solutions led by a well-crafted BBA. Most BBA proposals have serious shortcomings and usually include provisions that members of one party or the other cannot stomach. That is a bad strategy. A constitutional amendment typically requires two-thirds of both houses of Congress to propose and three-fourths of state legislatures to approve. Too many members of Congress use BBAs to posture as fiscally responsible even as they vote to grow the debt burden again and again.

Several BBA proposals do not have those design flaws or others (see Chapter 7). They are neutral, practical, and comprehensive; they have attracted bipartisan support. With enough time to familiarize members of Congress and their staff with them before a vote, either could become the 28th Amendment to the Constitution.

Over the last fifteen years, I have helped Reps. Amash, Brat, and other members of Congress develop and introduce proposals for well-written balanced budget amendments to the U.S. Constitution and other legislation to get the federal government back in the black.

In this author's view, the principles-based BBA has the edge. As re-introduced in 2023, it reads:

> Section 1. Expenditures and receipts shall be balanced, which may occur over more than one year. Expenditures shall include all expenditures of the United States except those for payment of debt, and receipts shall include all receipts of the United States except those derived from borrowing. Congress shall achieve balance within ten years following the ratification of this article.
> Section 2. For emergency situations, two-thirds of the House of Representatives and the Senate may for limited times authorize expenditures exceeding those pursuant to rules established under section 1. Debts incurred from such expenditures shall be paid as soon as practicable.

The following pages make the case for this principles-based BBA and complementary statutes.

Even if Congress moves quickly, it will take a few years to fix the way it budgets and for members of Congress to learn to be effective operators in these new and better budget institutions. To succeed, they will need to change policy while they change their practices, just as other fiscal turnarounds have done.

Yet constitutional change does not come easily. Congress has considered balanced budget amendment proposals many times starting in the Great Depression. The high-water mark was early 1995. Then, a BBA passed the House with nearly 73 percent support before failing by only one vote in the Senate. In 2011, similar language failed the House with only 61.3 percent support, and 67 senators split their votes between a conservative version and another from moderate Democrats.

Why have the BBAs kept failing? Did they have poorly constructed provisions that do not belong in the Constitution? Were tightly controlled processes that reduced member buy-in the problem? Or did proponents mess up the politics by failing to engage skeptics and opponents appropriately?

The answer: all of the above. BBA proposals are usually poorly written; the process tends to shut most members out of the discussion (let alone trying to improve the language); and Republicans have sometimes tried to jam Democrats instead of seeking consensus and building bridges.

Some BBA flaws are technical. Most would require balance between spending and revenue each year. Revenue is volatile and would interact with annual balance to cause unstable and unpredictable policy changes on both sides of the ledger. Other problems are political. Some Republicans pursue limited government goals with supermajorities to raise the debt limit, increase revenue, or spend above a share of the economy. Some Democrats try to exclude politically sensitive programs like Social Security and Medicare. Nearly all BBAs have numerous problems, as we will see in Chapter 5.

Congress has repeatedly missed windows of opportunity. Some observers have soured on a BBA and see failure as a reason to give up. But hope springs eternal, and BBAs seem to return to prominence every fifteen years or so.

In the early 1980s, states calling for an amendment convention, President Ronald Reagan's overwhelming victory, and the new Senate Republican majority led to BBA votes. In 1995, the Republican revolution's Contract for America demanded early action on a BBA. In 2011, resolving the debt limit impasse set up that year's BBA vote. Inflation fatigue, a debt limit deal, or an unforeseen shock could bring additional BBA votes in the late 2020s.

In such a moment, a BBA could succeed if it is well-designed and advances in a way that lets members of both parties contribute their ideas, express their preferences, and seek to build coalitions.[10] This competitive clashing is constructive. It promotes finding common ground on solutions to help the federal government serve the people better.

Beyond BBAs, most efforts to upgrade federal budgeting have been part of bipartisan deals to raise the statutory debt limit,[11] which usually happens at least once per two-year congressional term. Even then, the possibilities for change are shaped by public opinion, recent fiscal and economic context, geopolitical concerns, timing within the political cycle, congressional and presidential leadership, and the quality of existing legislation. Practical proposals with broad support have the best chances of Congress pulling them off the shelf and plugging them into a deal.

The Promise of a Principles-Based BBA

The emphasis on common ground differentiates this project from others on BBAs. Senator Mike Lee (R-UT) wrote a staunchly conservative book in 2011 called *The Freedom Agenda: Why a Balanced Budget Amendment is Necessary to Restore Constitutional Government*. Conservative commentator Mark Levin's 2014 book *The Liberty Amendments: Restoring the American Republic* is similarly written from a limited government perspective with a brash tone. Both have the curious idea that something requiring double supermajorities—in Congress and with state legislatures—can put a strong thumb on the scale for substantive policy preferences that may not have even bare majority support in Congress or with the American people.

Building consensus across a broad, bipartisan spectrum is the way for a BBA and related legislation to succeed. That is how our country best resolves problems—together. This is a practical guide to achieving a workable, sustainable, and politically viable BBA and the statutory supports needed to bring it to life as a tool for responsible governance.

A consensus BBA should be a neutral platform to help adjudicate competing proposals from members of Congress. Democrats, for example, should be able to propose tax increases for their colleagues' consideration just as easily as Republicans can propose spending cuts. Deciding what to enact and what not to is the point of vesting collective choice in a legislature.

Civilization advances in part from improvements to institutions, whether they address fiscal policy, dispute resolution, balance of powers, or much else. Better institutions can promote greater prosperity, peace, freedom, justice, opportunity, and many other aspects of human flourishing.

Yet some thinkers dismiss the viability or advisability of a BBA too quickly. For example, Allen Schick's comprehensive history and explanation of the federal budget process gives a handful of pages to a BBA.[12] He dismisses the concept based on the very real problems with the traditional BBA.

Similarly, former federal budget official Alice Rivlin wrote that "the Republicans continued to talk about their balanced budget amendment gimmick" in the late 1990s. She said it is "a bad idea for many reasons... because the federal government should run a small deficit in some years, run large deficits in some years, and strive for a zero deficit or a surplus in other years."[13]

I agree with the need for flexibility. Like Schick, Rivlin was mistaken to taint all possible approaches to a constitutional balance rule with the problems of the 1990s BBA. After all, constitutional and statutory balance rules have spread around the world in recent decades.

The principles-based BBA is, first, a flexible articulation of the widely supported balance principle. Americans overwhelmingly support a constitutional requirement for the federal government to stop spending more than it raises in revenue, and economists overwhelmingly prefer balance over the medium term or over the business cycle instead of every year. This BBA also has a reasonable safety valve for emergencies and a realistic time to reach balance. Many details would go in revisable statute built on a constitutional foundation.

Second, this BBA uses broad language like existing constitutional provisions. Recognizing the nature of what has worked before gives us clues about what is most likely to succeed again.

Third, the principles-based BBA avoids provisions with policy and political pitfalls that appear in other proposals. The consensus required to amend the U.S. Constitution leaves no room for provisions that many legislators oppose.

By sticking to principles, this unbiased BBA lets Congress fill in the details with normal legislation. The balance requirement, "which may occur over more than one year," would let Congress specify through statute for 1) operating balance over the medium term, 2) immediate emergency response with subsequent offsets, and, perhaps, 3) financing investments over their life cycle. It can accommodate several sorts of balance: for ongoing activities, for emergencies, and for investments.[14]

The principles-based BBA would let Congress choose full balance or primary balance. Primary balance excludes interest costs and would require much less deficit reduction, currently about half as much as full balance. Primary balance would be close to the 3 percent of GDP deficit limit that most countries in the European Union are expected to meet. The ambiguity in "payment of debt" in the second sentence of Section 1 makes this possible. That said, primary balance may not be enough to control the debt burden in the long run, but it could be a steppingstone to full balance or another balance-related target.

The BBA would let two-thirds of both houses of Congress spend for emergencies. That is the highest threshold that applies to legislating and is the same as overriding a president's veto. It does not define an emergency or mandate a repayment schedule, although it indicates that offsets should be forthcoming. The details are left to implementing legislation.

Finally, it would give Congress a full decade to reach balance. The federal budget has gotten way off track, and it is going to take time to set right.

This proposal would not put thumbs on the scale for policy outcomes, just that revenue and spending must somehow balance. It is neutral and would let spending and revenue float to the level deemed proper by the American people's representatives in Congress.

Perhaps these provisions seem reasonable and not especially controversial. That is the idea: well-designed constitutional rules should have those features. And much of the case for *this* version of a BBA is by avoiding the problems of the traditional BBA and its derivatives, which Chapter 5 explores.

Beyond these particulars, most of a constitutional amendment's value comes from establishing, or perhaps re-establishing, the norms stated in the provisions. For example, the 19th Amendment formalized the then-emerging idea that men and women should be equally able to participate in voting for members of Congress and presidents. Those who call for an airtight, self-enforcing BBA misunderstand the nature of constitutional language.

Congress and presidents once respected the idea that government debt should decline except during major crises. Restoring the political class's commitment to balance will not be easy. Members of Congress are always pulled in different directions. The permanent campaign of always thinking about the next election requires policymakers to devote a lot of time to fundraising and vote-getting, and neither encourages members to focus on the long term. Politicians of both parties live in fear of telling people no.

A BBA would help restore fiscal responsibility and representative government in several ways. First, the supermajorities required to enact it would produce an intense national conversation about short- and long-term spending and tax priorities and the associated roles of the federal government. A successful BBA would need to contain broadly acceptable principles and continue to build consensus among legislators, pundits, news and opinion contributors, and the public.

A BBA would give members of Congress political cover to disappoint some constituencies. Politicians could say they wanted to support something but there was no room in the budget this time; we can try again next year. They could deflect blame to the BBA.

Some believe that a well-crafted BBA alone would be sufficient to get Congress to find the political will to do the tough-but-necessary policy work. Probably not. Setting a goal of balance without an effective process could lead to frustration and missed targets.

But a newly ratified BBA would light a fire under Congress to figure out how to get to balance and how to stay there. Spending and revenue policy changes are necessarily part of those discussions, as are changes in the budget process and perhaps the power structures within Congress. We will explore options in the final chapters.

Process fixes may include 1) the core of implementing legislation to establish mechanisms for balancing over the medium term (NOT each year) with reasonable adjustments and offsetting emergencies; 2) leveraging the debt limit to help Congress stay on track; 3) a more effective approach to automatic budget enforcement; 4) a comprehensive congressional budget each year instead of just the 26 percent of spending in today's annual appropriations bills; 5) leveraging the president's State of the Union address to provide Congress information it needs to get started on time; and 6) getting Congress to complete each year's budgeting on schedule so agencies can do their jobs and so unfinished business does not keep Congress from moving on to the next budget cycle.

Those statutory pieces might come to be seen as doing the most to change the incentives in Congress, even if the shift in expectations from the BBA catalyzes Congress to adopt them in the first place. A national conversation on a BBA proposal and the prudential norm of fiscal responsibility could dramatically expand the political space for other aspects of congressional reform as well.

Years ago, I sat in as my then-boss Maya MacGuineas, president of the Committee for a Responsible Federal Budget, briefed the Problems Solvers Caucus, a bipartisan group of mostly moderate members of the U.S. House of Representatives. She pitched policy options to reduce the deficit. When she finished, one of the leaders said, maybe a little exasperated, "Maya, we know what we need to do. We just don't know how to do it and [politically] survive."

That is our mission: to help members of Congress survive—or even thrive—while keeping the American Dream alive. The details will be up to them.

This book makes the case for a set of best practices. They are meant to be neutral rules of the game that members of Congress could use to advance a more perfect union and a more robust deliberative process. They would help members harness the vast knowledge on which they can draw.

These proposals, of course, build on existing institutions that mostly work well. Congress relies on authoritative, objective, timely research and cost estimates from the Congressional Budget Office and the Joint Committee on Taxation. The executive branch produces insightful budget and management information, which would be far more powerful if Congress were better organized to make use of it.

Ultimately, a more effective Congress means a more representative government. As centrist Democrat Alice Rivlin wrote in her final book, "The best way to defend democracy is to make democracy work better."[15] The proposals outlined here are intended to have broad appeal so they can help preserve and protect what we all hold dear.

Plan for the Book

Chapter 2 lays out the dangers of today's federal fiscal path and how it came about. Chapter 3 explores how the U.S. federal government, state governments, and other countries have moved from dysfunction toward healthier budgeting. Chapter 4 traces the history of the drive for a BBA for the U.S. government.

Chapter 5 explains the flaws in traditional BBAs and their derivatives. Chapter 6 explores the nature of constitutional language. Chapter 7 tells the stories of the Business Cycle BBA and the Principles-based BBA. Chapter 8 considers objections to BBAs and their applicability to a principles-based BBA.

Chapter 9 delves into a principles-based BBA's direct implementing legislation. Chapter 10 outlines other upgrades to the federal budget process to help Congress reach and sustain balance. Chapter 11 concludes with procedural, organizational, and relational dynamics of advancing budget reforms.

The book is complete, but the story will continue. These concepts will evolve as we continue to learn how best to accommodate each other. Solving America's problems will require legislators of both parties, policy experts of diverse views, and others engaged in these discussions to develop and advance durable solutions for our country. The future can be brighter if we are willing to strive for it.

Notes

1. Paul Winfree, "The Looming Debt Spiral: Analyzing the Erosion of U.S. Fiscal Space," Economic Policy Innovation Center, https://epicforamerica.org/publications/the-looming-debt-spiral-analyzing-the-erosion-of-u-s-fiscal-space/, March 5, 2024.
2. The Default Clock Committee, "Two Minutes to Midnight: The Updated Federal Government 'Debt Default Clock,'" https://debtdefaultclock.us/debt-default-clock/, April 15, 2024, accessed June 9, 2024.
3. Harvard CAPS—Harris Poll, https://harvardharrispoll.com/wp-content/uploads/2023/07/HHP_July2023_KeyResults.pdf, July 2023, p. 57.
4. "Budget ceiling," 31 U.S.C. 1105, adopted in Pub. L. 97–258, September 13, 1982. The 1982 statute was part of a "positive law codification," in which various "organic statutes" are organized and set forth as a positive title of the United States Code. This provision derives from Sec. 7 of Public Law 95–435, an act to amend the Bretton Woods Agreements Act to authorize the United States to participate in the Supplementary Financing Facility of the International Monetary Fund. Section 7 stated that "Beginning with fiscal year 1981, the total budget outlays of the Federal Government shall not exceed its receipts.".
5. "Nearly three-fifths of the federal government's long-term structural fiscal imbalance derives from legislation enacted between 1965 and 1972, including the enactments of Medicare and Medicaid in 1965, expansions of Medicare and Medicaid in

1971–72, and substantial increases in Social Security benefits in 1972." in Charles Blahous, "Why We Have Federal Deficits: An Updated Analysis," Mercatus Center Research Paper, https://www.mercatus.org/research/research-papers/why-we-have-federal-deficits-updated-analysis, November 19, 2021.

6. C. Eugene Steuerle, *Dead Men Ruling: How to Restore Fiscal Freedom and Rescue Our Future*, The Century Foundation Press, 2014.
7. U.S. Government Accountability Office, "Sugar Program: Alternative Methods for Implementing Import Restrictions Could Increase Effectiveness," https://www.gao.gov/products/gao-24-106144, October 31, 2023.
8. See also, James M. Buchanan and Richard E. Wagner, *Democracy in Deficit*, In *The collected works of James M. Buchanan*, 1977/2000. James M. Buchanan, "The balanced budget amendment: Clarifying the arguments," *Public Choice*, 90 (1–4), 1997. Romina Boccia, "Fiscal Illusion and Deficit Spending," *Cato at Liberty*, https://www.cato.org/blog/fiscal-illusion-deficit-spending, December 14, 2022. Romina Boccia, "Apple Trees for Firewood: James Buchanan's Case for a Balanced Budget Amendment in the Context of U.S. Fiscal Policy," Research Paper, *Springer Nature Switzerland*, https://doi.org/10.1007/s41412-019-00089-2, October 7, 2019. Andrew T. Young, "Tax-Spend or Fiscal Illusion?" *Cato Journal*, Vol. 29, No. 3., September 14, 2009.
9. David Baumann, "When Procedure Matters as Much as Substance," Credit Union Times, https://www.cutimes.com/2017/03/03/when-procedure-matters-as-much-as-substance/, March 3, 2017.
10. Kurt Couchman, "A Well-Crafted Budget Amendment Can Succeed," The Hill, https://thehill.com/blogs/pundits-blog/the-administration/315423-a-well-crafted-budget-amendment-can-succeed/, January 20, 2017,
11. Committee for a Responsible Federal Budget, "Q&A: Everything You Should Know About the Debt Ceiling," https://www.crfb.org/papers/qa-everything-you-should-know-about-debt-ceiling#appendix, May 5, 2023.
12. Allen Schick, *The Federal Budget: Politics, Policy, Process*, Third Edition, Brookings 2007, pp. 35–38.

13. Alice Rivlin, *Divided We Fall: Why Consensus Matters*, Brookings, 2022, p. 159.
14. Some members of Congress and policy experts support a federal version of capital budgeting that is standard for state governments. This view is well-articulated in Alan M. Jacobs, "Budgeting for the Future: Public Investment as Intertemporal Politics," National Budgeting Roundtable, Working Paper #6, https://static1.squarespace.com/static/5445c4efe4b066b22fcf7611/t/578cdb7fd1758e37cc7705f3/1468849024175/Jacobs_Budgeting+for+Future.pdf, July 2016. On the other hand, the late Alice Rivlin, then associated with the Brookings Institution, as skeptical. She responded to a question on capital budgeting in a 2011 hearing on the federal budget process: "I do not think that a capital budget for the federal government would be particularly helpful and for a couple of reasons. Unlike states and cities, the federal government actually does not do much direct investing in capital goods except in the military. ... On the domestic side it is mostly grants to state and local governments, grants from the Highway Trust Fund or whatever, matching grants. That makes it much more difficult to have them in the capital budget, but the more important thing is immediately everybody who is conscious of not just the infrastructure deficit but the skills deficit and other deficits will say, 'But wait a minute infrastructure is an investment, but so is investment in the skills of the workforce.' And you get an ever-expanding definition of what is investment, which leads me to believe it is not a terribly useful concept at the Federal level." House Budget Committee, Hearing on "The Broken Budget Process: Perspectives from Former CBO Directors," https://www.congress.gov/event/112th-congress/house-event/LC3155/text, September 21, 2011. Nevertheless, this debate is far from settled, and a principles-based BBA would leave the question open for Congress to resolve as members prefer.
15. Alice Rivlin, *Divided We Fall: Why Consensus* Matters, Brookings, 2022, p. 286.

CHAPTER 2

Bad Budgeting Is Catching Up with Us

James Madison, a lead drafter of the U.S. Constitution, then-member of Congress from Virginia, and later America's fourth president, warned against government debt in a 1790 letter. He wrote, "I go on the principle that a public debt is a public curse and in a republican government more than in any other."

Many have the same intuition, if not Madison's gift for language. It seems wrong and dishonest for Congress routinely to spend more than it is willing to impose on the public with current taxes. This does not necessarily imply a need for higher taxes, of course. Perhaps a decent amount of government spending is not worth doing.

That said, sometimes incurring debt is part of responsible budgeting. Borrowing for emergencies like war or natural disasters is often justified. Debt financing for an investment may be worthwhile if returns will be sufficient, like President Thomas Jefferson's 1803 Louisiana Purchase for $15 million—then about 3 percent of GDP—or Secretary of State William Seward's "Folly" in buying Alaska from Russia in 1861 for $7 million—then less than one-tenth of one percent of GDP.

Even beyond emergencies and investments, temporary deficits can be a good thing. As we shall see, a structural balance rule to balance spending and revenue over the medium term implies that modest deficits during recessions can be fine if they are offset by surpluses during good years.

K. Couchman, *Fiscal Democracy in America*,
https://doi.org/10.1007/978-3-031-91938-1_2

Why? Because they let policy be stable and predictable. Budget balance in any given year matters much less than medium- and long-term trends.

Let us take stock of the federal government's fiscal health and examine how the growing debt burden is a barrier to better lives. It is not just a problem for the distant future anymore. The dead weight of debt finance undermines opportunities today while increasing the risks of a deep and traumatic debt crisis.

Sound budgeting requires more than a smart BBA, as we will see in Chapters 9, 10, and 11. Budgeting is fundamentally about tradeoffs within and between spending and revenue priorities in pursuit of careful stewardship of the people's resources for the public benefit.

America's Fiscal Health Is Poor

The federal government has a poor record on balancing the budget.

Over the last fifty years, spending has been chronically higher than revenue, as Fig. 2.1 shows. The only significant exception was 1998–2001, when spending was unusually low and revenue was unusually high as shares of the economy. These fleeting surpluses came from 1) a long period of economic growth, 2) the post-Cold-War peace dividend, 3) a technology bubble that produced exceptional capital gains tax receipts, and 4) multiple rounds of deficit reduction under Presidents Reagan, Bush, and Clinton across multiple Congresses with different arrangements of partisan control.

Deficits were low enough and economic growth was high enough, however, for the debt-to-GDP ratio to decline from post-World War II highs until 1973. Then the gap between spending and revenue grew the debt burden again until the late 1990s. After a brief reprieve, the debt started building up again. It has already reached harmful levels and is on a dangerous path.

U.S. debt held by the public—$28.3 trillion in October 2024[1]—has approached the entire annual economic output of the American people: $29.4 trillion in the third quarter of 2024.[2] The debt is six times all federal revenue: $4.9 trillion in Fiscal Year (FY) 2024.[3]

The debt is not just high. It is also growing. The Congressional Budget Office (CBO) expects the debt burden to grow over the next thirty years. It is already well above the point of undermining economic growth. The Organization for Economic Cooperation and Development (OECD) estimated in 2015 that debt would take a toll on U.S. growth between 60

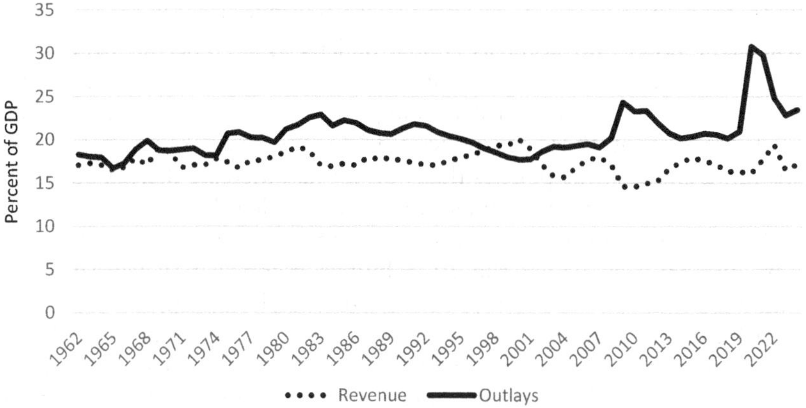

Fig. 2.1 Spending persistently exceeds revenue (*Source* CBO)

and 80 percent of GDP, while a 2021 meta-analysis in the *Cato Journal* found consensus that debt drag is evident by 80 percent of GDP and likely exists at lower levels.[4] Ever-higher debt burdens could choke off growth and bring stagnation.

These numbers are so huge that they do not seem real. Let us look at them a few other ways.

The debt in October 2024 was $213,667 per U.S. household and growing: $28.3 trillion divided by 132.5 million households. If each household took out a 15-year, fixed 6.50% APR mortgage to pay it off, it would cost $1,861 *per month*. Even a 30-year, fixed 7.50% APR mortgage would mean a monthly payment of $1,494. That is a big hole Congress has dug for us.

Divided equally over a population of 340 million, the debt was more than $83,000 per person. Most people do not have that much sitting around, and no one would be excited about forking that over to the government.

Fortunately, Congress does not have to pay off the debt, let alone do so in the next 15 or 30 years. It just needs to make sure the debt grows slower than the economy for the debt-to-GDP ratio—the standard measure of the debt burden—to shrink.[5]

Unfortunately, the deficits from new federal borrowing each year are on track to grow over the next decade and at an increasing rate (Fig. 2.2).

This shows the expected *new* debt each year. The overall stock of debt will grow faster and faster as annual deficits grow. The dip from 2025 to 2027 is based on the assumption that Congress will let temporary tax provisions expire instead of continuing most of them. In fact, Congress made permanent those tax policies and made many other changes to spending and revenue policies that will, on net, increase deficits but grow the economy in the 2025 budget reconciliation legislation.[6]

Even worse, debt will grow faster than the economy persistently in the next decade, even before the 2025 budget reconciliation legislation, as Fig. 2.3 shows. By definition, this is unsustainable. Facing an ever-higher debt burden as a share of the economy, sooner or later creditors will start to question the government's ability to guarantee timely payment of principal and interest. As creditors require higher interest rates to compensate for greater risk, the debt burden will grow faster in a vicious cycle until, most likely, a debt crisis forces painful tax hikes and spending cuts. If, however, the economy could grow faster than the debt, the debt burden would fall, and associated dangers would recede.

Sadly, these projections are all rosy. More plausible assumptions, as in Fig. 2.4, indicate a more rapid debt buildup. Instead of the debt burden rising to 119 percent of GDP in a decade, it could reach 141 percent. Or even more.

The differences between the baseline and this alternative scenario are that Congress would increase appropriated spending with the economy's growth instead of with inflation, would extend expiring tax provisions,

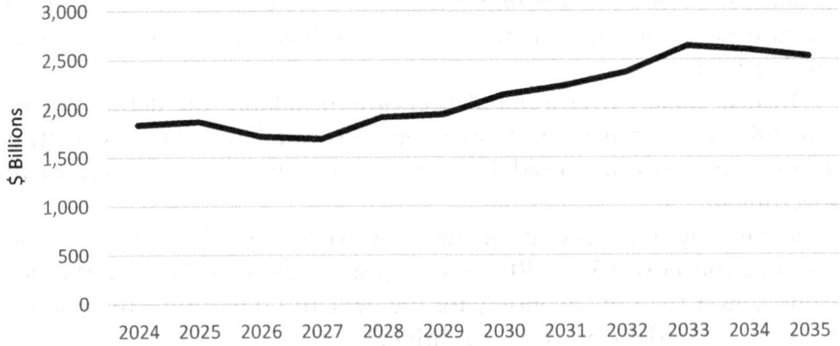

Fig. 2.2 Budget deficits are growing faster. (*Source* CBO)

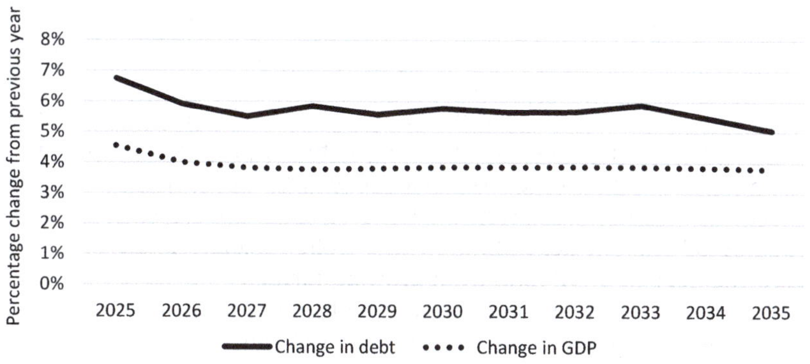

Fig. 2.3 Debt growing faster than the economy is unsustainable. (*Source* CBO)

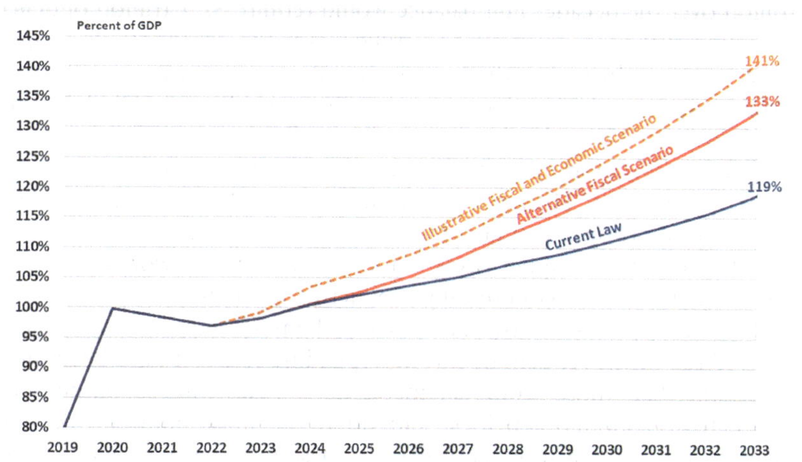

Fig. 2.4 Reality is worse than the official projections. (*Source* CRFB[7])

and would let various spending programs continue instead of phasing down or sunsetting them.

Even under the CBO's sunny projections, just bringing the debt growth down to economic growth by 2035—simply keeping the debt burden from growing further—would require deficits to be $620 billion lower *in* 2035. That is 7.7% more revenue, 5.9% less spending, or some of each. Policy changes that big would have to start small and grow. The

$620 billion deficit reduction would not be entirely direct policy changes: avoided interest costs from phased-in policy changes would contribute about 12 percent of overall savings.[8]

But that is just to stabilize the ratio of debt to the economy by 2035. The required savings are the difference between projected borrowing in 2035 and a deficit that equals economic growth that year. Overall deficit reduction—including interest effects—over the entire ten years would be roughly $3 trillion, depending on how policy changes phase in, just to keep the debt-to-GDP ratio from growing further.

Reaching balance under a balanced budget amendment would require even more savings. As we will explore, a well-crafted BBA should allow Congress to choose primary balance, which excludes interest costs from the balance calculation, or full balance, which includes everything.

Primary balance implies $920 billion in savings in 2035, or about $5 trillion over the decade. Full balance would require $2.7 trillion of deficit reduction that year, or about $13 trillion over the decade. If all changes were to come through reductions in spending growth, primary balance would require a 10% reduction in primary spending, and full balance would mean a 25% reduction in overall spending.

Debt stabilization entirely through tax increases would require even higher percentages. Hitting a savings target from the lower revenue base means a proportionately higher rate of change. It also reflects the different incentive effects, as higher taxes reduce the rewards of working, saving, investing, and other economically productive activities.

This all depends on the tax bases and rates,[9] but fiscal consolidations (AKA deficit reduction) through spending restraint have been more successful than those from tax increases.[10] Taxes impose burdens on productive economic activities, and often the most politically feasible tax increases are the most anti-growth. Despite a lower growth rate of nominal debt, slower economic growth may reduce revenue's impact on the debt burden. Reducing spending, however, avoids the deadweight losses of debt finance or from revenue increases, so the foregone spending translates almost directly into reductions in the debt-to-GDP ratio.

Of course, political optimization is not necessarily the same thing as economic optimization. Any politically viable path to balanced budgets could include both less spending and more revenue than anticipated under current law. Yet, waiting for a crisis to hit probably would mean massive and poorly considered tax hikes and spending cuts with far more damage than if we bit the bullet and balanced the budget sooner.

Waiting, however, lets politicians postpone the immediate pain needed for longer-term gains.

Excessive Public Debt Already Hurts Us

Too much government borrowing crowds out investment and other productive activity, increases inflation and interest rates, and corrupts our political culture. But before turning to economics, let us discuss intergenerational theft.

Stealing From the Kids

The Constitution's Fifth Amendment prohibits the government from taking private property for public use "without just compensation." The Ten Commandments that Moses brought the Israelites at Mount Sinai included: "You shall not steal." Philosopher John Locke considered "life, liberty, and property" to be the most fundamental rights.

It is bad enough when politicians take other people's money to buy votes and the support of special interests. It is even worse when they do it with debt. At least those burdened by high taxes can organize to push back on improper giveaways and the commensurate financing costs imposed on them.

But young adults do not vote as much as older adults, so younger generations have less political weight. Children and those yet to be born have no political power beyond what their current and future parents and grandparents might give them indirectly. If stealing from the weak is dishonorable, then theft from the powerless is reprehensible.

When so many prominent and influential people in our society make excuses for, dismiss, or even celebrate this thievery, it undermines the moral order that supports civilization. Regular reminders of this ethical failure fray the bonds connecting the body politic.

Interest Costs Magnify Political Strife

Too much debt makes politics worse. The interest on the national debt—$949 billion,[11] or $7,162 per household in FY 2024—crowds out competing policy priorities, whether they are tax cuts, new spending, or moving toward balancing the budget. Interest on the debt does not do anything for the present or the future. Interest merely pays the rent on funds that prior Congresses borrowed.

The federal government's cost of interest is growing by any measure. Rates are expected to increase, and the debt load keeps growing. Holding one constant while increasing the other would increase interest costs. Increasing both at the same time is driving rapid growth in interest costs.

In its latest projections, CBO expected interest costs to grow from $472 billion in FY 2022 to $1,783 billion in FY 2035, or from 1.9 percent to 4.1 percent of GDP.[12] In CBO's latest long-term budget outlook, interest costs could reach 6.3 percent of GDP by 2054.[13]

As concerning as this is, these projections may be optimistic. Annual appropriations may grow faster than inflation, expiring tax provisions have been extended, and emergencies could be more expensive than expected.

This puts enormous pressure on Congress. Fiscal hawks in Congress want to get the budget under control proactively with a balanced budget amendment and other reforms so we can avoid a big squeeze—and worse—later. Other members hope it will not happen during their time in office, or at least they will have someone else to blame if it does. This tension infuses every significant fiscal inflection point, and it is getting worse the longer Congress fails to address the festering problem.

Fiscal hawks are increasingly willing to use budget brinkmanship to get their colleagues to wake up. The agreements that brought conservative holdouts around to supporting Rep. Kevin McCarthy to be House Speaker in 2023 allegedly included commitments to seek structural changes in exchange for raising the debt limit. A few headlines from the start of the 118th Congress: "Debt limit battle set to dominate 2023 fiscal agenda" (*Roll Call*), "House GOP tempts fall government shutdown with impossible spending demands" (*Politico*), and "House Republicans prepare emergency plan for breaching debt limit" (*Washington Post*).[14]

Ultimately, the structural changes in the Fiscal Responsibility Act of 2023—the debt limit deal—were modest. It may have been the best outcome reasonably possible after President Joe Biden refused to negotiate until House Republicans forced him to the table. Even so, fiscal hawks were outraged that it did not do more. A handful of them ultimately made history by ejecting McCarthy from the speakership, though not entirely due to the FRA. After three weeks of one aspirant after another failing to get enough support on the floor, Rep. Mike Johnson (R-LA) got the unanimous support of House Republicans. Yet he soon ran into fiscal conservatives' discontent over a flat-funding continuing resolution in early 2025. Spending hawks were successful, however, in including substantial savings along with permanence for prosperity-boosting tax provisions in the 2025 budget reconciliation bill.

Proponents of sound budgeting have good intentions. Unfortunately, a shortage of well-crafted proposals with broad potential support has usually undermined their ability to make progress. This book and related efforts are meant, in part, to address this gap. Congressional leaders would be wise to fix this dysfunction out of self-interest and for the good of the country.

Tension from budget battles complicates putting Social Security and Medicare on sustainable paths. These programs can only pay out benefits from dedicated revenues and the reserves in their trust funds, which are special government bonds that reflect the prior surpluses that Congress borrowed to finance other programs. The Social Security Old Age and Survivors Insurance Trust Fund is expected to run dry in 2033.[15] When the funds are depleted, all beneficiaries face an across-the-board cut to benefit payments of about 23 percent.

Similarly, the Medicare Part A trust fund faces a 2033 depletion date.[16] This part of Medicare—health insurance for aged and disabled Americans—covers hospital-based care. Medicare would presumably delay payments rather than impose across-the-board cuts, but they do not have a clear plan. The Kaiser Family Foundation reports that "there is no automatic process in place or precedent to determine how to apportion the available funds or how to fill the shortfall."[17]

Social Security and Medicare have their own financing challenges, but they also drive the long-run deficit. Former Social Security trustee Charles Blahous attributes most of today's deficits to expansions in Social Security and federal health care programs decades ago.[18]Brian Riedl at the Manhattan Institute contends that the financing gaps for Social Security and Medicare, including interest costs attributable to them, equal nearly the entire projected budget deficit over the next thirty years.[19] The federal budget would be almost balanced in the long run except for Social Security and Medicare shortfalls.

Congress will have to change these programs eventually. This difficult task will almost certainly require a series of bipartisan agreements where members of both parties hold hands and jump together. Bringing their revenue and spending together is complicated by their overall budget impacts, as well as the tradeoffs between older beneficiaries, medical providers, and younger taxpayers who foot the bill.

In the meantime, however, these pressures make the routine business of federal budget and appropriations legislation more and more difficult. Appropriations and their conditions are hardly free of waste, corporate welfare, or encroachments on state responsibilities. Even so, appropriated programs are not the primary source of the long-term budget imbalances. Social Security and Medicare are.

But appropriated spending—discretionary spending—is the only part of the budget that Congress attempts to review and approve each year comprehensively. It is visible, so budget hawks focus disproportionately on appropriated spending.

Yet appropriations have fallen to 26 percent of overall spending, and the category is not growing faster than the economy. Rarely and only piecemeal do staffers review amendments for tax measures or direct spending programs, and members of Congress do not review or vote on the full collection each year. Direct spending and revenue programs are mostly out of sight, out of mind, and procedurally out of reach in the annual "budget" process. Appropriated spending is by far the most politically potent per dollar, so trying to achieve significant savings there has become a source of enormous conflict and frustration.

Debt Slows the Economy

In addition to fanning the flames of political strife, too much debt produces economic crowd-out. When the government borrows, it reduces the capital available for investment in private sector activities and increases interest rates. Market interest rates declined in recent decades until the Federal Reserve belatedly moved to address inflation in 2022.

Figure 2.5 shows the decline and recent spike in average 30-year fixed mortgage rates in the United States. Historically high home prices have compounded this shock. And yet, growing debt and a reversal of the global trends that have driven rates low could easily combine to push rates rapidly higher.

Rising global prosperity has dramatically improved the quality and length of life worldwide. With the rapid rise in income, global savings expanded faster than productive international investments could be found at previously prevailing interest rates. Interest rates dropped to unprecedented lows, encouraging borrowing, consumption, and investment while discouraging public and private savings.

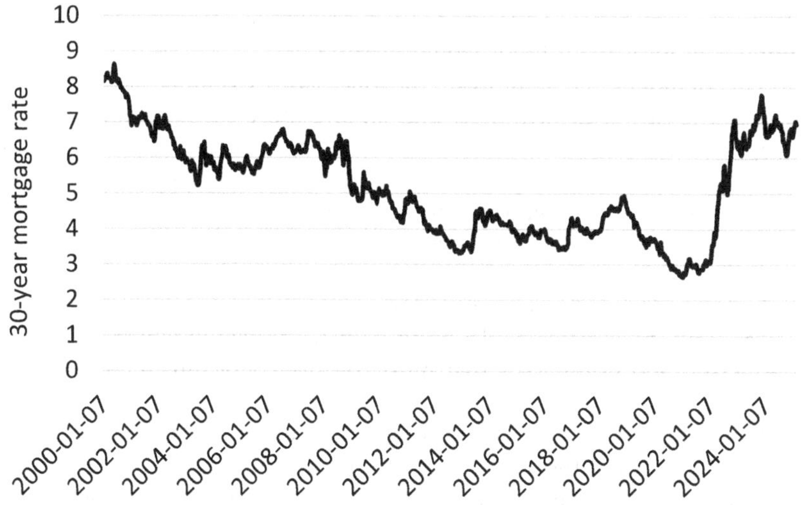

Fig. 2.5 Market interest rates have risen fast (*Source* Federal Reserve Economic Data)

Now, however, an aging global population seems to be reversing the global savings glut.[20] World population growth is slowing even as lifespans have increased dramatically,[21] in part as the spread of effective contraception has reduced fertility rates.[22] Older people produce less and consume more as they transition from the workforce to retirement.

Meanwhile, younger generations seem to be more willing to consume more of their income instead of saving it. Charles Goodhart and Manoj Pradhan's 2020 book *The Great Demographic Reversal: Ageing Societies, Waning Inequality, and an Inflation Revival* predicts a slew of problems for highly leveraged borrowers.[23]

At the same time, many countries have dramatically improved their business climates. The two most populous countries in the world, India and China, each improved their scores considerably on the World Bank's now-retired *Doing Business* report by about 19 and 17 points, respectively, on a 100-point scale from the 2014 to 2020 editions.[24]

Holding other factors constant, business climates that ease launching and operating a small or medium enterprise should increase the quantity of investment capital demanded. In economic jargon, it would shift the demand curve for loanable funds to the right, so interest rates and the amount of investment funds would increase.

The demographic shift from the once-fast-expanding saver population to the slower growth of savings among more consumption-oriented people would tend to increase interest rates by reducing the supply of loanable funds (technically, shifting the loanable funds supply curve to the left). Meanwhile, an improvement in business climates increases investment demand. Together, they imply significant global increases in interest rates.

It is wonderful that so many more people can live better in so many places. Still, their gains could bring pain to heavily indebted countries, businesses, and households that must roll over debt into higher interest rates.

How much more pain? CBO recently projected $14 trillion in federal interest costs over the next decade.[25] If interest rates are one percent (100 basis points) higher than expected, federal interest costs would be $3.3 trillion more.[26] In other words, modestly higher interest rates would push up federal interest expenses over the next decade from $104,000 to $129,000 per household.

A country carrying a heavy public sector debt burden will grow slower. Government borrowing diverts investment funds from more productive private sector uses. In addition, uncertainty about the ultimate path of fiscal consolidation imposes a risk premium on the economy, reducing investment and related opportunities.

Economists generally agree on these points but not necessarily on the size of the effects. A slight drag matters less than a significant drag. Fortunately, credible studies exist.

A 2013 World Bank paper estimated that economic growth slows in advanced countries by 0.017 percentage points per percentage point above a 77% debt-to-GDP ratio.[27] The U.S. debt-to-GDP ratio approaching 100 percent suggests that U.S. economic growth is about 0.35 percentage points lower than otherwise.

As noted above, a 2015 Organization for Economic Cooperation and Development paper estimated that most advanced countries suffer economic damage when the debt-to-GDP ratio reaches 60–80%.[28] They expected that the U.S. could have a little more room—70–90%—due to having the world's primary reserve currency for trade. The federal debt-to-GDP ratio is already 99 percent and rising. Meanwhile, the dollar's share of allocated reserve currencies has eroded to 58%.[29]

A survey of related studies found a broad consensus that too much public debt significantly slows economic growth.[30] In the wake of the post-pandemic rebound, slower growth may be our new reality.

In addition, for any given level of debt, a smaller economy means a higher debt-to-GDP ratio. This magnifies the economic burden of the debt, increasing the difficulty in restoring sustainable budgets solely through fiscal consolidation. Just like two heads are better than one, economic growth complements deficit reduction.

Unchecked Debt Growth Risks Severe Damage

If debt costs seem high in the near term, they worsen over time.

Lost Generation of Growth

A higher debt-to-GDP ratio crowds out private investments that improve productivity, worker compensation, and living standards. The longer this crowd-out persists, the larger the gap between actual living standards and what they could have been without the debt overhang.

To illustrate, we can use the World Bank's estimates: 0.017% slower growth for each percentage point that the debt-to-GDP ratio exceeds 77%. If the average debt-to-GDP ratio is 107%—30 percentage points above 77%—then growth is 0.51% slower than otherwise. Setting today's living standard at 100, over 30 years, the difference between 1.0 and 1.5 percent annual growth is a lot. In 30 years, 1.0% annual growth yields a 35% improvement in living standards. But 1.5% annual growth produces a 56% increase in living standards. Living standards improve in both cases, but the gap between the two scenarios is dramatic. What you, I, or anyone else planning to be around in 30 years would give up from refusing to tackle the debt now is enormous.

This is not hypothetical. From 1990 to 2020, the Japanese central government's debt-to-GDP ratio ballooned from 52.9% to 216.3%. From 1990 to 2021, Japan's GDP per capita, adjusted for buying power, grew from $19,972 to $42,940. In the same period, U.S. GDP per capita rose from $23,888 to $69,288.[31] U.S. economic output per person went from 1.2 times higher than Japan's to 1.6 times higher. That is the power of compound interest, or for Japan, of missing out due to debt drag and other issues.

Fiscal Crisis

Unless Congress changes course, the federal government risks a fiscal crisis. As CBO has written,[32]

> The likelihood of a fiscal crisis increases as federal debt continues to rise, because mounting debt could erode investors' confidence in the U.S. government's fiscal position. Such an erosion of confidence would undermine the value of Treasury securities and drive up interest rates on federal debt as investors demanded higher yields to purchase those securities. Concerns about the government's fiscal position could lead to a sudden and potentially spiraling increase in people's expectations for inflation, a large drop in the value of the dollar, or a loss of confidence in the government's ability or commitment to repay its debt in full, all of which would make a fiscal crisis more likely.

The economic and political consequences of a debt crisis would be traumatic. The Greek economy *still* has not fully recovered from the debt crisis that began in 2009, and that is with multiple rounds of bailouts and massive debt restructuring.

Yet, the scale is entirely different. In 2024, the United States produced 15.5 percent of global output, while Greece produced only 0.23 percent.[33] No one could—or would—bail out the United States. America would be on its own.

A debt crisis would be chaotic, and the particulars are unpredictable. Most spending would tighten, but less for programs directly supporting the most engaged American voters. Programs like Social Security, Medicare, and much of Medicaid would likely only tighten for wealthier retirees who could make do with fewer subsidies, for new retirees (though it would take time to phase changes in), and for medical providers through their payment rates.

Taxes would go up, especially on investment and high earners, reducing incentives to innovate and produce needed goods and services. A value-added tax could fall on everyone, and it would be such a money machine that a crisis-wracked Congress might find it irresistible.

Congress would slash spending on defense and foreign affairs. Reasonable cases exist for reducing the American military footprint abroad, downsizing foreign aid, and overhauling the State Department. But an immediate withdrawal of forces or capability from countries leaning on the U.S. could be destabilizing. A U.S. fiscal crisis could lead to war abroad, with immediate dangers for current allies and unknown risks for others in those regions and beyond.

National Security

That is not the only national security risk of growing debt and a possible fiscal crisis.

As I wrote a few years ago about the U.S.-China relationship[34]:

> China's ownership of $1.1 trillion in U.S. federal debt is also concerning and has eerie echoes of a time when America had geopolitical debt leverage. In 1956, U.S. President Eisenhower issued an ultimatum to heavily indebted Britain and France during the Suez Canal Crisis: "no ceasefire, no loan." This sped the end of Britain's already fraying empire and diminished its power for decades.
>
> China's leaders are unlikely to make such a threat unless they are sure it will have the desired impact. Imagine, however, if America faced stiff headwinds—from a recession, from reserve currency competition, the end of the global savings glut, or from a debt crisis—that pushed up U.S. interest rates. If that happened, relatively minor Chinese actions could create much larger problems for the United States and weaken America permanently. Some collateral economic damage would fall on China, but under certain circumstances, Beijing may decide that the benefits outweigh the costs.

Conclusion

Thomas Jefferson, lead author of the Declaration of Independence and America's third President, wrote while serving as vice president in 1798, "I wish it were possible to obtain a single amendment to our constitution; I would be willing to depend on that alone for the reduction of the administration of our government to the genuine principles of its constitution; I mean an additional article taking from the federal government the power of borrowing."[35]

Despite sincere efforts, 227 years later—nearly 250 years after the Declaration of Independence—America still lacks such an amendment. The world's greatest superpower ever remains dangerously dependent on debt. The following three chapters explore how U.S. states and other countries have reversed the curse of public debt, recount the pursuit of a BBA for the federal government, and review the shortcomings of most proposed balanced budget amendments.

Notes

1. U.S. Treasury, "Debt to the Penny," https://fiscaldata.treasury.gov/datasets/debt-to-the-penny/debt-to-the-penny, accessed January 28, 2025.
2. Bureau of Economic Analysis, "Gross Domestic Product (Third Estimate), Corporate Profits (Revised Estimate), and GDP by Industry, Third Quarter 2024," https://www.bea.gov/news/2024/gross-domestic-product-third-estimate-corporate-profits-revised-estimate-and-gdp-1, December 19, 2024.
3. Congressional Budget Office, "Monthly Budget Review: Summary for Fiscal Year 2024," https://www.cbo.gov/system/files/2024-11/60843-MBR.pdf, November 8, 2024.
4. Fall, F., et al. (2015), "Prudent debt targets and fiscal frameworks," OECD Economic Policy Papers, No. 15, OECD Publishing, Paris, https://doi.org/10.1787/5jrxtjmmt9f7-en, July 1, 2015. Jack Salmon, "The Impact of Public Debt on Economic Growth," *Cato Journal*, Vol. 41, No. 3 (Fall 2021), pp. 487–509.
5. Total debt is the sum of debt held by the public, which includes the Federal Reserve, and debt held in intragovernmental accounts like Social Security, Medicare, and other trust funds. As of June 17, 2024, total public debt outstanding was $34.8 trillion, debt held by the public was $27.6 trillion, and intragovernmental holdings were $7.1 trillion. Treasury Department, "Debt to the Penny," https://fiscaldata.treasury.gov/datasets/debt-to-the-penny/debt-to-the-penny, accessed June 20, 2024.
6. Rep. Jodey Arrington, H.R. 1, the One Big Beautiful Bill Act, Pub.L. 119–21, https://www.congress.gov/bill/119th-congress/house-bill/1, enacted July 4, 2025.
7. Committee for a Responsible Federal Budget, "Debt Explodes Under Alternative Scenarios," https://www.crfb.org/blogs/debt-explodes-under-alternative-scenarios, May 18, 2023.
8. Based on calculations using CBO's interactive tool, "How Changes in Revenues and Outlays Would Affect Debt-Service Costs, Deficits, and Debt," https://www.cbo.gov/publication/59937, February 16, 2024.

9. Christopher J. Conover, "Congress Should Account for the Excess Burden of Taxation," Policy Analysis No. 669, Cato Institute, https://www.cato.org/policy-analysis/congress-should-account-excess-burden-taxation, October 13, 2010.
10. Veronique de Rugy and Jack Salmon, "Flattening the Debt Curve: Empirical Lessons for Fiscal Consolidation," Mercatus Center at George Mason University, https://www.mercatus.org/research/research-papers/flattening-debt-curve-empirical-lessons-fiscal-consolidation, July 22, 2020. Falilou Fall, Debbie Bloch, Jean-Marc Fournier, and Peter Hoeller, "Prudent Debt Targets and Fiscal Frameworks," OECD Economic Policy Paper No. 15, https://www.oecd-ilibrary.org/economics/prudent-debt-targets-and-fiscal-frameworks_5jrxtjmmt9f7-en, July 1, 2015, p. 50.
11. Congressional Budget Office, "Monthly Budget Review: Summary for Fiscal Year 2024," https://www.cbo.gov/system/files/2024-11/60843-MBR.pdf, November 8, 2024.
12. Congressional Budget Office, "Budget and Economic Outlook: 2025 to 2035," https://www.cbo.gov/system/files/2025-01/51118-2025-01-Budget-Projections.xlsx, January 17, 2025.
13. CBO, "Long-Term Budget Projections: 2024 to 2054," https://www.cbo.gov/system/files/2024-03/51119-2024-03-LTBO-budget.xlsx, March 2024.
14. Paul M. Krawzak, "Debt limit battle set to dominate 2023 fiscal agenda," *Roll Call*, https://rollcall.com/2023/01/13/debt-limit-battle-set-to-dominate-2023-fiscal-agenda/, January 13, 2023. Caitlin Emma and Connor O'Brien, "House GOP tempts fall government shutdown with impossible spending demands," https://www.politico.com/news/2023/01/13/house-gop-government-spending-goals-00077762, January 13, 2023. Jeff Stein, Leigh Ann Caldwell, and Theodoric Meyer, "House Republicans prepare emergency plan for breaching debt limit," *The Washington Post*, https://www.washingtonpost.com/us-policy/2023/01/13/debt-ceiling-gop-plan/, January 13, 2023.
15. Social Security Trustees, "The 2025 Annual Report of the Board of Trustees of the Federal Old-Age and Survivors Insurance and Federal Disability Insurance Trust Funds," https://www.ssa.gov/OACT/TR/2025/tr2025.pdf, June 18, 2025.
16. The Board of Trustees for Federal Hospital Insurance and Federal Supplementary Medical Insurance Trust Funds, "2025 Annual

Report of the Boards of Trustees of the Federal Hospital Insurance Trust Fund and the Federal Supplementary Medical Insurance Trust Fund," https://www.cms.gov/oact/tr/2025, June 18, 2025.

17. Juliette Cubanski and Tricia Neuman, "FAQs on Medicare Financing and Trust Fund Solvency," Kaiser Family Foundation, https://www.kff.org/medicare/issue-brief/faqs-on-medicare-financing-and-trust-fund-solvency/, June 17, 2022.
18. Charles Blahous, "The Failure to Establish Effective Rules for Financing U.S. Federal Entitlement Programs," Mercatus Center at George Mason University, July 19, 2022.
19. Brian Riedl, "Fix Social Security And Medicare To Protect Other Priorities," Peter G. Peterson Foundation, https://www.pgpf.org/expert-views/americas-fiscal-and-economic-outlook/fix-social-security-and-medicare-to-protect-other-priorities, November 8, 2021.
20. Ben S. Bernanke, "Why are interest rates so low, part 3: The Global Savings Glut," Brookings Institution, https://www.brookings.edu/blog/ben-bernanke/2015/04/01/why-are-interest-rates-so-low-part-3-the-global-savings-glut/, April 1, 2015.
21. The World Bank, "Life expectancy at birth, total (years)," https://data.worldbank.org/indicator/SP.DYN.LE00.IN, accessed January 16, 2023.
22. UN Department of Economic and Social Affairs, "World Fertility and Family Planning 2020," https://www.un.org/en/development/desa/population/publications/pdf/family/World_Fertility_and_Family_Planning_2020_Highlights.pdf, United Nations 2020.
23. Charles Goodhart and Manoj Pradhan, *The Great Demographic Reversal: Ageing Societies, Waning Inequality, and an Inflation Revival*, Palgrave MacMillan, 2020.
24. World Bank, "Historical Data - Doing Business—with scores," https://www.doingbusiness.org/content/dam/doingBusiness/excel/db2020/Historical-data---COMPLETE-dataset-with-scores.xlsx, accessed January 16, 2023.
25. CBO, "The Budget and Economic Outlook: 2025 to 2035," https://www.cbo.gov/publication/60870, January 17, 2025.

26. Based on calculations from CBO, "Workbook for How Changes in Economic Conditions Might Affect the Federal Budget: 2024 to 2034," https://www.cbo.gov/publication/60074, April 9, 2024.
27. Thomas Grennes, Mehmet Caner, and Fritzi Koehler-Geib, "Finding The Tipping Point – When Sovereign Debt Turns Bad," https://elibrary.worldbank.org/doi/abs/10.1596/1813-9450-5391, June 22, 2013.
28. Falilou Fall, Debbie Bloch, Jean-Marc Fournier, and Peter Hoeller, "Prudent Debt Targets and Fiscal Frameworks," OECD Economic Policy Paper No. 15, https://www.oecd-ilibrary.org/economics/prudent-debt-targets-and-fiscal-frameworks_5jrxtjmmt9f7-en, July 1, 2015.
29. International Monetary Fund, "Currency Composition of Official Foreign Exchange Reserves (COFER)," https://data.imf.org/?sk=E6A5F467-C14B-4AA8-9F6D-5A09EC4E62A4, accessed June 20, 2024.
30. Jack Salmon, "The Impact of Public Debt on Economic Growth," *Cato Journal*: Vol. 41, No.3, https://www.cato.org/cato-journal/fall-2021/impact-public-debt-economic-growth, Fall 2021.
31. World Bank, "GDP per capita, PPP (current international $)—Japan, United States," https://data.worldbank.org/indicator/NY.GDP.PCAP.PP.CD?locations=JP-US, accessed December 31, 2022.
32. CBO, "The 2022 Long-Term Budget Outlook," https://www.cbo.gov/publication/58340, July 2022.
33. International Monetary Fund, "GDP based on PPP, share of world," https://www.imf.org/external/datamapper/PPPSH@WEO/OEMDC/ADVEC/WEOWORLD, accessed June 20, 2024.
34. Kurt Couchman, "Debt Damage: How America's Spending Hurts U.S. Security," The National Interest, https://nationalinterest.org/feature/debt-damage-how-americas-spending-hurts-us-security-70426, July 31, 2019.
35. Thomas Jefferson, "Extract from Thomas Jefferson to John Taylor," https://tjrs.monticello.org/letter/178, November 26, 1798.

CHAPTER 3

Coming Back from the Brink

The federal government's fiscal outlook is troubled. The growing debt burden slows economic growth, reduces opportunity, stifles innovation, incubates toxic politics, and risks a devastating debt crisis.

Yet hope remains. Governments—including the U.S. federal government—have turned themselves around and have thrived. Others have not, and they have stagnated or worse (e.g., Japan, Greece, pre-WWII Germany). Here, we highlight success stories.

A common part of formalizing commitments to fiscal recovery is reasonable budget targets. Usually, this combines constitutional and statutory rules that aim for balanced budgets. The rules may formally target debt, deficits, or spending relative to revenue, but all have the same objective: controlling debt accumulation.

American Independence Brought a Mountain of Debt

On July 4, 1776, the Declaration of Independence distilled the grievances that had produced long-simmering rebellions, uprisings, and general discontent toward European overlords, especially the British throne. The Revolutionary War had begun in April the year before, and it ended soon after the major American victory in the Battle of Yorktown, Virginia, in October 1781.

K. Couchman, *Fiscal Democracy in America*,
https://doi.org/10.1007/978-3-031-91938-1_3

By the war's end, the young republic had bought its freedom. In addition to deaths, injuries, displacement, and general misery, the colonies had borrowed deeply. "The United States debt, foreign and domestic, was the price of liberty," wrote founding father Alexander Hamilton.[1]

Financing war—especially when defending the homeland against foreign aggressors—is the most justified reason to borrow. According to the Declaration of Independence, governments are created to secure "certain unalienable Rights, that among these are Life, Liberty and the pursuit of Happiness" for the people.[2] War threatens everything. Preserving the option to borrow in case of war and other crises is a major reason why debt burdens must be low otherwise.

But there was not yet a national government of any consequence. The thirteen American colonies, not the federal government, borrowed heavily during the War of Independence. Each colony was sovereign and independent, bound to the others by little more than a common purpose. Each was primarily responsible for its military needs. Each took on debt—a promise to pay, on schedule, both principal and interest—from its own citizens and from foreign powers, including France, Spain, and the Netherlands.[3]

The Articles of Confederation, the first attempt at a legal union between the States, went into effect on March 1, 1781. It did not infringe on the sovereignty of the States to any practical degree. The Continental Congress was more of a diplomatic forum between thirteen sovereigns than a legislating body. It lacked the power to raise revenue or to compel the states to contribute to the general welfare, so it printed vast sums of paper money and produced severe inflation approaching 30 percent in 1778.[4]Inflation, as Americans rediscovered in the early 2020s, happens when the money supply grows faster than economic output.

The States ended the Revolutionary War with different levels of war debt. All gained political freedom from Britain, but they bore the costs unevenly. Politicians and the people in heavily indebted states thought the price of liberty—the debt—should be the responsibility of all. Naturally, officials in states not so burdened were unenthusiastic about imposing tax burdens on those who elected them for the benefit of out-of-staters. Lacking a way to resolve the conflict under the Articles of Confederation, disunion was a constant threat.

The national government needed the independent ability to raise revenue to pay the debts of the United States and to borrow in times of need. Among many defects in the Articles of Confederation, this compelled the states to send delegates to a convention to improve on the existing constitution. The new constitution—proposed by convention on September 17, 1787, ratified on June 21, 1788, and effective when the First Congress convened on March 4, 1789—included those powers.[5]

Even then, it took years and far-reaching political maneuvers to get the debt under control. A crucial early step was the deal between Secretary of the Treasury Alexander Hamilton, then-Rep. James Madison, and Thomas Jefferson. All sides got a win. Or as it would be called later, they did some log rolling. Hamilton got the federal government to take on the states' Revolutionary War debts, among other provisions to establish good credit for the federal government, through the Funding Act of 1790.[6] Section 13 of the Act authorized a federal loan of $21.5 million to finance the assumption of state debts then existing in 1786 in the amounts listed in Table 3.1.

In exchange, Madison and Jefferson got a permanent seat for the federal government on the banks of the Potomac River, one part in Maryland and the other in their native Virginia. The Residence Act of 1790 provided that the new national capitol building should be ready by the first Monday in December of 1800, at which point the federal government would relocate there. Furthermore, the Maryland (eastern)

Table 3.1 Federal assumption of state debts

State	*Amount*
New Hampshire	$300,000
Massachusetts	$4,000,000
Rhode Island and Providence Plantations	$200,000
Connecticut	$1,600,000
New York	$1,200,000
New Jersey	$800,000
Pennsylvania	$2,200,000
Delaware	$200,000
Maryland	$800,000
Virginia	$3,500,000
North Carolina	$2,400,000
South Carolina	$4,000,000
Georgia	$300,000

Source Funding Act of 1790

side would be the location for "suitable buildings for the accommodation for Congress, and of the President, and for the public offices of the government of the United States."[7]

Extraordinary institutional redesign and creation laid the groundwork to turn a poor, lightly populated fringe on the edge of the Atlantic Ocean into a globe-striding powerhouse: 1) replacing the feckless Articles of Confederation with the Constitution of the United States, 2) subsequent political agreements, 3) building the capacity of the executive branch, and 4) state and citizen adjustment to new practices.

As Fig. 3.1 shows, federal debt held by the public declined from nearly 30 percent of GDP in 1790—a dangerous level for an underdeveloped country—to only 5.7 percent before the War of 1812. Fiscal prudence, rising prosperity, and a growing population contributed. After that, it generally declined again and was extinguished entirely during Andrew Jackson's presidency (1829–1837). It stayed in the low single digits until the Civil War.

The federal government had no formal statutory, let alone constitutional, balance rule, but the shared norm to pay down government debt whenever possible was powerful. Though unwritten, the rule existed. The founding generation's herculean institutional, political, and administrative achievements put the federal government on a path of declining debt burdens and fostered rapid growth of the nation's economy, population, and territory. Many states were not so prudently managed.

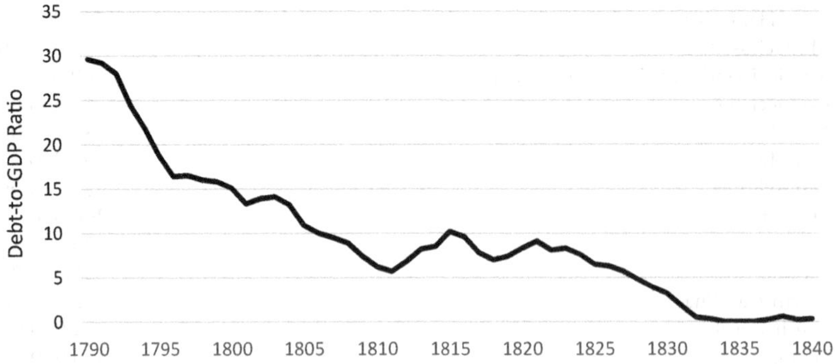

Fig. 3.1 The federal debt burden declined after independence (*Source* CBO[8])

America's Young States Get into Debt Trouble

During the 1820s and 1830s, northern states including Ohio, Indiana, New York, and Pennsylvania invested heavily in canal construction and other internal improvements to support migration and to promote shipping furs and other resources from the frontiers to the population-dense coastal regions. This infrastructure required large sums upfront before it could generate revenue from tolls. The borrowing relied on the promises of future profits.

Meanwhile, many southern states including Arkansas, Mississippi, and Alabama borrowed to capitalize local banks. In those times, states generally prohibited branch banking (multiple locations), so each bank was a stand-alone entity. It shielded them from competition with big city banks but also made them vulnerable to swings in the local economy, panics, and bank runs.

The crucial element here is that states lacked formal and informal fiscal constraints. They had taken the politically easy route. They borrowed deeply and accumulated substantial public debt to build up banking and infrastructure in their states instead of focusing on creating the conditions for the private sector to determine the best bets. Bearing risks while pursuing profits tends to promote considered judgment, but that is not what state legislatures did.

Even as Congress and the Jackson Administration paid off the federal debt, state borrowing for internal improvements was about to collide with the Panic of 1837. The Panic was a financial crisis with bank runs and related turmoil that became a major depression and a long-lived recession. The factors that created the Panic and subsequent economic trouble included foreign creditors, financial sector fragility, federal and state policy changes, and crop failures.

After years of economic weakness, eight states and the territory of Florida had defaulted by 1842 (see Fig. 3.2).[9] States began to adopt annual balance requirements of various forms in the 1840s under pressure from creditors as well as anti-aid provisions meant to keep taxpayers from backing private enterprises. The political and economic fallout led many states to enact hard budget constraints through balanced budget rules, debt limits, and related fiscal controls. Other existing and subsequently established states adopted similar rules, despite uneven uptake. Some states required additional prods.[10]

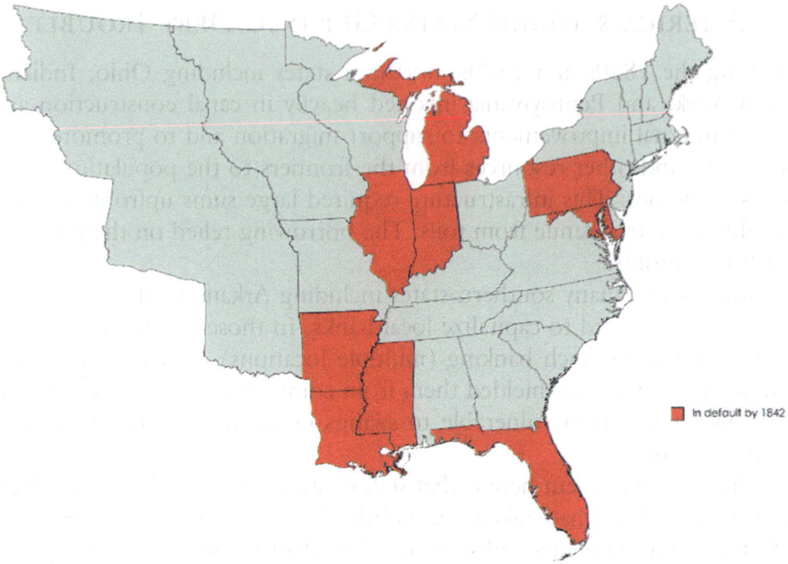

Fig. 3.2 Eight states and the Florida territory had defaulted by 1842 (*Source* Wallis et al.)

Policy responses, including new fiscal rules, supported another economic boom until the Civil War began in 1861. Another major round of state defaults emerged in the post-Reconstruction period as southern states repudiated Reconstruction government debts. The U.S. economy has experienced numerous booms and busts since, yet the trends toward greater prosperity and better institutions including balanced budget rules have moved together.

Though better than what came before, state business climates[11] and fiscal rules still leave much room for improvement. Just because most states have annual balance rules does not mean it is a good approach. Annual balance became the norm long before legislators understood the pattern of economic booms and busts that we now call the business cycle. As experience has shown, however, a strict annual balance rule would force state policymakers into one or more of three undesirable options:

1. Fiscal Consolidation During Recessions: Revenue growth slows or even shrinks during recessions due to stagnant or declining income and employment. Annual balance can also let policymakers spend too much during the boom years when revenue is abundant. Then, when a recession comes, bringing policies that would produce high spending back in line with revenue requires significant and disruptive changes through spending cuts, tax increases, or both, adding to the uncertainty and stress of the recession faced by the public and by elected officials.

2. Deviation from the Balance Rule: Rather than changing policy dramatically during recessions, states might not balance the budget. Some states generally require annual balance but allow tapping into reserve funds to cover a shortfall, but that is not the only option. As former New York State Comptroller Edward Regan testified to the Judiciary Committee of the U.S. Senate,[12] state annual balance rules "have tended to push public officials into manipulative actions and outright deceptions," like:

> Shifting expenditures off budget; manipulating receipt and payment activities; accelerating tax revenues; postponing expenditures; delaying refunds to taxpayers and salaries to employees into the following fiscal year; delaying vendor payments; reducing contributions to pension funds by forcing changed actuarial assumptions; and, borrowing repeatedly against the same assets by refinancing them after the original debt has been mostly repaid.

One study found that states with annual balance rules "frequently reported deficits in their adopted budgets and relied on sizeable and favorable expenditure variances to close budget gaps before the end of the budget period."[13]

In other words, they cook the books. Many in the public interpret news coverage of these juggling tricks as mismanagement, corruption, or worse. These practices are toxic to impressions of policymakers' commitment to the rule of law and sound governance. Even if they approximate reasonable fiscal practices overall, questionable kernels find fertile ground for accusations and nasty narratives that can persist long after budgets are back on track.

3. Federal Bailouts: Receiving funds from the federal government may seem like the most attractive option of all, as it avoids ill-timed fiscal consolidation and disreputable finagling. Federal bailouts are uncertain to arrive, however, and they tend to bring conditions that stick around much longer than the money lasts. These strings can distort the balance of powers between state and federal governments. Even so, state annual balance requirements make it more difficult for states to resist handouts during tough times and for their members of Congress to oppose them.

Annual balance produces messy budget management. The scramble for adjustments, transfers, bailouts, and other coping devices feels anarchic. It also makes planning more difficult for residents, businesses, and state and federal policymakers.

Despite ongoing shell games and juggling tricks, annual balance has helped states control debts enough to avoid defaulting again, at least so far, and bond markets generally provide another layer of discipline. Yet annual balance does not support predictable, reasonable ways to build up and draw on reserves over the business cycle without undermining state powers. Annual balance has served decently well, but it is time for an upgrade.

Structural Balance Is the Future for State Budget Rules

Some think Colorado's multi-faceted Taxpayer's Bill of Rights (TABOR) is the gold standard of fiscal rules[14] and should be that upgrade. TABOR is a constitutional provision to limit the amount of revenue that state and local governments can retain and spend, generally to the prior year's spending adjusted for changes in inflation and population. Revenue exceeding the limit is refunded to taxpayers unless voters approve the government retaining and expending surplus revenue.[15]

Coloradans is among the 18 states where initiatives to amend state constitutions are possible.[16] Voters adopted TABOR through initiative in 1992 after unsuccessful efforts in 1986, 1988, and 1990.[17] The people hired to specialize in managing the government—the legislature—were sidestepped through direct democracy, and TABOR lacked support when adopted from many legislators charged with making it work, but it is popular with the public.

In addition to other restraints on government growth, TABOR's spending rule is supposed to limit spending growth to inflation and population unless voters approve otherwise. That rule would mean gradually but inexorably reducing spending as a share of state GDP, as Fig. 3.3 shows, by excluding the productivity factor of GDP growth. A mechanically followed TABOR-style spending growth cap starting in 1970 or 1990 from an initial 10 percent of GDP would mean a more than 60

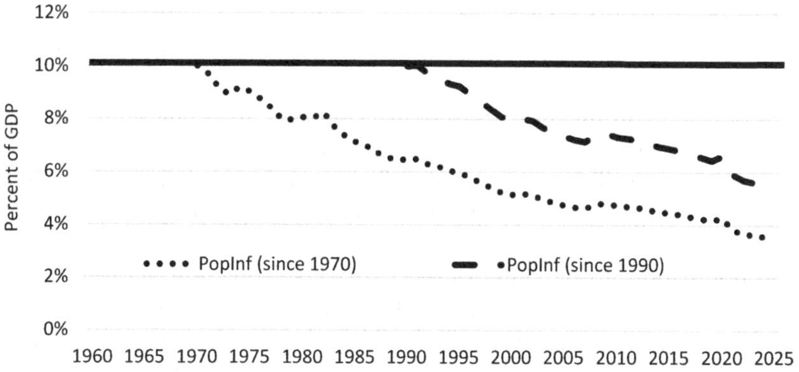

Fig. 3.3 An inflation-and-population-based spending growth limit requires persistent cuts (*Source* Federal Reserve Bank of St. Louis, author's calculations)

percent or 40 percent decrease in spending as a share of GDP, respectively, by today.

To the extent that a state budget is bloated with programs that do not add value for the people, spending reductions can be beneficial. At some point, however, a state could reach a healthy equilibrium between services rendered and the revenue policies needed to finance them. Further spending cuts after that would reduce well-being because the public services foregone would be more valuable than the revenue reductions made possible.

Back to Colorado, between a voter-approved referendum to loosen the cap and the legislature's creative use of TABOR's enterprise provision (entities with only a small share of state or local government funding), from FY 1999–2000 to 2022–2023, total state spending grew from 6.5 percent of the state economy to 9.0 percent. Over the same period, the general fund, which is subject to the TABOR limit, only increased from 3.0 percent to 3.2 percent, and that was largely due to a successful referendum in 2005 to suspend and rebase the cap.[18] Other spending, including enterprise funds, grew by 2.3 percent of state GDP, about 11 times faster than spending subject to the limit. Over the last 23 years, state spending covered by the TABOR cap fell from 46 to 36 percent today.

All that said, TABOR has almost certainly limited government growth as Colorado has shifted from favoring Republicans to favoring Democrats in public office.

Elsewhere, an inflation-and-population-based spending limit has been difficult to replicate or sustain. Washington state limited spending growth to a rolling average of inflation and population from 2000 to 2007 and then switched to a rolling average of growth in state personal income.[19] In Pennsylvania, a proposed constitutional inflation-and-population-growth limit of the Taxpayers Protection Act failed in the Republican-controlled House in 2022 when moderate Republicans and all Democrats voted it down.[20] At this point, a supermajority of states has tried and failed at least once to enact TABOR-like spending caps.

Instead, states are increasingly seeking to replace annual balance rules with structural balance.[21] Structural balance means a spending growth rule ensures budget balance over the medium term, with surpluses during good years set aside to offset deficits in bad years. Switzerland already does this successfully, and we will look at the mechanics of a bill in Congress along the same lines in Chapter 9. In addition to Washington State, Indiana, Connecticut, Florida, and other states already smooth spending over the business cycle, and interest is growing elsewhere.

The American Legislative Exchange Council, a national organization whose public sector members are largely conservative state legislators, has approved a Statement of Principles on Balancing Budgets Over the Business Cycle and Model Policy for a Next-Generation Tax and Expenditure Limitation, both based on structural balance spending rules.[22]

Arkansas Representative David Ray and Senator Ben Gilmore proposed legislation along these lines in 2021.[23] After years of frustration trying to approve various iterations of a population-and-inflation spending growth limit, legislators in diverse states are actively considering structural balance rules to balance their budgets over the medium term.

As noted, tax and expenditure limitations like TABOR are more than just spending growth limits, of course. They often require voter approval for borrowing or for tax increases. These add another layer of protection from political incentives that push for more expansive government activities than the public interest may require.

The U.S. government and many states have turned themselves around through better budget rules and institutions. The rest of the world has many such lessons, though we will limit it to two cases here.

Sweden: Beyond a Bloated Welfare State

Long envied by self-styled social democrats in the United States, Sweden is reputed to be a wealthy welfare state. Yet that reputation is outdated. Extensive social welfare commitments impose heavy tax burdens and increase debt fatigue when taxes cannot keep up. Reality caught up to Sweden in the forms of higher taxes, higher unemployment, and lower growth. The people demanded changes, and the government acted.

Sweden's debt-to-GDP ratio was a healthy 32 percent in 1991. It had been as high as 62 percent in 1985, up from just 12.5 percent in 1970. But by 1997, it was 88 percent, well into the zone of slowing economic growth and risking fiscal crisis. Following rounds of reforms, by 2019, it had dropped below 39 percent before slightly increasing in 2020 due to the pandemic, and then falling again in 2021 and 2022 to 37 percent.[24]

From 1990 to 1993, Sweden's growth rate in per capita GDP was well below average, with those four years seeing no growth or negative growth. Per capita GDP growth did not return to trend until the late 1990s.[25] We can resolve the debate about whether low growth drives debt buildup or vice versa by recognizing that causation runs both ways.

Swedish central government spending jumped from 34 percent of GDP in 1989 to 44.2 percent in 1993 before returning to a 31–34 percent band since 2001. This spending is still well above the early 1970s level of around 23 percent.[26] The spending jump of the early 1990s drove most of the debt spiral, and controlling spending reversed it.

Swedish revenue was relatively stable from 1987 to 2000, around 37 percent of GDP, except in 1991 and 1992, when it fell as low as 31 percent. For the last 20 years, it has floated around 33 percent with a modest downward trend, plus or minus a percentage point.[27]

Sweden's return to fiscal responsibility has dramatically reduced interest costs. In 1994, just as the turnaround began, 12.8 percent of central government spending went to interest payments. By 2019, interest expense was only 1.1 percent of spending.[28] As Fig. 3.4 shows, the decline in Sweden's debt burden has helped reduce the country's interest expenses by reducing the debt burden and securing lower average interest rates, exactly the opposite of the current U.S. experience.

The story behind those topline figures includes both policy reform and ongoing institutional changes. Sweden did not do everything all at once.

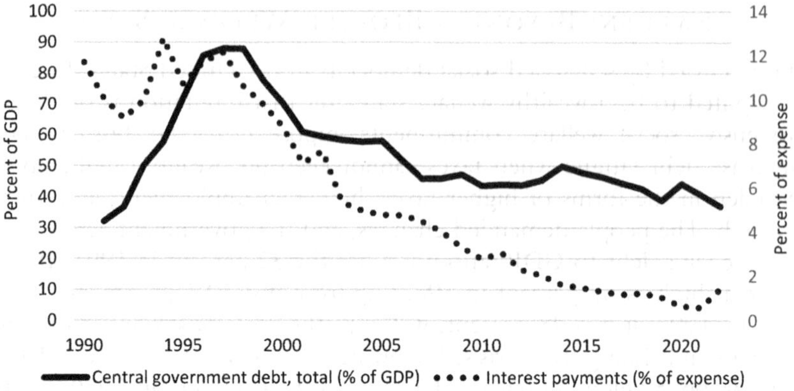

Fig. 3.4 A declining Swedish debt burden brought lower interest costs (*Source* World Bank)

Sweden's officials did what the politics of the day would allow. But policymakers kept coming back to fine-tune policies and processes. Sustained efforts over three decades have produced impressive results.

Sweden's macroeconomic goals of spending control and reducing the debt burden have been consistent since reform began in the mid-1990s, and the fiscal framework has evolved. Starting in 1993, the legislature set topline primary spending levels (excluding interest costs) for the current budget year and several additional years. In 1997, Sweden adopted a phased-in surplus target to ensure it would pay down the debt.

In 2000, Sweden enacted a balanced budget requirement for local governments. In 2007, it set up an independent fiscal policy council to monitor the government's compliance with fiscal rules. In 2016, Sweden adopted a debt anchor to target a debt-to-GDP ratio of 35 percent, plus or minus five percentage points. Collectively, these reforms provide "clear rules for the level of expenditures, the budget balance, and government debt and supervision."[29]

Swedish fiscal scholars Lars Jonung and Fredrik N. G. Andersson attribute the success of the Swedish framework to four factors: 1) leading politicians remember the debt buildup of the 1990s and the difficulty in reversing it, 2) the evolution toward flexibility has kept public support high, 3) financial markets have rewarded fiscal probity with lower interest rates, and 4) Swedes developed the framework through internal political processes instead of facing external imposition.[30]

As time passes, Sweden will not have leading politicians who remember the unpleasant lessons of debt buildup. Fortunately, it has created new institutions to promote better budgeting. Time will tell if those systemic upgrades are enough to keep new generations of Swedes from having to learn those lessons all over again.

Switzerland's Rules Have Been Exceptionally Successful

Commonly called the Swiss debt brake, Switzerland's budget targets get rave reviews from proponents of sound budgeting. Economist Daniel J. Mitchell may be America's #1 cheerleader for bringing it here.[31] As we will see, the combination of the Principles-based Balanced Budget Amendment and the Responsible Budget Targets Act resembles the main themes of the Swiss rules.

A January 2002 paper published by the International Monetary Fund described this innovative proposal to "maintain *structural* budget balance while allowing a variation of the actual balance with the business cycle,"[32] as Fig. 3.5 illustrates. It promotes saving (or reducing debt) with the above-trend revenue during the good years and drawing down reserves (or borrowing) during recessions and emergencies. Structural balance lets spending and revenue policies grow steadily with the economy, as the expenditure line indicates.

Switzerland's BBA and its implementing legislation came from necessity. In the 1990s, its central government's debt-to-GDP ratio was growing. It grew from only 12.3 percent in 1990 to 27.1 percent in 1998, fell from 1999 through 2001, then jumped to its all-time high of 29.7 percent in 2002.[34]

Compared to American red ink, even Switzerland's highest debt burden does not seem so high. Yet, the Swiss Confederation is more decentralized than the United States. In addition, revenue raising requires the electorate's approval through referenda, which bond buyers recognize as a constraint on fiscal consolidation. In other words, bond markets might get jumpy at lower debt levels in a small, highly decentralized country where raising revenue is difficult.

After years of deliberation and options development by the federal legislature, the federal council (the executive branch), the cantons (Swiss

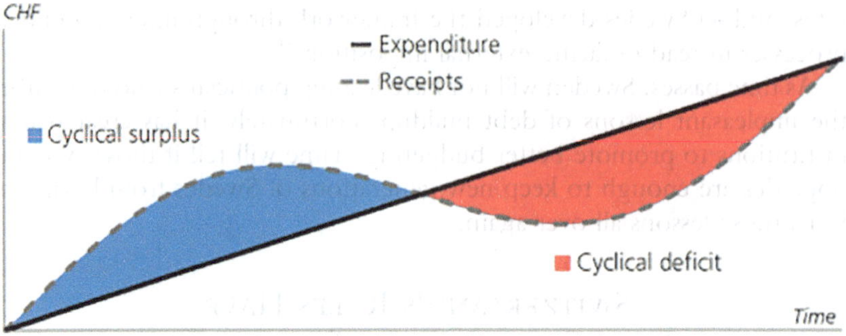

Fig. 3.5 Consistent path of expenditure and cyclically dependent receipts (*Source* Swiss Confederation[33])

versions of states), and the people,[35] the federal council referred a proposed constitutional amendment to the people. On December 2, 2001, nearly 85 percent of Swiss voters approved the language in box 3.1 to replace Article 126 of the Constitution.[36]

Box 3.1 Swiss constitutional provision for balanced budgets **Article 126: Financial management**

1 The Confederation shall maintain its income and expenditure in balance over time

2 The ceiling for total expenditure that is to be approved in the budget is based on the expected income after taking account of the economic situation

3 Exceptional financial requirements may justify an appropriate increase in the ceiling in terms of paragraph 2. The Federal Assembly shall decide on any increase in accordance with Article 159 paragraph 3 letter c

4 If the total expenditure in the federal accounts exceeds the ceiling in terms of paragraphs 2 or 3, compensation for this additional expenditure must be made in subsequent years

5 The details are regulated by law.

These principles provide few details, as Sec. 5 acknowledges. After several years of budgeting under the constitutional language alone, the Swiss Federal Assembly enacted a statute in October 2005 to fill in the details and mechanisms to bring the constitutional principles to life with clear rule-of-law standards.[37]

Budget experts have written warmly about the Swiss debt brake for years. For example, in the 2016 book *Can the Debt Growth Be Stopped?* academics Barry Poulson and John Merrifield sought to synthesize it and the Business Cycle BBA into a sophisticated proposal for a federal fiscal rule.[38] Also in 2016, Law Library of Congress expert and native German speaker Jenny Gesley wrote a brief report summarizing the constitutional and statutory provisions with complete translations of both in the appendix.[39]

The Swiss debt brake provides economic and policy stability in the near term while controlling the debt over the medium and long term. It does so by limiting most spending to what revenue would be if economic growth were on trend or at potential GDP, and it tracks deficits with the notional compensation account. It lets the assembly increase the spending limit for emergencies as well, and it must offset such spending in subsequent years depending on the size of the emergency spending. Another notional account, the amortization account, keeps stock of emergency balances. The Swiss Federal Audit Office tracks the two accounts and other budget metrics to ensure compliance.

The results have been remarkable. Switzerland's debt-to-GDP ratio began to turn around soon after. It ticked down from 29.7 percent in 2002 to 29.4 percent in 2005 and then dropped below 18 percent by 2022.[40] The Swiss debt burden continued to decline even during the 2008–2009 global financial crisis and fiscal troubles elsewhere in Europe. Like most other governments, Swiss debt increased in 2020 during the COVID-19 pandemic but only by a reasonable amount that did not trigger excessive inflation.[41] This prudence is especially noteworthy considering that higher-inflation countries surround Switzerland, and that the entire continent suffered an energy shock from Russia's 2022 invasion of Ukraine.

During a December 2020 meeting on Zoom between authors of contributions to an edited volume, a German fiscal expert even described Switzerland's debt-to-GDP ratio as falling too fast. It is difficult for Americans to imagine such a thing. His concern came from recognizing that a modest debt can have greater benefits than costs. A relatively low level of debt provides a safe medium of exchange to promote liquidity in domestic and international financial markets, including converting currencies on the financial side of goods and services trade. A low supply of a high-demand debt instrument also implies low interest rates.

In addition to the debt brake, Switzerland's debt decline was partly due to the reasonable idea that agencies can return funds to the treasury if the funds do not have good uses. If the Swiss legislature gives an agency more funds than it can productively use for its missions and activities, it does not have to spend all of it. Many U.S. states do likewise, but not the federal government. In addition, Switzerland's revenue forecasts have been consistently lower than actual revenue. They have since adjusted for both factors and expect the debt to shrink more slowly and stabilize.[42]

Yet Switzerland's political culture differs from America's. At an April 2018 Heritage Foundation discussion on budget rules with Jan-Egbert Sturm, Chairman of the Swiss Debt Brake Group of Experts, an attendee asked what automatic enforcement measures Switzerland has in place to ensure the budget hits the targets. He paused for a moment and then said they do not have automatic enforcement. The government follows the rules because the people expect them to.[43]

Switzerland's deficit reduction (fiscal consolidation) came primarily from spending restraint. Swiss federal government spending fell from 19.5 percent of GDP in 2002 to 16.7 percent in 2022.[44] Revenue increased from 9 percent of GDP in 2002 to as high as 10.1 percent in 2021 but returned to 9.1 percent in 2022.[45] This fiscal responsibility, combined with a welcoming business climate, has made this small, landlocked country with few natural resources one of the most prosperous countries in Europe and the world.

Switzerland's successful fiscal institutions include a principles-based constitutional balanced budget rule and a statutory component. The constitutional provision had nearly 85 percent support when the people adopted it, and it continues to have strong public support. The statutory complement fills in the details so Swiss legislators have clear instructions for turning the constitutional principles into governance guidelines through the annual budget.

The Swiss budget rules codified a commitment to reduce the debt burden after a period of substantial accumulation. They have subsequently tilted budget debates toward those favoring sustainable levels of central government debt and away from those less committed to that goal. The key has been to maintain momentum for sound budgeting for the long term while providing fiscal flexibility and policy stability in the short term.

The European Union's Framework for Responsible Budgeting

European Union countries are expected to practice prudent budgeting. Initially, they were supposed to keep their debt-to-GDP ratios below 60 percent and deficits below 3 percent of GDP. Breaches of those thresholds trigger reporting, expectations of corrective measures, requirements for plans, and eventually fines if a country does not make progress toward meeting its commitments. More recently, targets have shifted to include more complicated, medium-term balance goals that vary with countries' situations.[46]

These EU rules are in addition to national-level rules. Other than Greece and Spain, every EU country has a national balanced budget rule, and many also have national spending limits, revenue floors, debt limits, or combinations thereof. Non-EU members Iceland, Norway, Switzerland, and the UK require budget balance, some with additional requirements.[47] Not all EU countries are fully compliant, but observers seem to think that additional oversight has improved outcomes.

America is failing the EU test for sound budget outcomes. The United States government has a debt-to-GDP ratio of around 100 percent and a FY2024 deficit exceeding 6 percent of GDP, and both are set to grow. A fiscal turnaround that includes well-written constitutional and statutory rules could help America change course, however. In fact, the EU's new medium-term, cyclically adjusted framework fits the proposals outlined here.

**

Many governments have gotten themselves into debt trouble. Many have gotten themselves back out. It may not be easy, but it is possible. In addition to the countries discussed above, Argentina, Canada, New Zealand, Ireland, Germany, Denmark, Chile, Finland, and others can inspire hope that America—and other countries struggling with debt—can turn things around.[48] Contra the special interest doom narrative, governments that get their fiscal houses in order tend to benefit politically.[49]

Adopting and holding to well-designed budget targets and debt controls in both constitutions and statutes has often been a common element in fiscal turnarounds. That does not mean that the specific rules and institutions that worked in nineteenth-century U.S. states or in other countries can be grafted directly onto the United States federal government.

It is easy for Americans to overlook the importance of professional, independent fiscal councils to monitor budget information and to report compliance with rules. The U.S. Treasury, other executive branch agencies, the Government Accountability Office, the Congressional Budget Office, and the Joint Committee on Taxation produce vast amounts of high-quality data and regular reports on the government's fiscal outlook.

The United States has excellent information. Now it needs good rules and better incentives.

We can learn from other countries' experiences. Their solutions can inspire us. Yet the design of a better fiscal constitution for the U.S. federal government must reflect America's contemporary policy, process, and, most of all, political needs in the third decade of the twenty-first century.

Notes

1. Alexander Hamilton, "Report Relative to a Provision for the Support of Public Credit," Treasury Department, https://founders.archives.gov/documents/Hamilton/01-06-02-0076-0002-0001, January 9, 1790.
2. "U.S. Declaration of Independence," https://www.archives.gov/founding-docs/declaration-transcript, July 4, 1776.
3. Office of the Historian, "U.S. Debt and Foreign Loans, 1775–1795," U.S. Department of State, https://history.state.gov/milestones/1784-1800/loans, accessed February 18, 2023.
4. Samuel H. Williamson "Annual Inflation Rates in the United States, 1775 - 2022, and United Kingdom, 1265 - 2022," MeasuringWorth, https://www.measuringworth.com/calculators/inflation/index.php, accessed February 18, 2023.
5. United States Constitution, https://www.senate.gov/about/origins-foundations/senate-and-constitution/constitution.htm.
6. U.S. Congress, "An Act making provision for the [payment of the] debt of the United States," 1 Stat. 138, August 4, 1790.
7. U.S. Congress, "An Act for establishing the temporary and permanent seat of the Government of the United States," 1 Stat. 130, July 6, 1790.

8. Congressional Budget Office, "Historical Data on Federal Debt Held by the Public," https://www.cbo.gov/sites/default/files/111th-congress-2009-2010/reports/2010_08_05_federaldebt.pdf, July 2010.
9. John Joseph Wallis, Richard E. Sylla, and Arthur Grinath III, "Land, Debt, and Taxes: Origins of the U.S. State Default Crisis, 1839 to 1842," Atlanta Federal Reserve Bank, https://www.atlantafed.org/-/media/documents/news/conferences/2011/sovereign-debt/papers/Wallis.pdf, September 2006.
10. Jeremy Horpedahl, "U.S. State Debt Defaults and Constitutional Reform in Historical Perspective," in *New Perspectives on State Fiscal Challenges*, eds. Barry Poulson and John Merrifield, Lexington, 2023.
11. William Ruger and Jason Sorens, "Freedom in the 50 States," https://www.freedominthe50states.org/.
12. Senate Judiciary Committee, "Balanced-Budget Constitutional Amendment," Senate Report 104–5, https://www.congress.gov/104/crpt/srpt5/CRPT-104srpt5.pdf, January 24, 1995.
13. Sharon N. Kioko and Michelle L. Lofton, "Balanced Budget Requirements Revisited," *Public Finance Review*, *49*(5), 635–672, https://doi.org/10.1177/10911421211054977, December 1, 2021.
14. Jonathan Williams and Nicholas Stark, "Colorado Offers Gold Standard for Fiscal Restraint: ALEC in *National Review*," https://alec.org/article/colorado-offers-gold-standard-for-fiscal-restraint-alec-in-national-review/, November 3, 2022.
15. Article X, Sec. 20, Constitution of Colorado.
16. Ballotpedia, "States with initiative or referendum," https://ballotpedia.org/States_with_initiative_or_referendum, accessed February 1, 2025.
17. Ballotpedia, "List of Colorado ballot measures,"https://ballotpedia.org/List_of_Colorado_ballot_measures, accessed February 1, 2025.
18. Colorado General Assembly, "Explore the Colorado State Budget," https://leg.colorado.gov/explorebudget/, accessed February 4, 2023.
19. Washington State Economic and Revenue Forecast Council, "Fiscal Growth Factors," https://erfc.wa.gov/fiscal-growth-factors, accessed February 4, 2023.

20. Motion to discharge House Bill 71, the Taxpayer Protection Act, Pennsylvania General Assembly, https://www.legis.state.pa.us/cfdocs/billinfo/bill_votes.cfm?syear=2021&sind=0&body=H&type=B&bn=71, June 21, 2022.
21. Kurt Couchman, "Structural Balance Can Help States Unleash Freedom and Reclaim Sovereignty," Americans for Prosperity, https://americansforprosperity.org/new-afp-report-structural-balance-can-help-states-unleash-freedom-and-reclaim-sovereignty/, February 7, 2023.
22. American Legislative Exchange Council, "Statement of Principles on Balancing Budgets Over the Business Cycle," https://alec.org/model-policy/statement-of-principles-on-balancing-budgets-over-the-business-cycle/, introduced December 3, 2021, finalized December 16, 2021. American Legislative Exchange Council, "A Next-Generation Tax and Expenditure Limitation Act," https://alec.org/model-policy/a-next-generation-tax-and-expenditure-limitation-act/, introduced November 30, 2022, finalized December 23, 2022.
23. Rep. David Ray, "HB1902: To Limit The Increase In General Revenue Expenditures From Year To Year; And To Create A Nexus Between The Amount Of General Revenue Expenditures And The Growth Of The State Disposable Personal Income," https://www.arkleg.state.ar.us/Bills/Detail?id=HB1902&ddBienniumSession=2021, introduced April 12, 2021.
24. World Bank, "Central government debt, total (percent of GDP)—Sweden," https://data.worldbank.org/indicator/GC.DOD.TOTL.GD.ZS?locations=SE, accessed October 12, 2024.
25. World Bank, GDP per capita growth (annual percent)—Sweden, https://data.worldbank.org/indicator/NY.GDP.PCAP.KD.ZG?locations=SE, accessed February 1, 2025. World Bank, "GDP per capita (constant 2015 US$) - Sweden," https://data.worldbank.org/indicator/NY.GDP.PCAP.KD?locations=SE, accessed February 1, 2025.
26. World Bank, "Expense (percent of GDP)—Sweden," https://data.worldbank.org/indicator/GC.XPN.TOTL.GD.ZS?locations=SE, accessed February 1, 2025.

27. World Bank, "Revenue, excluding grants (percent of GDP)—Sweden," https://data.worldbank.org/indicator/GC.REV.XGRT.GD.ZS?locations=SE, accessed February 1, 2025.
28. World Bank, "Interest payments (percent of expense)—Sweden," https://data.worldbank.org/indicator/GC.XPN.INTP.ZS?locations=SE, accessed February 1, 2025.
29. Fredrik N. G. Andersson Lars Jonung, "Preparing for the Next Crisis: Lessons from the Successful Swedish Fiscal Framework," in *Public Debt Sustainability: International Perspectives*, eds. Barry W. Poulson, John Merrifield, and Steve H. Hanke, Lexington, 2022, pp. 69–100.
30. Ibid.
31. Dan Mitchell, "The Continuing Success of Switzerland's Spending Cap," International Liberty, https://danieljmitchell.wordpress.com/2018/06/26/the-continuing-success-of-switzerlands-spending-cap/, June 26, 2018. Dan Mitchell, "Visualizing the Difference Between Switzerland and Europe's Welfare States," International Liberty, https://danieljmitchell.wordpress.com/2022/08/28/visualizing-the-difference-between-switzerland-and-europes-welfare-states/, August 28, 2022.
32. Stephan Danninger, "A New Rule: 'The Swiss Debt Brake,'" https://www.imf.org/external/pubs/ft/wp/2002/wp0218.pdf, IMF Working Paper, January 2002.
33. Swiss Federal Department of Finance, "The debt brake," https://www.efd.admin.ch/efd/en/home/fiscal-policy/the-debt-brake.html, accessed February 5, 2023.
34. The World Bank, "Central government debt, total (percent of GDP)—Switzerland," https://data.worldbank.org/indicator/GC.DOD.TOTL.GD.ZS?locations=CH, accessed January 22, 2023. Some commentators rely on the total government debt of Switzerland, that is, adding the central government debt to that of the cantons. Yet the Swiss Confederation's highly decentralized model with substantial fiscal autonomy for the cantons suggests that combining them would be an analytical error when considering the political economy of fiscal reform at the central government level.
35. Schweizerischen Bundesrat, "Botshaft zur Schuldenbremse," https://swissvotes.ch/attachments/bf389de6579d1c11eae169e67484624628ea550652318a0a362c3e741db70dfc, July 5, 2000.

36. Bundesratsbeschluss über das Ergebnis der Volksabstimmung vom 2. Dezember 2001, https://www.fedlex.admin.ch/eli/fga/2002/150/de, February 4, 2002. Technically, the German, French, and Italian versions of that language.
37. Die Bundesversammlung der Schweizerischen Eidgenossenschaft, "Bundesgesetz uber den eidgenossischen Finanzhaushalt," https://fedlex.data.admin.ch/filestore/fedlex.data.admin.ch/eli/cc/2006/227/20220101/de/pdf-a/fedlex-data-admin-ch-eli-cc-2006-227-20220101-de-pdf-a.pdf, October 7, 2005, as of January 1, 2022.
38. John D. Merrifield and Barry W. Poulson, *Can the Debt Growth Be Stopped? Rules-Based Policy Options for Addressing the Federal Fiscal Crisis*, Lexington, 2016.
39. Jenny Gesley, "Switzerland: Implementation of Article 126 of the Swiss Constitution—The 'Debt Brake,'" Law Library of Congress, https://tile.loc.gov/storage-services/service/ll/llglrd/2016591729/2016591729.pdf, June 2016.
40. The World Bank, "Central government debt, total (percent of GDP)—Switzerland," https://data.worldbank.org/indicator/GC.DOD.TOTL.GD.ZS?locations=CH, accessed February 1, 2025.
41. Bastian Benrath, "Swiss Inflation Slows to 2.8 percent Before Likely Jump in January," https://www.bloomberg.com/news/articles/2023-01-04/swiss-inflation-slows-to-2-8-before-likely-jump-in-january, January 4, 2023.
42. Swiss Confederation, "The debt brake," https://www.efd.admin.ch/efd/en/home/fiscal-policy/the-debt-brake.html, accessed February 4, 2023.
43. Heritage Foundation, "Hitting the Brakes on Overspending and Debt," https://www.heritage.org/debt/event/hitting-the-brakes-overspending-and-debt, April 4, 2018.
44. The World Bank, "Expense (Percent of GDP) - Switzerland," https://data.worldbank.org/indicator/GC.XPN.TOTL.GD.ZS?locations=CH, accessed February 1, 2025.
45. The World Bank, "Tax Revenue (Percent of GDP)—Switzerland," https://data.worldbank.org/indicator/GC.TAX.TOTL.GD.ZS?locations=CH, accessed February 1, 2025.
46. European Council, "Excessive deficit procedure," https://www.consilium.europa.eu/en/policies/excessive-deficit-procedure/, accessed October 12, 2024.

47. International Monetary Fund, "Fiscal Rules Dataset: 1985–2021," https://www.imf.org/external/datamapper/fiscalrules/matrix/matrix.htm, January 2022, accessed October 12, 2024.
48. Committee for a Responsible Federal Budget, "Fiscal Turnarounds: International Success Stories," https://www.crfb.org/papers/fiscal-turnarounds-international-success-stories, February 22, 2010.
49. Falli Falilou, Debra Blochi, Jean-Marc Fournieri, and Peter Hoelleri, "Prudent debt targets and fiscal frameworks," OECD Economic Policy Papers, No. 15, OECD Publishing, Paris, https://doi.org/10.1787/5jrxtjmmt9f7-en, July 3, 2015, pp. 49–50.

CHAPTER 4

The Rise of the Balanced Budget Amendment

America's founders worried about government debt. James Madison called it a "public curse." Thomas Jefferson had seen debt troubles in Europe, and he worried about it in the new United States. In fact, his wish for an amendment to prohibit federal debt reflected his sense of extravagant spending during John Adams' presidency.

The founders' antipathy toward excessive debt was no philosophical abstraction. That generation had witnessed crippling government debts in England and France that sometimes consumed more than half of those countries' revenues, imposed heavy burdens on the people, and incited unrest.

Peacetime Debt Reduction Held Firm for 150 Years

Fortunately, the U.S. federal government did not need a constitutional constraint on borrowing for a long time (see Fig. 4.1). The Constitution granted few and defined powers to the federal government, and elected officials held close to them for a while.

Congress and presidents also followed the norm of prudence. They reduced the debt burden except during emergencies—mostly wars—or when exceptional opportunities arose, like the Louisiana Purchase. Reducing debt burdens during normal times expanded their ability to

K. Couchman, *Fiscal Democracy in America*,
https://doi.org/10.1007/978-3-031-91938-1_4

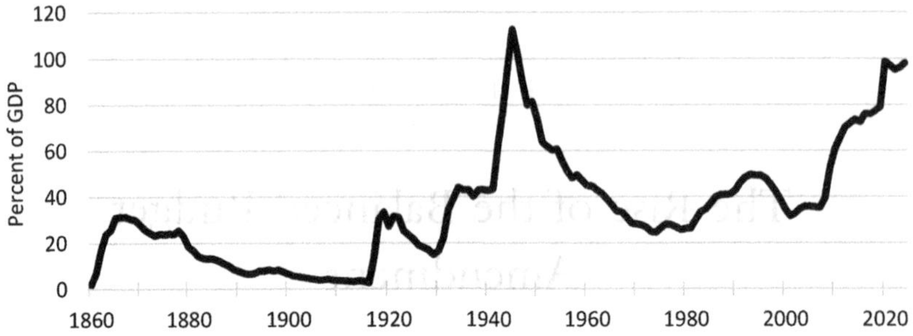

Fig. 4.1 Federal debt used to fall after emergencies (*Source* CBO)

borrow during extraordinary periods. Sound finances are an asset during crises.

Even the Civil War followed this pattern. The federal debt-to-GDP ratio escalated to save the Union and recover. The debt burden peaked at 31.4 percent in 1866 and 1867 before gradually falling to 2.7 percent in 1916.

It took off again as the federal government's size and scope grew. That growth came as President Woodrow Wilson's (1913–1921) progressive concepts of government and new economic ideas spread, especially under the shadow of the triple disasters of the Great War, the Great Depression, and the Second World War. As Fig. 4.1 shows, from the end of 1916 to the end of 1919, the debt jumped from 2.7 to 33.4 percent of GDP. It was 16.5 percent of the economy at the end of 1930, 43.3 percent at the end of 1941, and 102.6 percent at the end of 1946.

Between the First World War and the Great Depression, President Calvin Coolidge (1921–1929) worked with Congress to control the debt. He said, "there is no dignity quite so impressive and no independence quite so important, as living within our means."[1] The debt burden fell by half.

The 1920s brought peace, prosperity, and declining debt in the United States. That ended with the stock market crash of 1929, which began in early September, reached extreme levels in late October, and resolved in November. Federal Reserve, congressional, and President Herbert Hoover's (1929–1933) mismanagement turned a bursting bubble into the Great Depression, which President Franklin Delano Roosevelt (1933–1945) and congressional allies made even worse.[2] The economic downturn and the federal response led to an unprecedented peacetime debt-to-GDP increase of 27 percentage points from 1930 to 1941.

On May 8, 1935, U.S. Senator Millard Tydings (D-MD) introduced Senate Joint Resolution 123 (see Exhibit 1 in the Appendix) to reassert the norm of balanced budgets.[3] S.J.Res.123 would have required the president to submit a detailed budget request to Congress, barred Congress from enacting other legislation before the budget bill, prohibited net spending increases unless offset by new revenue, and provided an exemption during times of war. It was not a proposal for a constitutional amendment, but it had similar goals.

During the same term of Congress, U.S. Representative Harold Knutson (R-MN) introduced the first proposal for a balanced budget amendment to the Constitution on May 4, 1936, as House Joint Resolution 579 (see Appendix, Exhibit 2).[4] H.J.Res.579 proposed that "The public debt of the United States shall be limited in peacetime on a basis of population in each decennial census to twenty billions of dollars on a basis of the census of 1930." After hitting that per capita cap, additional spending would have to be covered in full by new revenue.[5]

This proto-BBA proposal reflected angst about President Roosevelt's New Deal borrowing binge. It probably would have been too stringent to last, however. From the end of 1929 to the end of 1935, the federal debt burden had jumped from 14.9 to 42.9 percent of GDP. With a 1930 population of 123.2 million, the limit would have been $162 per person. By the end of 1936, however, the debt burden was already $264 per capita and would keep rising in nominal terms all the way to nearly $82,000 at the end of FY 2024.[6]

In a House with 332 Democrats and allied minor parties and only 103 Republicans,[7] however, Rep. Knutson's resolution got neither a hearing nor a vote. With the Great Depression still in full swing, congressional leaders had other priorities. As Table 4.1 shows, however, Knutson's BBA was the first in a series of milestones.

The Senate hit the next milestone: a committee hearing. Senators Harry Byrd (D-VA) and Styles Bridges (R-NH) introduced S.J.Res.126 on January 25, 1956 (Appendix, Exhibit 3). They had proposed a similar resolution on July 13, 1954, but it came too late in the 83rd Congress to make progress. They had been developing and making the case for a BBA for a decade.

A proponent of the Byrd-Bridges BBA summarized it[8]:

Table 4.1 Milestones for BBA proposals

Year	*Joint Res. #*	*Sponsor(s)*	*Hearing(s)*	*Markup*	*House Vote*	*Senate Vote*
1936	H.J.Res.579	Knutson	n/a			
1956	S.J.Res.126 S.J.Res.133	Byrd/ Bridges Curtis	June 1956			
1981	S.J.Res.58	Thurmond	April 1981	May 1981		69–31 (8/4/ 1982)
1982	H.J.Res.350	Jenkins/ Conable	May/Aug 1982		236–187 (10/1/ 1982)	
1995	S.J.Res.1	Dole	Jan. 1995	15–3 (Jan. 1995)		
1995	H.J.Res.1	Barton	Jan. 1995	20–13-1 (Jan. 1995)	300–132 (1/26/ 1995)	66–34 (3/2/ 1995)
2011	H.J.Res.2	Goodlatte	n/a	n/a	261–165 (11/18/ 2011)	
2011	S.J.Res.10	Hatch	n/a	n/a		47–53 (12/14/ 2011)
2011	S.J.Res.24	Udall	n/a	n/a		21–79 (12/14/ 2011)

Source Library of Congress

The President is required to transmit to Congress on or before the fifteenth day after the beginning of each regular session a balanced budget for the ensuing fiscal year under the laws then existing. If Congress authorizes expenditures to be made in excess of the President's estimated receipts, Congress is forbidden to adjourn for more than three days at a time until action has been taken necessary to balance the budget for such ensuing fiscal year. In case of war or other grave national emergency, if the President shall so recommend, the Congress by a vote of three fourths of all the members of each House may suspend the foregoing provisions for balancing the budget for periods, either successive or otherwise, not exceeding one year each.

The Senate had a narrow Democratic majority, and Republican Dwight Eisenhower (1953–1961) was president.[9] The Subcommittee on Constitutional Amendments of the Senate Committee on the Judiciary held a hearing on June 14, 1956, on S.J.Res.126 and on S.J.Res.133 by Sen. Carl T. Curtis (R-NE), a related proposal.[10]

Sen. Bridges made the case. He stated in part:

> I am not one, Mr. Chairman, who feels that a balanced budget is a matter of merely bookkeeping figures. To me it represents the integrity of the dollar and the responsibility of our Government toward our citizens in the protection of the purchasing power of their dollars, the value of their investments and securities and the value of our social-security program.

He observed that "we are going to have to meet cold war economic competition and we certainly cannot do so unless we put our financial house in order first."

A Treasury Department statement supported "bringing expenditures and revenues into balance and reducing the public debt." The Department, however, recommended "against the relatively inflexible methods" of the proposed amendments. The Byrd-Bridges and Curtis BBAs did not get a vote.

The following year, 1957, the Indiana General Assembly made the first application to Congress for an amendment convention for a balanced budget provision in the Constitution. In addition to proposing the language of the Byrd-Bridges resolution, the application proposed a time and place for the convention as well as procedural expectations and requirements.[11]

During this early groundswell for a BBA, the pattern of peacetime reductions in the debt burden repeated. The debt-to-GDP ratio fell to 24.6 percent by 1974. But then it stopped.

Several factors prevented further debt reductions. Spending for federal transfer programs was growing. Cold War competition between Marxist totalitarianism and market democracies was in full force. The oil supply crises of the 1970s shocked the system. Congress had a new budget process that bifurcated the management of annually appropriated spending from the rest of the budget. It also required the president and the agencies to spend virtually all funds that Congress had appropriated.

The end of debt reduction coincided with an inflation-driven tax revolt in many states. That is when BBAs began to get serious traction.

State Legislatures Dance with Congress

Every state but Vermont has a balanced budget requirement. They vary—constitutional, statutory, or both—requiring balance for a governor's proposed budget, for the enacted budget, for the executed budget (at the end of the fiscal year or biennium), or at multiple points; they also vary on the scope of coverage: the operating budget, the general fund, or everything. Some limit debt, with exceptions, while others tie spending to revenue directly, or both, or they limit spending or revenue growth to economic or income growth.

Bond markets have helped keep states in line as well. Poor management leads to bond buyers requiring risk premiums that drive up interest costs. State legislators are used to keeping government spending close to available revenue. Many believe the federal government should do likewise.

The Article V Library has compiled all state applications for an amendment convention.[12] For BBAs, Indiana's legislature went first in 1957. Wyoming was second in 1961. In 1963, Idaho proposed limiting federal debt to $350 billion with exceptions for emergencies and at least $3 billion per year in debt principal retirement.

Applications for amendment conventions to consider balanced budget and debt limit rules intensified in the 1970s.

- 1973: Virginia
- 1975: Virginia, Alabama, Louisiana, Mississippi, Arkansas
- 1976: Pennsylvania, Nebraska, Florida, Alabama, Oklahoma, Georgia, Indiana, Virginia, South Carolina, Delaware
- 1977: Oregon, Texas, Maryland, Tennessee
- 1978: South Carolina, Colorado, Kansas, Wyoming, Tennessee
- 1979: Indiana, Arizona (twice), Utah, Arkansas, Idaho, South Dakota, North Carolina, North Dakota, New Mexico, Nevada, Mississippi, Louisiana (twice), Iowa, New Hampshire
- 1980: Nevada
- 1982: Alaska
- 1983: Missouri

In all, state legislatures have applied 85 times for an amendment convention for a BBA and another four times for a limit on federal debt. A debt limit component has been part of 21 of the 85 BBA applications. Several states made multiple applications, and some have since rescinded all or some such applications.

In addition, state legislatures have sought other amendments to reduce federal power. Barring the federal government from coercively leveraging federal funds inspired eight applications. Convention applications have addressed revenue sharing nineteen times, tax limitations nearly sixty times, and a presidential line-item veto four times.

Petitions specific to a BBA have not yet met the threshold of two-thirds of state legislatures. Some claim, however, that Congress can and must add active plenary convention calls—applications calling for an amendment convention without specifying the subject or subjects in the operative language—to petitions for a BBA or another fiscal responsibility amendment. If so, they say that states met the threshold in 1979 and that Congress has refused its duty to call a convention.[13]

Others argue that Congress cannot aggregate plenary applications with the balanced budget or debt limit applications. They observe that legislative history and the non-binding "whereas" clauses of these unbounded applications show that they were sought for other purposes, even if the operative clauses were ambiguous.[14] We will return to this topic.

Meanwhile and not coincidentally, in the 1970s and 1980s, members of Congress were busy with BBAs and related statutory proposals. This was the middle of a long period of Democratic control of the U.S. House of Representatives that began in 1955 and ended in 1995.[15]

In the 93rd Congress (1973–1975), members of both parties introduced 25 balanced budget or spending limit constitutional amendment proposals. None got a vote or a hearing, and the most popular version—H.J.Res.1064 by Rep. Floyd Spence (R-SC)—had only 23 cosponsors (Appendix, Exhibit 4).[16] Most BBA proposals during this period had similar features with mostly cosmetic variations.

Most BBA activity that term happened before Congress enacted the Congressional Budget and Impoundment Control Act on July 12, 1974. The Act established the Congressional Budget Office, the House and Senate Budget Committees, and a new system of congressional budgeting intended to manage appropriations and, separately, direct spending and revenue according to a comprehensive annual plan laid out in a concurrent resolution on the budget.[17] Concurrent resolutions require the agreement of the House and the Senate but are not presented to the president, so they do not become law.

Partly a reaction to President Richard Nixon's attempted refusal to spend up to one-third of appropriated funds,[18] the 1974 Act also took the wind out of congressional BBA proponents' sails. The 94th Congress (1975–1977) saw BBA proposals in Congress fall to eight, perhaps in the hope that a newly empowered Congress would finally have the statutory tools to eliminate deficits and control the debt. If only.

The 95th Congress (1977–1979) saw 40 balanced budget or spending limit amendment proposals, though none exceeded 24 cosponsors. These proposals reflected the same angst about persistent federal deficits that drove state legislators to apply for an amendment convention and the prospect of states taking matters into their own hands.

The National Taxpayers Union was a major driving force for BBAs in both the states and Congress.[19] NTU lobbied and organized state legislators, providing support for proponents and countering arguments offered by opponents. A 1979 article in *The New York Times* notes that "NTU began coordinating the effort" at a 1975 organization meeting in Kansas City, Missouri.[20]

> A model resolution was written and sponsors were sought in the legislatures. After the first four states in 1975, eight states passed resolutions in 1976, five in 1977, five in 1978 and eight so far this year, making a total of 30, or four short of two-thirds.

Organizations that provide intellectual, coordinating, and political support are vital to advancing sound public policy. We will return to the practical business of non-governmental organizations supporting principled policymakers in Chapter 11.

In 1978 and 1979, the National Tax Limitation Committee convened an eminent collection of scholars for a "Federal Amendment Drafting Committee." Members included Milton Friedman, James Buchanan, Paul McCracken, Bill Niskanen, Lew Uhler, Craig Stubblebine, Walter Williams, Robert Bork, Robert Nisbet, and Robert Carleson. They published their proposal (Appendix, Exhibit 5) on January 30, 1979.[21] Their complex proposal addressed multiple issues, including deficits, debt, inflation, and unfunded mandates.[22]

The first-introduced BBA of the 96th Congress (1979–1980) had 53 original cosponsors—cosponsors at the time of introduction—in the House: 42 Republicans and 11 Democrats.[23] Another had 43 cosponsors. A third had 121 cosponsors: 97 Republicans and 24 Democrats.[24] All in all, members of the 96th Congress introduced a whopping 100 BBA or related proposals.

In the 1980 elections, Ronald Reagan trounced Jimmy Carter with an electoral college vote of 489–49 and a popular vote of 50.8% to 41.0%. Republicans flipped 12 Senate seats. Senate Democrats' 59–41 majority in the 96th Congress turned into a 53–47 Republican majority. Democratic control of the House dropped from 278–157 to 243–192.

Finally, BBAs would get floor votes. Even though presidents have no formal role in proposing constitutional amendments to the states, President Reagan harnessed public angst about deficits, inflation, and economic malaise from the Jimmy Carter years to advocate for a BBA. He enthusiastically encouraged state legislatures to call for an amendment convention while pushing Congress to act.

The Senate moved first with S.J.Res.58 (Appendix, Exhibit 6), one of 14 BBAs proposed in the Senate. Sen. Strom Thurmond (R-SC) introduced the resolution—his third BBA proposal during that Congress—on March 27, 1981. Following hearings in April 1981, a Judiciary Committee markup in May 1981, and a robust floor amendment process in July and August 1982, the Senate passed the resolution by a vote of 69–31 on August 4, 1982.[25] Having cleared the two-thirds threshold for a constitutional amendment, a chamber of Congress had voted on and approved a BBA for the first time.

Turning to the House, H.J.Res.350 (Appendix, Exhibit 7) by Rep. Edgar Jenkins (D-GA) and Rep. Barber Conable (R-NY) was one of 70 BBA proposals. It became the consensus version with 231 cosponsors. Democratic leaders did not schedule it for a floor vote, so members forced the vote through a discharge petition, a special process in the U.S. House in which a majority of members sign a petition to bring a measure out of the committees of jurisdiction for a floor vote. Discharge petitions are rare and only occur when House leaders refuse to let a piece of legislation come to the floor. Its hand forced, the House Judiciary Committee held 14 days of hearings in May and August before ordering the resolution reported.

The floor debate showed the pressure Congress felt from the states. Rep. Del Latta (R-OH) said, "Thirty-one states have now petitioned for a constitutional convention. Only three more need to petition. Then we are going to have a convention, and the door will be open. The door will be open to all sorts of amendments to that Constitution." Several other speakers echoed that observation.[26] Members of Congress generally prefer to avoid having decisions that affect them taken out of their hands.

On October 1, 1982, the BBA failed to obtain two-thirds support.[27] After several hours of debate and several procedural motions, the House voted 236–187 with just 55.8% supporting.

Democrats picked up House seats in the 1982 election and would hold a comfortable margin of control through 1994. BBA proposals (Appendix, Exhibit 8) by Rep. Charlie Stenholm (D-TX) in the 100th (1987–1988), 101st (1989–1990), 102nd (1991–1992), and 103rd (1993–1994) Congresses attracted 239, 252, 278, and 264 cosponsors, respectively. His proposals got House votes but always fell 10–15 votes short of two-thirds.[28]

After four more years of a Republican-led Senate, Democrats had the majority until 1995. Senators continued to consider BBAs in markups, hearings, and floor votes. Sen. Strom Thurmond's (R-SC) S.J.Res.225 (Appendix, Exhibit 9) narrowly failed on a 66–34 vote in 1986,[29] as did Sen. Paul Simon's (D-IL) S.J.Res.41 (Appendix, Exhibit 10) in March 1994 with a 63–37 vote.[30]

Congress had not proposed a BBA to the states, but it was not deaf to the American people's demand for responsible budgeting. Congress had enacted statutory deficit targets with sequestration enforcement—automatic across-the-board spending cuts—in the Balanced Budget and Emergency Deficit Control Act of 1985.

But BBEDCA 1985 had a constitutional problem. Congress directed the Comptroller General, the head of the U.S. Government Accountability Office (then the U.S. General Accounting Office), a legislative branch agency, to carry out the sequester. The Supreme Court struck down the enforcement in *Bowsher v. Synar*, ruling that legislative branch entities cannot perform executive branch functions.[31] Congress then enacted the Balanced Budget and Emergency Deficit Control Reaffirmation Act in 1987, directing the Office of Management and Budget in the Executive Office of the President to carry out the sequester.

Like the Congressional Budget and Impoundment Control Act of 1974, BBEDCA in 1985 and BBEDCRA in 1987 undermined the push for a BBA.

Lacking a constitutional mandate, however, Congress kept missing its statutory deficit caps and loosening them with new statutes. They tried a different approach in the Budget Enforcement Act of 1990. The BEA replaced BBEDCA's deficit caps with caps on appropriated spending and added the Statutory Pay-As-You-Go Act to control deficit increases from changes to revenue and direct spending policies. Each included enforcement through sequester mechanisms.

These approaches likely helped in the short term, but they had design flaws and were bound to unravel sooner or later.[32] Still, they and the BBAs reflected the same impulse: a Cold War Congress where a generation of members had faced the voters as the federal government grappled with deficits and debt that many Americans connected to elevated inflation levels.

During this period, BBA proponent Senator Orrin Hatch (R-UT) offered the Constitutional Convention Implementation Act seven times, first in 1979 and last in 1991.[33] It sought to clarify procedures by which states could apply for and rescind applications for a constitutional convention, how states could ratify and rescind ratifications, how Congress would aggregate applications by subject matter, basic rules of conventions, and more.

Though well intended, many provisions likely would have exceeded Congress' proper authorities for an amendment convention and intruded on the powers of state legislatures or the commissioners serving in a convention. The Senate Judiciary Committee marked up and reported the bill in 1984 and 1985, but the full Senate never voted on it. Some senators may have feared that greater clarity would encourage more states to apply for a convention and would, therefore, increase the chance that one would happen.

Looking back, state applications for a Convention of States for a BBA crested in the early 1980s. States began to rescind their petitions under intense lobbying by the John Birch Society on the right and a constellation of organizations on the left.

The 1994 Republican Revolution Revives the BBA

The BBA was down but not out. Republicans' stunning victories in the 1994 mid-term elections brought new energy. Republicans picked up 54 House seats, turning a 258–176 Democratic majority into a 230–204 Republican majority. In the Senate, 9 Republican pickups turned the advantage from 57–43 Democrat to 52–48 Republican.

The final stage of the Republicans' 1994 campaign push included a Contract with America.[34] House Republican leaders Newt Gingrich and

Dick Armey wrote it, building on themes from President Reagan's 1985 State of the Union address. The Contract called for a BBA:

> A balanced budget/tax limitation amendment and a legislative line-item veto to restore fiscal responsibility to an out-of-control Congress, requiring them to live under the same budget constraints as families and businesses.

With an electoral mandate and a bold vision, Republican leaders were ready to move. Immediately at the start of the new Congress in 1995, Rep. Joe Barton (R-TX) proposed H.J.Res.1 (Appendix, Exhibit 11), and Senate Majority Leader Bob Dole (R-KS) introduced S.J.Res.1 (Appendix, Exhibit 12). These were the lead proposals among another two dozen BBAs offered that Congress.

Dole's BBA had 38 Republican and 8 Democratic cosponsors by the end of January 1995.[35] Introduced on January 4, it had a Senate Judiciary Committee hearing the following day and markup sessions each of the next two weeks. The Judiciary Committee ordered it reported on January 18 on a 15–3 vote with support from all ten Republicans and five Democrats, including Joe Biden and Diane Feinstein, and with opposition from only three Democrats.[36]

Extrapolating from the committee vote to the full Senate implied support from around 82 senators. But much can happen between a markup and floor consideration. Members sometimes support reporting legislation from committees even if they consider it flawed and would oppose it on the floor. They generally say it is to keep the process moving so they can fix problems before final passage. Chapter 8 will carefully consider the views of the Senate Judiciary Committee Democrats who opposed the resolution.

The House moved even faster. Barton also introduced his BBA on January 4, and the House Judiciary Committee marked it up and ordered it reported on January 11. The 20–13 party-line vote had all Democrats opposing except for Rep. Sheila Jackson Lee (D-TX), who voted "present."[37]

Membership on the House Judiciary Committee, however, tends to overrepresent the ideological wings of each party—the true believers—and has few moderates. When the Judiciary Committee reported it, the resolution's cosponsors included 171 Republicans and 6 Democrats.

On January 18, the Judiciary Committee filed the markup report, and a week later, the House of Representatives considered H.J.Res.1 on the floor. After substitute amendment votes through a Queen of the Hill process where the amendment with the most votes becomes the text for final passage, the House approved a BBA for the first time on January 26, 1995. The 300–132 vote was 69.4% of members present and voting. 228 Republicans and 72 Democrats voted for it, and 129 Democrats, 1 Independent (Bernie Sanders), and 2 Republicans voted against it.

House passage plus a solid bipartisan vote in the Senate Judiciary Committee boded well for Senate approval, which would send the BBA to state legislatures for ratification. The Senate took up the House-passed resolution at the end of January. BBA debate and amendment consideration consumed February 1995.

On March 2, 1995, the Senate vote on final passage failed by a single vote. The 66 Yea votes included 52 Republicans and 14 Democrats, while the 34 Nays were 33 Democrats and 1 Republican: Mark Hatfield of Oregon. Some blame Hatfield for the BBA's failure, but others say several Democrats were willing to vote Nay to keep the amendment from being proposed to state legislatures. They were, however, content to claim the mantle of fiscal responsibility if the BBA was not approved.

The record shows Senate Majority Leader Bob Dole, the sponsor of the leading Senate BBA, voting Nay, but that was purely strategic. Senate rules let a member voting in the negative on a measure later move for its reconsideration. That is precisely what Dole did the following year. In June 1996, the BBA failed again, with two more Democrats joining most of their fellow partisans in the Nay column.

1995 was the high-water mark for congressional consideration of BBA proposals. So far.

The other part of the BBA plank in the Contract with America did not fare much better. Congress enacted the statutory Legislative Line-Item Veto Act in 1996, but the Supreme Court struck it down 6–3 in 1998.[38]

In addition, the late 1990s tech bubble produced a flood of capital gains revenue. At the same time, the post-Cold War peace dividend and multiple rounds of fiscal restraint brought four years of federal budget surpluses in FY 1998–2001. Maybe a BBA was not needed after all?

Congress gave BBAs little attention in the late 1990s and 2000s. Members kept the issue warm by re-introducing proposals each year, typically with just one or two getting more than notional support. The Senate was even less active. True, Sen. Orrin Hatch's (R-UT) BBA again failed by one vote in 1997. After that, however, BBAs attracted few cosponsors.

No state legislature applied to Congress for a BBA-focused convention of states during this period. Not one.

Elected Republicans in DC were not doing well otherwise. During six years of mostly unified control during the George W. Bush administration, Congress and Bush let earmarks run rampant, expanded spending, grew the federal regulatory footprint in primary education with the No Child Left Behind Act, added new Medicare benefits in the Medicare Modernization Act of 2003, and launched the disastrous invasion of Iraq.

Republicans also passed deficit-increasing tax cuts in 2001 and 2003 through budget reconciliation, a fast-track process meant to enable deficit reduction. That push made more sense during Clinton's presidency when Republicans sought to return surpluses to taxpayers instead of spending them. Tax cuts without spending restraint made less sense as the economy softened in 2001 and even less so in 2003, but one-party control makes the chance to use reconciliation almost irresistible.

In addition to Bush's unilateral push to reform Social Security in 2005, a mismanaged response to the same year's Hurricanes Katrina and Rita, and revelations that House GOP leaders had protected alleged pedophile Rep. Mark Foley (R-FL), these factors fueled a Democratic wave in 2006.

Democrats had another wave election in 2008 amid a financial crisis. Senator Barack Obama (D-IL) defeated Senator John McCain (R-AZ) to become president, the House Democratic majority swelled from 233 to 257, and Senate Democrats expanded from 51 seats to 59. Senate Democrats obtained a filibuster-proof 60 members when Arlen Specter (PA) switched parties from Republican to Democrat on April 30, 2009.

The debt ballooned due to bipartisan bailouts of the financial sector in 2008 and Democratic big spending in the 111th Congress. Suddenly, congressional interest in BBAs was back. Sen. Jim DeMint's (R-SC) conservative-oriented 2010 BBA got 16 cosponsors. Goodlatte's version bumped up to 179 cosponsors, while joint resolutions from Reps. Jeb Hensarling (R-TX) and Bobby Bright (D-AL) had 53 and 42, respectively.[39]

Another wave of related state applications for an amendment convention started in 2010 with Florida and continued until 2022 with Alabama, North Dakota, Louisiana, New Hampshire, Ohio, Tennessee, Georgia, Alaska, Michigan, Utah, South Dakota, West Virginia, Indiana, Oklahoma Texas, Missouri, Arizona, Wisconsin, Wyoming, Mississippi, Arkansas, South Carolina, and Nebraska all submitting applications.

In this latest wave, convention calls have often included multiple topics in addition to a BBA. The unifying theme is reducing the federal government's power generally and specifically over the states, as well as fiscal prudence. For example, Nebraska's 2022 application included a balanced budget, congressional term limits, federal taxation restrictions, the federal debt limit, repeal of the income tax amendment, selection and tenure of federal judges, and the Convention of States project.

Tea Party Energy Was Not Enough to Approve Flawed BBAs

Tea Party strength peaked in 2011. Republicans had taken back the House by flipping 64 seats.

The first sign of a building wave was Republican Scott Brown winning a special election for the open U.S. Senate seat in Massachusetts following Senator Ted Kennedy's death. Brown was sworn in on February 4, 2010. Despite losing winnable races in Nevada, Delaware, and West Virginia, Republicans flipped six more Senate seats that year, but Democrats would hold a 53–47 majority in the 112th Congress.

The Tea Party was a reaction to Democratic overreach. In just two years of unified Democratic control, they had rammed through the American Rescue and Recovery Act's bailout bonanza for automakers, local governments, and many others, a regulatory takeover of the financial sector, and a hugely disruptive tax, transfer, and regulatory program in Obamacare: the Patient Protection and Affordable Care Act and its reconciliation sidecar, the Health Care and Education Reconciliation Act of 2010. They failed to enact a cap-and-trade scheme in the name of climate change, and they failed to get a union-boss-boosting card check bill through as well.

The debt-to-GDP ratio rocketed from 39.2 percent at the end of September 2008 to 65.5 percent by September 2011. Some came from the bank bailouts in the last months of the Bush administration in response to the 2008 financial crisis, but most came from an aggressive spending expansion during unified Democratic control. California progressive Nancy Pelosi was Speaker of the House during this period.

Rep. Bob Goodlatte (R-VA), a senior member of the House Judiciary Committee who had been in Congress since 1993, introduced two BBAs at the start of the Congress. H.J.Res.1 was the conservative BBA with supermajorities to raise the debt limit, to increase revenue, or to exceed spending as a certain percentage of GDP. H.J.Res.2 (Appendix, Exhibit 13) was closer to neutral: it was essentially what had passed the House in 1995, previously sponsored by Joe Barton (R-TX), Ernest Istook (R-OK), and others.

Congress had to raise the federal debt limit that year. Posturing by all sides is typical in the early phases, but serious negotiations between leadership and the White House usually happen quietly in the background. The Tea Party energy that swept many new Republicans into Congress gave the GOP the upper hand. Many look back on that period as a missed opportunity, wondering what might have been if members had been more focused and had well-developed proposals available.

A BBA was part of the early positioning. The House Judiciary Committee marked up H.J.Res.1, the conservative BBA, on June 23, 2011. Democrats offered amendments to exclude old-age entitlement programs from balance, to strike supermajorities to raise the debt limit or to increase revenue, to exempt taxes on oil and gas companies from the revenue restrictions, to waive balance when the economy is weak, to waive balance during any military contingency, and to require a supermajority to privatize Social Security or Medicare. All were defeated, mostly in party-line votes. Republicans proposed amendments to reduce the percent-of-GDP spending cap from 20 to 18% and to increase the threshold for revenue increases from three-fifths to two-thirds. Both were adopted. The motion to report the resolution favorably was a party-line, 20–12 vote.[40]

On July 15, 2011, as the drop-dead date for raising the debt limit neared, Rep. Jason Chaffetz (R-UT) introduced the Cut, Cap, and Balance Act of 2011. The bill proposed limits on both appropriated (discretionary) and direct (mandatory) spending and percentage-of-GDP caps on spending. It would have made a $2.4 trillion debt limit increase contingent on Congress approving a BBA with specific provisions including annual balance. The House passed it on July 19, 2011, with 229 Republicans and 5 Democrats supporting and 9 Republicans and 181 Democrats opposing. The Senate would vote to table it (kill it) 51–46 on July 22.[41]

On July 21, 2011, Rep. Justin Amash (R-MI) introduced the first version of the Business Cycle BBA (Appendix, Exhibit 16).

Soon thereafter, congressional leaders and President Obama finished negotiating a debt limit deal with the Budget Control Act of 2011. The BCA raised the debt limit, set caps on appropriated spending for almost a decade, established a "super committee" to pursue an ambitious deficit reduction deal, and required both houses to hold votes on one or more BBAs by the end of the year, among other provisions. The BCA became law on August 2, 2011.[42]

On November 15, the House Rules Committee reported a resolution for considering H.J.Res.2—the traditional BBA, not the conservative version—under suspension of the rules but with five hours of debate instead of the customary 40 minutes, equally divided between proponents and opponents.[43] Suspension of the rules requires a two-thirds vote to pass, the same threshold as a constitutional amendment, and no amendments are possible. No one had a chance to offer a substitute amendment or any amendment to address the many flaws in that version (see Chapter 5), neither in committee nor on the floor.

The November 18 vote was 261–165, or 61.3 percent of the House, well short of the two-thirds needed. Four Republicans opposed it: freshman Justin Amash, Budget Committee Chair Paul Ryan, Rules Committee Chair David Dreier, and Judiciary Committee member Louie Gohmert. 25 Democrats voted for it, while 161 opposed it.[44]

Soon thereafter, two-thirds of senators split their votes for two different BBAs, but neither had enough to pass.[45]For the rest of the 112th Congress and the 113th Congress, Amash kept advocating for the Business Cycle BBA. But Congress moved on. The window was closing.

In 2015, Rep. Dave Brat (R-VA) proposed a different version, the Principles-based BBA, as H.J.Res.55 (Appendix, Exhibit 20). Again, Chapter 8 has the details. Neither house voted on a BBA in the 114th Congress.

The House would next vote on a BBA on April 12, 2018. This time, it came a mere two months after Congress had wiped the Statutory Pay-As-You-Go scorecards of the deficit increases from the Republican-only Tax Cuts and Jobs Act. Section 30102 of the Bipartisan Budget Act of 2018, a deal to increase the caps on appropriated spending, did the wiping.[46] The BBA vote was a fiscal fig leaf to distract from Republicans taking a mulligan on deficits. The vote was a disappointing 233–184 (55.9%), with Republicans voting 226–6 for it and Democrats voting 7–178 against it.[47]

Amash kept re-introducing the BCBBA throughout his service in Congress, which ended on January 3, 2021. In 2022, Senator Mike Braun (R-IN) and Representative Jodey Arrington (R-TX) introduced an updated BCBBA (Appendix, Exhibit 19).

On March 15, 2023, Sen. Braun instead introduced an update of the Principles-based BBA (Appendix, Exhibit 21), which is harmonious with the statutory Responsible Budget Targets Act (see Chapter 9). Rep. Nathaniel Moran (R-TX) introduced the Principles-based BBA in the House on July 6, 2023. Rep. Nancy Mace (R-SC) proposed the BCBBA with three-fourths for emergencies on September 18, 2023, and Rep. Arrington re-introduced the BCBBA with a two-thirds emergency threshold on February 7, 2024.[48]

The runup in the federal debt during the COVID-19 pandemic and subsequent inflation and interest rate increases have put fiscal responsibility and BBAs back on the agenda. The House Judiciary Committee had a subcommittee hearing on constitutional amendment proposals including BBAs in 2023, but a rumored markup was displaced by other issues. Keeping better BBAs warm and in the minds of members of Congress and the public sets them up for the best chance of success when the window of opportunity opens again.

Congress may not observe the norm of budget balance these days, but restoring it remains an aspiration of many members. Some pursue it directly in their votes on policy, while others would like to vote that way but need something to help them push back on the grasping hands of special interests.

That is why the push for a BBA is so essential. It had broad, bipartisan support when the first versions were proposed in the 1930s, 1940s, and 1950s, and even for most of the 1970s. That started to change in the 1980s, especially after House Republicans made it a central theme of the 1994 elections. Ultimately, a well-crafted balance rule should appeal broadly to members on both sides of the aisle.

As we will see, versions that have gotten votes have had serious political and policy flaws. They fail to distinguish between the need for specifics in statute and the pragmatism of principles in constitutional provisions. But there is a better way.

Notes

1. Calvin Coolidge, *Autobiography of Calvin Coolidge*, p. 159.
2. Amity Shlaes, *The Forgotten Man: A New History of the Great Depression*, Harper Perennial, 2008.
3. Sen. Millard Tydings, S.J.Res. 123 (74th Congress), "To provide for a balanced budget," introduced May 8, 1935.

4. Senate Judiciary Committee, "Balanced-Budget Constitutional Amendment, Senate Report 104–5, 104th Congress, https://www.congress.gov/104/crpt/srpt5/CRPT-104srpt5.pdf, January 24, 1995.
5. Rep. Harold Knutson, H.J.Res. 579 (74th Congress), "Proposing an amendment to the Constitution of the United States," introduced May 4, 1936.
6. Debt held by the public. Gross federal debt per capita exceeded $102,500 by the end of FY2024. U.S. Treasury, "Debt to the Penny," https://fiscaldata.treasury.gov/datasets/debt-to-the-penny/debt-to-the-penny, accessed October 13, 2024.
7. Office of the Historian, "Party Divisions of the House of Representatives, 1789 to Present," U.S. House of Representatives, https://history.house.gov/Institution/Party-Divisions/Party-Divisions/, accessed March 25, 2023.
8. Robert B. Dresser, "Balancing the Federal Budget: The Proposed Byrd-Bridges Amendment," American Bar Association Journal, Vol. 43, No. 1 (January 1957), https://www.jstor.org/stable/25719864, pp. 35–37.
9. United States Senate, "Party Division," https://www.senate.gov/history/partydiv.htm, accessed March 25, 2023.
10. Senate Judiciary Committee, "Balancing of the Budget: Hearing before a Subcommittee of the Committee of the Judiciary, United States Senate, Eighty-Fourth Congress, Second Session, on S. J. Res. 126, Proposing an Amendment to the Constitution of the United States Relative to the Balancing of the Budget and S. J. Res. 133, to Limit the Spending Powers of the Congress and to Provide for the Reduction of the National Debt," June 14, 1956.
11. Indiana General Assembly, House Concurrent Resolution 9, adopted March 12, 1957, Congressional Record, 103 Cong. Rec. 6475–76, May 8, 1957, https://www.congress.gov/85/crecb/1957/05/08/GPO-CRECB-1957-pt5-11-1.pdf.
12. Article V Library, http://article5library.org/, accessed June 27, 2023.
13. Fred Lucas, "House measure says Congress obligated to call convention for fiscal responsibility amendment," FoxNews.com, https://www.foxnews.com/politics/house-measure-congress-obligation-call-convention-balance-budget-amendment, July 19, 2022.

14. Robert G. Natelson, "Counting to Two Thirds: How Close Are We to a Convention for Proposing Amendments to the Constitution?" *Federalist Society Review*, https://fedsoc.org/commentary/publications/counting-to-two-thirds-how-close-are-we-to-a-convention-for-proposing-amendments-to-the-constitution, Vol. 19, May 9, 2018.
15. Office of the Historian, "Party Divisions of the House of Representatives, 1789 to Present," U.S. House of Representatives, https://history.house.gov/Institution/Party-Divisions/Party-Divisions/, accessed April 8, 2023.
16. Rep. Floyd Spence, H.J.Res. 1064 (93rd Congress), "A resolution proposing an amendment to the Constitution of the United States relative to the balance of the budget," https://www.congress.gov/bill/93rd-congress/house-joint-resolution/1064, introduced June 18, 1974.
17. U.S. Congress, Congressional Budget and Impoundment Control Act of 1974, Public Law 93–344, https://www.congress.gov/93/statute/STATUTE-88/STATUTE-88-Pg297.pdf, July 12, 1974.
18. John R. Kasich and G. William Hoagland, "Lawmakers five decades ago passed a big budget fix. It made a difference (for them)," Los Angeles Times, https://www.latimes.com/opinion/story/2024-07-12/federal-budget-and-impoundment-control-act-presidential-spending-power, July 12, 2024.
19. Tom Coburn, *Smashing the DC Monopoly: Using Article V to Restore Freedom and Stop Runaway Government*, WND Books, 2017, pp. 191–198.
20. Charles Mohr, "Tax Union Playing Chief Role in Drive," *The New York Times*, https://www.nytimes.com/1979/05/15/archives/tax-union-playing-chief-role-in-drive-aides-refer-to-our.html, May 15, 1979.
21. National Tax-Limitation Committee, "About Us," https://limittaxes.org/about/, accessed April 20, 2023.
22. Federal Amendment Drafting Committee, "A Proposed Constitutional Amendment to Limit Federal Spending," National Tax Limitation Committee, Washington, DC, January 30, 1979, reprinted in Milton Friedman and Rose Friedman, *Free to Choose: A Personal Statement*, Harcourt Books, 1980, Appendix B, pp. 313–314.
23. Rep. Thomas E. Coleman, H.J.Res. 2 (96th Congress), "A joint resolution proposing an amendment to the Constitution of the

United States to provide that appropriations made by the United States shall not exceed its revenues, except in time of war or national emergency; and to provide for the systematic paying back of the national debt," https://www.congress.gov/bill/96th-congress/house-joint-resolution/2/, introduced January 3, 1979.

24. Rep. L. A. Skip Bafalis, H.J.Res. 14, "A joint resolution proposing an amendment to the Constitution of the United States to provide that appropriations made by the United States shall not exceed its revenues, except in time of war or national emergency; and to provide for the systematic paying back of the national debt," https://www.congress.gov/bill/96th-congress/house-joint-resolution/14/, introduced January 15, 1979.
25. Sen. Strom Thurmond, S.J.Res. 58 (97th Congress), "A joint resolution proposing an amendment to the Constitution altering Federal fiscal decision-making procedures," S. Rept. 97–151 https://www.congress.gov/bill/97th-congress/senate-joint-resolution/58, introduced March 27, 1981.
26. The Congressional Record, October 1, 1982, Vol. 128, Part 20, https://www.congress.gov/97/crecb/1982/10/01/GPO-CRECB-1982-pt20-1-2.pdf, pp. 27,171–27,435.
27. Rep. Edgar Jenkins, H.J.Res. 350, "A joint resolution proposing an amendment to the Constitution altering Federal budget procedures," https://www.congress.gov/bill/97th-congress/house-joint-resolution/350, introduced October 29, 1981.
28. Rep. Charlie Stenholm, H.J.Res. 321 (100th), https://www.congress.gov/bill/100th-congress/house-joint-resolution/321?s=1&r=1, H.J.Res. 268 (101st), https://www.congress.gov/bill/101st-congress/house-joint-resolution/268?s=1&r=2, H.J.Res. 290 (102nd), https://www.congress.gov/bill/102nd-congress/house-joint-resolution/290?s=1&r=3, H.J.Res. 103 (103rd), https://www.congress.gov/bill/103rd-congress/house-joint-resolution/103?s=1&r=4, "A joint resolution proposing an amendment to the Constitution to provide for a balanced budget for the United States Government and for greater accountability in the enactment of tax legislation," introduced June 17, 1987, introduced May 11, 1989, introduced June 26, 1991, and introduced February 4, 1993, respectively.
29. Sen. Strom Thurmond, S.J.Res. 225, "An original joint resolution proposing an amendment to the Constitution relating

to a Federal balanced budget," https://www.congress.gov/bill/99th-congress/senate-joint-resolution/225?s=3&r=12, introduced October 23, 1985.
30. Sen. Paul Simon, S.J.Res. 41, "A joint resolution proposing an amendment to the Constitution of the United States to require a balanced budget," https://www.congress.gov/bill/103rd-congress/senate-joint-resolution/41, introduced February 4, 1993.
31. U.S. Supreme Court, *Bowsher v. Synar*, 478 U.S. 714 (1986).
32. Kurt Couchman, "Better budget targets can help Congress balance near- and long-term needs," Americans for Prosperity, https://americansforprosperity.org/wp-content/uploads/2022/07/Americans-for-Prosperity-White-Paper-Better-budget-targets-can-help-Congress-balance-near-and-long-term-needs.pdf, September 12, 2022.
33. Sen. Orrin Hatch, "Constitutional Convention Implementation Act" of 1979, 1981, 1984, 1985, 1987, 1989, and 1991, S. 1710 (96th Congress), introduced September 5, 1979; S. 817 (97th Congress), introduced March 26, 1981; S. 119 (98th Congress), introduced January 26, 1983; S. 40 (99th Congress), introduced January 3, 1985; S. 589 (100th Congress), S. 204 (101st Congress), introduced February 6, 1989; S. 214 (102nd Congress), introduced January 15, 1991.
34. House Republican Conference, "Contract with America," https://global.oup.com/us/companion.websites/9780195385168/resources/chapter6/contract/america.pdf, 1994.
35. Rep. Joe Barton, H.J.Res.1, "Proposing a balanced budget amendment to the Constitution of the United States," https://www.congress.gov/bill/104th-congress/house-joint-resolution/1, introduced January 4, 1995. Sen. Robert Dole, S.J.Res. 1, "A joint resolution proposing an amendment to the Constitution of the United States to require a balanced budget," https://www.congress.gov/bill/104th-congress/senate-joint-resolution/1, introduced January 4, 1995.
36. Senate Judiciary Committee, S.Rept. 104–5, "Balanced-Budget Constitutional Amendment," https://www.congress.gov/104/crpt/srpt5/CRPT-104srpt5.pdf, January 24, 1995.
37. House Judiciary Committee, H.Rept. 104–3, "Balanced Budget Constitutional Amendment," https://www.congress.gov/104/crpt/hrpt3/CRPT-104hrpt3.pdf, January 18, 1995.

38. Supreme Court of the United States, *Clinton v. City of New York*, 524 U.S. 417 (1998).
39. Sen. Jim DeMint, S.J.Res. 27, "A joint resolution proposing a balanced budget amendment to the Constitution of the United States," https://www.congress.gov/bill/111th-congress/senate-joint-resolution/27, introduced February 4, 2010. Rep. Jeb Hensarling, H.J.Res. 79, "Proposing an amendment to the Constitution of the United States to control spending," https://www.congress.gov/bill/111th-congress/house-joint-resolution/79, introduced March 3, 2010. Rep. Bobby Bright, H.J.Res. 78, "Proposing a balanced budget amendment to the Constitution of the United States," https://www.congress.gov/bill/111th-congress/house-joint-resolution/78, introduced March 2, 2010.
40. House Judiciary Committee, "Balanced Budget Constitutional Amendment," House Report 112–117, https://www.congress.gov/112/crpt/hrpt117/CRPT-112hrpt117.pdf, June 23, 2011.
41. Rep. Jason Chaffetz, H.R. 2560, "Cut, Cap, and Balance Act of 2011," https://www.congress.gov/bill/112th-congress/house-bill/2560/, introduced July 15, 2011.
42. Sen. Tom Harkin, S. 365, "Budget Control Act of 2011," Public Law 112–25, https://www.congress.gov/bill/112th-congress/senate-bill/365, enacted August 2, 2011.
43. Rep. Richard Nugent, H.Res.466, "Providing for consideration of motions to suspend the rules," https://www.congress.gov/bill/112th-congress/house-resolution/466, adopted November 17, 2011.
44. Rep. Bob Goodlatte, H.J.Res.2, "Proposing a balanced budget amendment to the Constitution of the United States," https://www.congress.gov/bill/112th-congress/house-joint-resolution/2/, introduced January 5, 2011.
45. Sen. Orrin Hatch, S.J.Res. 10, "Joint resolution proposing a balanced budget amendment to the Constitution of the United States," https://www.congress.gov/bill/112th-congress/senate-joint-resolution/10, introduced. Sen. Mark Udall, S.J.Res. 24, "Joint resolution proposing a balanced budget amendment to the Constitution of the United States," https://www.congress.gov/bill/112th-congress/senate-joint-resolution/24, introduced August 2, 2011.

46. Rep. John Larson, H.R.1892, "Bipartisan Budget Act of 2018," Public Law 115–123, https://www.congress.gov/bill/115th-congress/house-bill/1892, enacted February 9, 2018.
47. Rep. Bob Goodlatte, H.J.Res. 2, "Proposing a balanced budget amendment to the Constitution of the United States," https://www.congress.gov/bill/115th-congress/house-joint-resolution/2, introduced January 3, 2017.
48. Rep. Jodey Arrington, H.J.Res.77, "Proposing a balanced budget amendment to the Constitution of the United States," https://www.congress.gov/bill/117th-congress/house-joint-resolution/77, introduced March 17, 2022; Sen. Mike Braun, S.J.Res.42, "A joint resolution proposing a balanced budget amendment to the Constitution of the United States," https://www.congress.gov/bill/117th-congress/senate-joint-resolution/42, introduced March 17, 2022; Sen. Mike Braun, S.J.Res.19, "A joint resolution proposing a balanced budget amendment to the Constitution of the United States," https://www.congress.gov/bill/118th-congress/senate-joint-resolution/19, introduced March 15, 2023; Rep. Nathaniel Moran, H.J.Res.80, "Proposing a balanced budget amendment to the Constitution of the United States," https://www.congress.gov/bill/118th-congress/house-joint-resolution/80, introduced July 6, 2023. Rep. Nancy Mace, H.J.Res.90, "Proposing a balanced budget amendment to the Constitution of the United States," https://www.congress.gov/bill/118th-congress/house-joint-resolution/90, introduced September 18, 2023. Rep. Jodey Arrington, H.J.Res.113, "Proposing a balanced budget amendment to the Constitution of the United States," https://www.congress.gov/bill/118th-congress/house-joint-resolution/113, introduced February 7, 2024.

CHAPTER 5

Flawed BBAs Cannot Deliver

It is time to dig into the problems with most BBA proposals. Congress has only voted on BBAs with fatal flaws. Other versions that have not had votes have additional defects. Nearly all proposals are unacceptable as policy and are usually nowhere close to viable politically.

Here we will explore why BBAs keep failing or would fail, even when the public and members of Congress are open to the concept. Those insights help design one that can succeed, as we will see in the next few chapters.

The Traditional BBA Has Many Problems

Let us start with the version from the last serious vote: House Joint Resolution 2 (H.J.Res.2), as proposed by Rep. Bob Goodlatte (R-VA) on January 3, 2011, at the beginning of the 112th Congress.[1] It got 61.3 percent support in the House that November[2] and had 226 Republican and 16 Democratic cosponsors.

It was similar to what passed the House and narrowly failed the Senate in 1995 and failed the House again in 2018. H.J.Res.2 contains the most common weaknesses, so let us make it the base case. Then we will look at other BBAs.

House Joint Resolution 2 (112th Congress)

K. Couchman, *Fiscal Democracy in America*,
https://doi.org/10.1007/978-3-031-91938-1_5

Proposing a balanced budget amendment to the Constitution of the United States.

That the following article is proposed as an amendment to the Constitution of the United States, which shall be valid to all intents and purposes as part of the Constitution when ratified by the legislatures of three-fourths of the several States within seven years after the date of its submission for ratification:

> Article —
> Section 1. Total outlays for any fiscal year shall not exceed total receipts for that fiscal year, unless three-fifths of the whole number of each House of Congress shall provide by law for a specific excess of outlays over receipts by a rollcall vote.
> Section 2. The limit on the debt of the United States held by the public shall not be increased, unless three-fifths of the whole number of each House shall provide by law for such an increase by a rollcall vote.
> Section 3. Prior to each fiscal year, the President shall transmit to the Congress a proposed budget for the United States Government for that fiscal year in which total outlays do not exceed total receipts.
> Section 4. No bill to increase revenue shall become law unless approved by a majority of the whole number of each House by a rollcall vote.
> Section 5. The Congress may waive the provisions of this article for any fiscal year in which a declaration of war is in effect. The provisions of this article may be waived for any fiscal year in which the United States is engaged in military conflict which causes an imminent and serious military threat to national security and is so declared by a joint resolution, adopted by a majority of the whole number of each House, which becomes law.
> Section 6. The Congress shall enforce and implement this article by appropriate legislation, which may rely on estimates of outlays and receipts.
> Section 7. Total receipts shall include all receipts of the United States Government except those derived from borrowing. Total outlays shall include all outlays of the United States Government except for those for repayment of debt principal.

> Section 8. This article shall take effect beginning with the later of the second fiscal year beginning after its ratification or the first fiscal year beginning after December 31, 2016.

First, note that H.J.Res.2 is 313 words over eight sections. That is quite a mouthful on which to seek constitutional-level consensus. We will talk more about that in the next chapter. Onto the particulars, one section at a time.

Annual Balance—and Other Errors—Would Produce Instability

Section 1's most significant error would be to require yearly balance: spending in a year could not exceed revenue that year. But first, let us tackle the lesser problems.

It approaches spending the wrong way by using *outlays*. Outlays is a term in statute that means funds have passed legally from a federal government agency to a non-federal entity.[3] A TSA employee gets paid. A military contractor cashes the check. A state receives a grant.

Congress does not control outlays directly. Congress provides budget authority, which lets the agencies make contracts that eventually result in outlays. *Budget authority* is "the authority provided by Federal law [enacted by Congress for federal agencies] to incur financial obligations."[4]

A constitutional requirement aimed at outlays instead of budget authority would create unnecessary complications for Congress when enacting fiscal policy and for executive branch financial management. These challenges would only be amplified by the existing legal requirement for agencies to spend all funds Congress gives them.

A more general term would provide more flexibility. The Constitution already includes the word *expenditures* to describe spending, and it would work for a BBA as well.

The term *fiscal year* is also a statutory construction, currently for the period beginning October 1 and ending September 30.[5] A BBA should say *year* and let implementing legislation provide the precision.

Next, the escape clause from annual balance is only "three-fifths of the whole number of each House of Congress." The Senate already needs three-fifths to pass anything, and it does not provide much discipline.

That fraction is also historically sensitive. Now defunct, it once required counting "three fifths of all other Persons," that is, enslaved people, when apportioning representatives and direct taxes to reduce the share of House seats to states where slavery remained legal.[6]

The *whole number* means all members of the body, even if they are absent. That phrase already appears in the Constitution, but not for any congressional procedure. It is only for deciding how many representatives each state gets in the U.S. House and how the President and Vice President are selected. Applying the whole number to Congress' legislative actions would be a novelty.

Now we return to *annual balance*. Annual balance would create big management problems, made even worse by using outlays. Revenue and spending can only be estimated for an upcoming year and even less accurately during the budget and appropriations process that begins six months before each fiscal year. Only when the fiscal year is complete can the Department of the Treasury verify spending and revenue outcomes.

Many states nominally have annual balance requirements, but they have tools to soften the edges. As discussed in Chapter 3, state balance rules vary considerably, and states also have a range of flexibilities. In addition, the states get a lot of their budgets from the federal government: about one-third of their revenue and spending during normal times.

In addition, the federal government often expands safety net spending during recessions, even as revenue collections decline. Unemployment insurance, Medicaid, the Supplemental Nutrition Access Program (food stamps), and other programs automatically spend additional sums as more people become eligible during hard times.

As Fig. 5.1 shows, federal spending and revenue are unstable. This graphic shows their volatility through percentage changes from year to year. Revenue has been more volatile than spending, but both vary quite a bit from year to year, and they often move in opposite directions. These are percentage changes, not levels (see Fig. 2.1).

Those who embrace economist John Maynard Keynes' view that government can actively manage the overall economy to keep growth close to trend call the collective set of programs that increase deficits during recessions *automatic stabilizers*. They believe the drop in revenue collections and automatic increases in government spending help stabilize the broader economy, prevent a deeper recession, and accelerate economic recovery. In their terminology, annual balance is a destabilizing, pro-cyclical rule that would amplify the booms and the busts.

You do not need to be a Keynesian to see the problems with annual balance, however. Balancing the budget yearly despite these autopilot

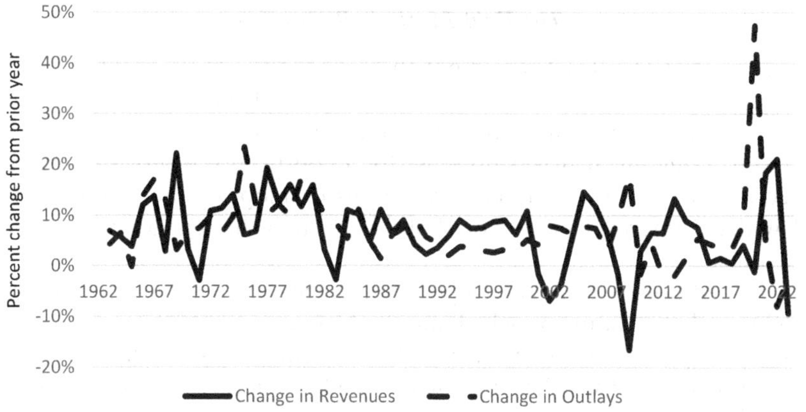

Fig. 5.1 Federal revenue and spending are volatile from year to year (*Source* CBO, author's calculations)

policies would force significant changes elsewhere. During recessions, policy instability—big spending cuts, revenue increases, or both—would be a political nightmare. Policymakers and the public would quickly tire from rampant uncertainty as the government tried to make changes reactively. Congress would soon find or create loopholes in an annual balance rule or even start to ignore it.

In a 2000 poll of economists, 87.7 percent agreed (some with provisos) with the statement, "If the federal budget is to be balanced, it should be done over the course of the business cycle rather than yearly."[7] In other words, the economic consensus is that annual balance is a dud.

Many Democrats worry that the freeze–thaw cycle of annual balance would erode longstanding policy priorities. Some Republicans fear it would interact with recessions to ratchet up a bigger government with temporary spending reductions and long-lasting revenue increases. Members of both parties worry about making big policy changes when times are tough.

The alternative in the traditional BBA to pro-cyclical, destabilizing annual balance is waiving the requirement with a three-fifths vote. Recessions happen about every five years but with great variability, and Congress tends to hesitate to restore normal policy after a downturn. How long would it take before Congress had a well-stocked excuses bank and made annual balance almost meaningless?

The Debt Limit Is Redundant

Section 2 of H.J.Res.2 would put the debt limit in the Constitution and require three-fifths of the whole number of each house to raise it. The debt limit is already in statute and does not need to be in the Constitution. Logically, it makes no sense for a constitutional provision, which requires an exceptional level of consensus to adopt or alter, to refer to a law that Congress can alter or abolish[8] through the regular, much easier process.

In addition, a BBA and implementing legislation should control the debt, and the statutory debt limit would become an annoying vestigial organ. Suppose, for example, that the debt subject to the statutory limit is 106 percent of GDP at the initial overall balance. After about 20 years of full balance (more or less), the economy would have doubled, so the debt burden would fall to around 53 percent of GDP, yet the nominal debt would remain right at the dollar-amount limit.

The Government Accountability Office (GAO) does not even consider the debt limit to be a fiscal rule. It "only restricts the Department of the Treasury's authority to borrow and finance the decisions already passed by Congress and signed into law by the President; it does not restrict Congress's ability to pass spending and revenue legislation that affects the level of debt."[9]

Many members of Congress dislike the debt limit and want it to disappear. That is an opportunity. In a BBA-related political deal, Congress could set up a trigger to repeal the statutory debt limit when the 38th state legislature ratifies the BBA or when Congress enacts initial implementing legislation. Alternatively, the debt limit could increase automatically whenever the budget meets BBA-derived goals. Any such trade could be an essential part of a BBA's initial congressional approval process.

The President's Budget Request in the Constitution Would Threaten the Balance of Powers

Section 3 repeats using fiscal year, outlays, and annual balance in enshrining the president's budget proposal in the Constitution. Doing so would risk the balance of powers, especially Congress's primacy in fiscal policy.

The Constitution vests in Congress the powers "to lay and collect Taxes, Duties, Imposts, and Excises, to pay the Debts and provide for the common Defence [sic] and general Welfare of the United States," among others. It says, "No Money shall be drawn from the Treasury [by the president or other executive branch officials] but in Consequence of Appropriations made by Law" by Congress.

The president's main fiscal policy power is to approve and sign budget-related legislation into law, though two-thirds of both houses of Congress can overcome vetoes. Otherwise, the president's other relevant job is to "take Care that the Laws be faithfully executed" and "Commission all the Officers" necessary to carry out those laws.

Congress already requires by statute that the president submit a budget each year that meets various requirements,[10] but this is a convenience to Congress. Given the extraordinary claims of "inherent Article II authorities" propounded by devotees of a super-powered executive branch,[11] expanding the foundation for such claims to a BBA in the Constitution carries far more risk than benefit. It is safer for our system to keep the president's budget request solely in statute.

Hurdles to Tax Increases Are Politically Problematic

Section 4 marginally increases the difficulty of enacting any "bill to increase revenue." It would require such a bill to be "approved by a majority of the whole number of each House by a rollcall vote." So, for example, assuming no vacancies in the House or Senate, a revenue-raising bill would need 218 and 51 votes. Even if, say, ten representatives and four senators were absent for the votes, those numbers would still be the thresholds even though a simple majority would be 213 and 49 votes, respectively, due to the absences.

On the other hand, and contrary to BBA proponents' intentions, this language might make revenue raising easier in the Senate. Budget reconciliation only requires a bare majority to raise revenue, but that only happens during one-party control. Otherwise, Senate rules usually require 60 votes to pass legislation. Yet a constitutional provision for a majority of the whole number for a bill to increase revenue would give advocates for revenue raising a strong argument that the Constitution supersedes Senate rules, thus dropping a 60-vote threshold to a bare majority or slightly above for tax hikes.

The ambiguity of a "bill to increase revenue" is not a concern. Definitions belong in statute, just as for *year* and *expenditures*. This provision's practical impact might be negligible. Even so, the asymmetry between increasing revenue and reducing spending complicates budgeting without clear benefits. It also irritates key blocs in Congress, making it harder to pass the BBA in the first place.

Low and Multiple Emergency Thresholds Can Encourage War

Section 5 would set a lower bar to spend for military emergencies than for other crises. It would create an automatic blanket waiver whenever a declaration of war is in effect. Otherwise, Congress would have to pass a joint resolution declaring the existence of "an imminent and serious military threat to national security [which is] adopted by a majority of the whole number of each House."

Declaring a war or engaging in major military activity would let Congress deficit spend, raise the debt limit, and otherwise turn off the proposed BBA with mere majorities, again, perhaps superseding the Senate's 60-vote filibuster rule. Without such military contingencies, the three-fifths requirement for suspending the provisions would prevail. This conflict-contingent, lower bar creates a powerfully perverse incentive for war. Sometimes military force is necessary, but Congress should consider it separately without it being a sweetener for loose budgeting.

To his credit, Rep. Goodlatte took this problem seriously when he became aware of it. Upon re-introducing his BBA in 2013 and thereafter, Rep. Goodlatte narrowed the exemption only to military-related funding.[12] Unfortunately, this problem persists in other BBAs.

Implementing Legislation Is Needed, and It Is Okay to Say So

Section 6 states that Congress can pass implementing legislation. It is acceptable to include. Technically, that power already exists through the *necessary and proper clause* in Article I, Sec. 8, clause 18 of the Constitution.[13] It is redundant, but several existing amendments have similar language. It explicitly allows inherently uncertain estimates, but that is unavoidable when planning for annual balance in the upcoming year.

Full Balance Would Mean Massive Policy Changes

Section 7 is a straightforward definition of terms. It defines the scope of receipts to include everything except what is derived from borrowing. If not for this provision, the budget would be "balanced" despite borrowing, contrary to the purpose of a BBA, since the federal government treats debt as a means of financing. The provision excludes repayment of debt principal from outlays.

Except during emergencies or other waivers, this language requires total balance: revenue must cover all spending, including interest costs. Full balance is a respectable goal, and reaching it would rapidly reduce the debt burden as the economy grows. The political reality, however, is that Congress lacks a consensus that so much deficit reduction is possible within any tangible transition period.

We will return to it, but a more ambiguous phrase like *payment of debt* could accommodate full and primary balance, depending on implementing legislation. Primary balance excludes net interest costs, whereas full balance includes them. The difference in political viability is significant because primary balance requires less than half as much deficit reduction as full balance.

Too Little Time to Balance

Section 8 would set a tight deadline to reach balance. If the BBA had been approved by Congress and ratified by three-fourths of state legislatures by the end of March 2011, balance would have been required by the start of FY 2018 on October 1, 2017: "the first fiscal year beginning after December 31, 2016." (This is just an illustration—Congress did not vote on BBAs until much later that year.)

This most generous transition would have been 6 ½ years. According to the January 2011 CBO baseline, which assumed the expiration of the Bush tax cuts and various other policies that Congress has extended, the deficit needing to be closed by FY 2018 through some combination of spending cuts and tax increases would have been $610 billion that year.[14] The actual deficit in FY 2018 was $779 billion.[15]

The least generous timeline would come from "the second fiscal year beginning after its ratification." Let us say that the 38th state legislature would have ratified the BBA in September 2016. The first fiscal year beginning after ratification would start the following month in October

2016. By then, Congress should have finalized all appropriations, and the second fiscal year would begin on October 1, 2017. Congress would have *a single budget cycle* between ratification and balance.

In January 2016, CBO projected a deficit of $572 billion in FY 2018.[16] The policy changes needed to eliminate that entire deficit in a single year would have been enormous, disruptive, and unpopular. That much change all at once could trigger a nasty recession due to rapid shifts in the anticipated patterns of financial flows for households and markets.

Back to the generous case, House Budget Committee Chair Paul Ryan's (R-WI) budget resolution for FY 2012—approved by the House Budget Committee on April 6, 2011—would have reached balance sometime around 2038.[17] This assumes that Congress would enact all proposed policy changes. Under Chairman Jim Jordan (R-OH), the even more conservative FY 2012 budget from the House Republican Study Committee, which got only 119 votes (28 percent of House members voting),[18] would have reached balance in FY 2020,[19] again assuming full enactment.

Those budget resolution votes all fell far short of two-thirds. Granted, policy changes do not require two-thirds, but when members are thinking about a constitutional amendment, they are also considering what would be required of them.

Bad BBA Ideas from Democrats

Having seen all the problems in the traditional BBA with decent bipartisan support, let us turn to Democrat-proposed BBAs. Democrats have introduced and supported BBAs from the 1940s to the present.

Then-Rep. Ben McAdams (D-UT) sponsored the Blue Dog Coalition's BBA in the 116th Congress (2019–2021).[20] Senator Jon Tester (D-MT) proposed something similar in the Senate.[21] In addition to many issues already discussed, these BBAs would try to soften annual balance's pro-cyclical nature and would exclude Social Security and Medicare.

> Section 4. Section 1 of this article shall not apply during a fiscal year if, during that fiscal year or the preceding fiscal year, the economy of the United States grew by less than an annualized rate of 0.0 percent in real gross domestic product during 2 or more consecutive quarters or the unemployment rate was more than 7 percent during 2 or more consecutive months.

> Section 2 of this article shall not apply to a fiscal year if, during the 1-year period ending on the date on which the President transmits to Congress a proposed budget for the United States Government for that fiscal year, the economy of the United States grew by less than an annualized rate of 0.0 percent in real gross domestic product during 2 or more consecutive quarters or the unemployment rate was more than 7 percent during 2 or more consecutive months.
> Section 6. Except as provided in the second clause, total receipts shall include all receipts of the United States Government other than those derived from borrowing, and total outlays shall include all outlays of the United States Government other than those for repayment of debt principal.
> For each fiscal year, the receipts (including attributable interest) and outlays of the Federal Old-Age and Survivors Insurance Trust Fund, the Federal Medicare Hospital Insurance Trust Fund, the Federal Disability Insurance Trust Fund, or any fund that is a successor to any such fund, shall not be considered to be receipts or outlays for purposes of this Article.
> Section 7. No court of the United States or of any State shall enforce this article by ordering any reduction in Social Security or Medicare payments authorized by law, including any amounts paid from the Federal Old-Age and Survivors Insurance Trust Fund, the Federal Medicare Hospital Insurance Trust Fund, the Federal Disability Insurance Trust Fund, or any fund that is a successor to any such fund, unless the receipts (including attributable interest) and other amounts available for that fund for the applicable fiscal year are not sufficient to cover the outlays that would otherwise occur during that fiscal year if the fund were fully solvent.

In addition to exempting Social Security and Medicare, as above, the Tester version would also exempt natural disaster funding.

> For any fiscal year, outlays relating to a natural disaster shall not be considered to be outlays for purposes of this article if the law making the amounts available explicitly exempts the outlays from this article and is agreed to by a majority of the whole number of each House.

Recessions Toss All the Rules

Let us look closer at the waiver during times of economic weakness. The provision's authors recognized (correctly) that annual balance would drive policy instability during both booms and busts.

Their choice to target annual balance, however, left them with little alternative to their long and messy jumble of statutory constructs and a recap of putting the president's budget request in the Constitution. The recession provision undermines the balance rule by adding to the conditions (also military situations and whenever else Congress can muster three-fifths) when it would not be in force. It would set up brutal policy fights to regain balance as recessions ended. Annual balance truly is the original sin of BBAs.

Social Security and Medicare Get a Pass

Now, let us consider the idea of exempting Social Security and Medicare from balance. It may be reasonable to exempt programs with dedicated funding from rules applicable to programs funded by the general fund. Other countries like Switzerland and Sweden do so, but their social insurance programs have supplementary rules to maintain intra-program solvency.

Unfortunately, Social Security and Medicare lack pro-solvency mechanisms. CBO expects Social Security's larger trust fund, the Old Age and Survivors Insurance program, to be depleted in 2033 and Medicare's Part A Hospital Insurance trust fund in 2033.[22] When trust fund assets are all gone, current law limits trust fund spending to incoming revenue. Medicare has several other trust funds, but only Hospital Insurance is limited to dedicated funding; the Treasury automatically backfills the others with transfers from the general fund.

Congress can address these statutory programs through implementing legislation. A BBA does not need to include them. In addition, BBA implementing legislation can certainly treat different programs differently. Social insurance programs with dedicated funding sources could be exempt from automatic fiscal consolidation or have custom-made budgetary controls. As discussed further in Chapter 9, it may be possible for Social Security *automatic fiscal stabilizers* in statute to reduce incrementally the funding gap through pre-selected adjustments to provisions of existing law.[23]

Tying the Hands of the Courts

Likewise, the prohibition on courts ordering automatic changes to Social Security and Medicare funding—except for general revenue transfers—is not necessary in a BBA. Implementing legislation can address that too. Following decades of agitation against "activist courts," the federal judiciary's culture seems to have shifted decisively against blatant judicial usurpation of legislative powers.

Furthermore, courts are a vital part of federal checks and balances. A constitutional provision should preserve the possibility for courts to have some role. The precise shape of potential court involvement in budget enforcement is a tricky topic best reserved for relatively easy-to-amend statutes, and the Constitution lets Congress shape the judiciary's jurisdiction "with such Exceptions, and under such Regulations as the Congress shall make."[24] We will come back to this as well.

A Special Exemption for Disasters

Rounding out this cluster of bad ideas is an exemption for natural disaster response. In practice, it is entirely reasonable to address disasters immediately and then account for the budget consequences later.[25] The problem, maybe not surprising by now, is that putting an annual balance requirement in the Constitution would not provide that flexibility, at least without triggering the general emergency provision. An additional emergency provision for natural disasters would be redundant.

It is surprising that these BBAs did not also carve out investments, often called *capital expenditures*. Some think the federal government should have a capital budget that spends up front to build things and recoups user fee revenue over assets' useful lives. These annual balance BBA proposals would not make room for them, but a principles-based BBA could let statute decide.

Bad BBA Ideas from Conservatives

Let us finish with problematic, conservative-favored provisions: a supermajority to raise taxes, a GDP-based spending limit, no court-ordered adjustments, and state-approved federal debt issuances.

We will begin with excerpts from Sen. Cindy Hyde-Smith's (R-MS) 2023 proposal[26]:

> Section 2. Total outlays for any fiscal year shall not exceed 18 percent of the gross domestic product of the United States for the calendar year ending before the beginning of such fiscal year, unless two-thirds of the duly chosen and sworn Members of each House of Congress shall provide by law for a specific amount in excess of such 18 percent by a rollcall vote.
> Section 4. Any bill that imposes a new tax or increases the statutory rate of any tax or the aggregate amount of revenue may pass only by a two-thirds majority of the duly chosen and sworn Members of each House of Congress by a rollcall vote. For the purpose of determining any increase in revenue under this section, there shall be excluded any increase resulting from the lowering of the statutory rate of any tax.
> Section 8. No court of the United States or of any State shall order any increase in revenue to enforce this article.

Another provision on standing to sue comes from Sen. Mike Lee's (R-UT) 2021 proposal[27]:

> Section 6. Any Member of Congress shall have standing and a cause of action to seek judicial enforcement of this article, when authorized to do so by a petition signed by one-third of the Members of either House of Congress. No court of the United States or of any State shall order any increase in revenue to enforce this article.

GDP-based Spending Limits

Sen. Hyde-Smith's GDP-based spending limit also includes a set-aside by a percentage of the "duly chosen and sworn" members of Congress, which means the same thing as the whole number and would be an unnecessary novelty. Her 18-percent-of-GDP spending cap would apply to the calendar year that ends before the applicable fiscal year. That is, the dollar amount of the cap would come from GDP in a one-year period that ends fully nine months before the later one-year period to which it would apply.

For example, the spending cap for FY 2024—October 2023 through September 2024—would be 18 percent of national output from January 2022 through December 2022. The midpoints of those periods—June 30, 2022, and March 31, 2024—are twenty-one months apart.

Yet, output from almost an entire congressional term ago would bind spending without regard to revenue, though that is in a separate provision. Intervening nominal growth from an expanding population, improving productivity, and inflation would reduce the retrospective 18 percent cap to something below 17 percent during the fiscal year to which it would apply.

We can use CBO's February 2023 economic projections[28] to illustrate meeting this requirement for FY 2024. The BBA would cap FY 2024 spending (October 2023 through September 2024) at 18 percent of GDP for calendar year 2022. CY 2022 GDP was $25.42 trillion, so 18 percent would be $4.576 trillion. That is 16.6 percent of the projected FY 2024 GDP.

Many would say that is an adequate share of the economy for the federal government to spend. Some would like federal spending to consume even less of the American people's income. But when FY 2024 federal spending would be about 23.5 percent of GDP under those projections, a BBA that would require one-third lower spending no matter what else Congress might do would be a tough sell.

Moreover, some may worry that such a cap would also, in practice, become a floor. After that, Congress might spend that much whether it made sense or not. Many on the left, however, would consider that spending level to be grossly inadequate for what they regard as the proper roles of the federal government.

Supermajority to Raise Taxes

Let us consider a two-thirds supermajority to raise taxes. It is understandable. Many believe the federal government spends too much on more activities than it can reasonably do well. It seems logical to reduce extraneous spending before imposing additional tax burdens.

Even so, a constitutional provision's durability rests on political consensus. Congress can do a lot to hollow out provisions while stopping short of repealing them. A rule that puts a big thumb on the scale toward a policy outcome that many members of Congress oppose could soon show itself to be nothing but a parchment barrier without staying power.

That said, such a rule has no chance of adoption in the first place. Constitutional amendments require broad bipartisan support—two-thirds of both houses of Congress and three-fourths of state legislatures—and therefore need approval from wide swaths of both parties' political coalitions. Increasing the difficulty of raising revenue compared to cutting spending is simply a non-starter for many of the congressional and state legislator votes needed to propose and ratify a BBA.

Courts Cannot Increase Revenue

Let us turn to Sen. Lee's provision prohibiting courts from raising revenue. Again, the lack of symmetry between spending and revenue is a political problem. More fundamentally, courts play a key role in our system of checks and balances. Judicial review of legislation is a bedrock of American governance. The U.S. Supreme Court is the final arbiter of constitutional questions, and Congress and presidents give it broad deference. Of course, some elected officials go too far and end up abdicating their responsibility to preserve and defend the Constitution.

The courts likely have a positive role to play. Its precise form belongs outside the Constitution, however. Congress has the power to enact legislation guiding court jurisdiction and practices under both the necessary and proper clause in Article I, Section 8, clause 18 of the Constitution and more directly in Article III, Section 2, clause 2, which states that the Supreme Court shall operate "under such Regulations as the Congress shall make."

It may be appropriate for the courts to order the executive branch to take policy actions specified in implementing legislation for the balanced budget rule. It may be right and proper for the Supreme Court to uphold the conviction of a budget official who refuses to carry out the law. Some actions may be necessary at one point but not later, or they may not initially appear needed—or even imagined—but become imperative later. In any case, the precise nature of court activities concerning a BBA belongs in the arena shaped by ordinary legislation.

Senator Lee did not just propose a BBA, however. He also published a book in 2011, *The Freedom Agenda: Why a Balanced Budget Amendment Is Necessary to Restore Constitutional Government*. Yet he erred in seeking to advance his limited government policy preferences in the context of a BBA. He laid out his views on five critical elements for a BBA: (1) full, annual balance, (2) percent of GDP spending caps, (3) a supermajority vote to circumvent (his word) elements 1 and 2, (4) a supermajority vote to raise the debt ceiling, and (5) a supermajority vote to increase taxes.

As we have seen, four of these five have substantial political or policy problems or both. Only the third element holds up.

Like Senator Lee, many BBA proponents put their limited government hopes and dreams into their proposals. A realistic and feasible BBA is not a silver bullet for limited government. A well-crafted BBA and its implementing legislation are tools for responsible and sustainable government, and both rely on broad, bipartisan support to be adopted and sustained. Whether that government is more limited or more expansive depends on other factors.

Other conservative proposals have additional poorly considered provisions. Section 3 of Rep. Mark Green's (R-TN) 2019 BBA[29] says if the president's budget request does not meet annual balance, then executive actions can be overturned by a simple majority vote in both houses until such a budget is submitted. Rep. John Ratcliffe's (R-TX) 2019 proposal [30] would require a three-fourths vote (above the two-thirds needed to override a veto) in both houses to raise the debt limit (Sec. 3), withhold pay to the president unless he submits a balanced budget request (Sec. 4), and withhold congressional compensation until Congress passes a balanced budget (Sec. 5), which is problematic given that Congress does not do an actual budget (see Chapter 10). Rep. Scott Perry's (R-PA)[31] would put agency budget justifications into the Constitution (Sec. 5).

Let us not beat this dead horse anymore. Provisions like these do not belong in the Constitution.

State Approval for Federal Borrowing Courts Disaster

An especially notable overreaction to excessive federal debt comes from Compact for America's BBA proposal.[32] In addition to various already-noted defects, their language would subject new federal borrowing to approval by the states. The lack of an independent power for revenue raising was a devastating problem under the Articles of Confederation. It was a major factor that drove the founding generation to replace the Articles with the present Constitution. This provision would dangerously undermine federal sovereignty.

In this proposal, Congress would have to request state approval for a specific amount of debt authority. If a majority of state legislatures—many of them part-time[33]—would fail to approve the borrowing within 60 days, it could not occur. Congress would not even be able to fall back on borrowing under a higher supermajority threshold. This fiscal straitjacket would overcorrect today's leading source of fiscal imprudence—high and growing debt—and create another kind of budget irresponsibility—the inability of Congress to provide for emergencies unless it enacts sizable, immediate changes to other budget areas.

To their credit, however, Compact for America has developed an ingenious way to invigorate the never-successfully-used state convention route for constitutional amendments. The approach would eliminate the purported risks of a runaway convention by tightly limiting an in-person convention to deliberating pre-approved BBA language. We will get further into a Convention of States in the next chapter.

Compact for America's model policy would embed their BBA proposal in legislation for each state to adopt individually. Each state would approve that identical language. Upon the 38th state legislature adopting the same legislation, a limited convention would occur quickly to approve the specified BBA, for which Congress would have given pre-approval, and which the thirty-eight state legislatures would have already approved ratification in the original legislation.

This procedural shell around the BBA is a notable innovation. Nonetheless, only five states have signed up, and Congress has not pre-approved the Compact for America scheme. It is going nowhere fast.

Inflation, State Grants, and Unfunded Mandates

As mentioned in the last chapter, the National Tax Limitation Committee (NTLC) convened a Federal Amendment Drafting Committee in 1979. Like many of the congressional BBAs that followed, its proposed BBA[34] would try to do too many things, including many already discussed (Appendix, Exhibit 5).

The NTLC-convened committee's BBA would reduce the spending growth rate following inflation more than three percent. It would bar state and local grants from declining as a percentage of spending for six years, and then it would keep Congress from balancing at the expense of state and local governments. It would prohibit Congress from imposing unfunded mandates on state and local governments. Outside of emergency spending (two-thirds required), Congress could only spend more than revenue with a three-fourths vote and permission from the majority of state legislatures. Finally, members of Congress could sue the Secretary of the Treasury to enforce the BBA, but the court could not order any specific actions.

As with other topics, controlling inflation and keeping Congress from commandeering the states are important issues. That does not mean they belong in the Constitution, at least in this form. Congress already has the power "To coin Money [and] regulate the value thereof," and the laws establishing the Federal Reserve System and its duties are supposed to limit inflation. The federal government's relationship with state and local governments is supposed to be shaped by the former's limited and enumerated powers and the reservation of most other powers to the states or the people under the Tenth Amendment. Those issues are beyond the scope of this book, however.

Finally, conservative proponents of a "strong" BBA should more carefully consider the potential political ramifications. Fiscal responsibility is popular with swing voters, as are various other issues that cut differently toward the major parties. Suppose swing voters think a BBA is strong enough to guarantee fiscal responsibility. In that case, more would vote with greater weight to different issues, with the ironic outcome of fewer actual proponents of sound budgeting in the legislature.

Voters need an ongoing reason to support those who would deliver good outcomes. Otherwise, close elections and legislative control can quickly go the other way.

The "Term Limit" BBA

In July 2011, as Congress was fighting about the debt limit, businessman and investor Warren Buffett off-handedly suggested during a television interview that any time the deficit exceeded three percent of GDP, no sitting member of Congress could run for reelection.[35] A variation would prohibit members of the majority party in Congress from running for reelection if the budget was not balanced. These and related suggestions have been passed around the Internet but have not been proposed in Congress.

Still, they are bad ideas. Sometimes borrowing a lot is the right thing to do, like during wars. Replacing the entire membership of Congress would be a disaster for institutional knowledge and the ability of the people's representatives to make policy instead of the permanent political class in Washington, D.C. Only punishing the majority party would encourage the minority party to be even more irresponsible than it already is, and the president might get in on the action during divided government.

These examples should empower readers to evaluate other BBA provisions and those in other constitutional proposals. As we have seen, most BBA proposals have room to improve. They include provisions that do not belong in the Constitution. They would create unnecessary and harmful economic and policy uncertainty. Some would encourage war. And most cannot hope to attract the necessary coalition of support, or if one were somehow pushed through during a fiscal crisis, it would not stand the test of time.

Writing federal constitutional language is fundamentally different from state constitutional or federal statutory language. It is unlike federal statutes and even less like federal regulations. Before coming to the better BBAs in Chapter 7, we must first examine constitutional language, its purposes, and the procedures by which Congress and state legislatures can change it.

Notes

1. Rep. Bob Goodlatte, H.J.Res. 2 (112th), "Proposing a balanced budget amendment to the Constitution of the United States," https://www.congress.gov/bill/112th-congress/house-joint-resolution/2/text, introduced January 5, 2011.
2. Clerk of the House, Roll Call 858, H.J.Res. 2, https://clerk.house.gov/Votes/2011858, November 18, 2011.
3. Congressional Budget and Impoundment Control Act of 1974, §3, (§622, Title 2, United States Code).
4. Ibid.
5. §631, Title 2, United States Code.
6. U.S. Constitution, Article I, Sec. 2, clause 3.
7. Dan Fuller and Doris Geide-Stevenson, "Consensus on Economic Issues: A Survey of Republicans, Democrats, and Economists," Eastern Economic Journal, Vol. 33, No. 1, Winter 2007, pp. 81–94, https://cclark.gcsu.edu/Survey%20of%20Republicans,%20Democrats,%20and%20Economists.pdf.
8. Rep. Brendan Boyle, H.R.6724 (117th), "Debt Ceiling Reform Act," https://www.congress.gov/bill/117th-congress/house-bill/6724, introduced February 15, 2022; Rep. Jodey Arrington, H.R.6393, "Responsible Budgeting Act," https://www.congress.gov/bill/117th-congress/house-bill/6393, introduced January 13, 2022.

9. GAO, "The Nation's Fiscal Health: Effective Use of Fiscal Rules and Targets," GAO-20–561, https://www.gao.gov/assets/710/709576.pdf, September 2020.
10. U.S. Code, "Budget contents and submission to Congress," 31 USC 1105, https://uscode.house.gov/view.xhtml?req=granuleid:USC-prelim-title31-section1105&num=0&edition=prelim, accessed January 3, 2021.
11. Gene Healy, *The Cult of the Presidency: America's Dangerous Devotion to Executive Power*, Cato, 2009.
12. Rep. Bob Goodlatte, H.J.Res. 2 (113th), "Proposing a balanced budget amendment to the Constitution of the United States," https://www.congress.gov/bill/113th-congress/house-joint-resolution/2/text, introduced January 3, 2013. Rep. Bob Goodlatte, H.J.Res. 2 (115th), "Proposing a balanced budget amendment to the Constitution of the United States," https://www.congress.gov/bill/115th-congress/house-joint-resolution/2/text, introduced January 3, 2017.
13. Kurt Couchman, "Congress has substantial powers—if it claims them," *The Hill*, https://thehill.com/opinion/white-house/369006-congress-has-substantial-powers-if-it-claims-them, January 15, 2018.
14. CBO, 10-Year Budget Projections, https://www.cbo.gov/sites/default/files/recurringdata/51118-2011-01-budgetprojections.xls, January 2011.
15. CBO, Historical Budget Data, https://www.cbo.gov/system/files/2020-01/51134-2020-01-historicalbudgetdata.xlsx, January 2020.
16. CBO, 10-Year Budget Projections, https://www.cbo.gov/sites/default/files/recurringdata/51118-2016-01-budgetprojections3.xlsx, January 2016.
17. House Budget Committee, Report 112–58 on H.Con.Res. 34, the Concurrent Resolution on the Budget for Fiscal Year 2012, https://www.congress.gov/112/crpt/hrpt58/CRPT-112hrpt58.pdf, April 11, 2011.
18. Clerk of the House, Roll Call 275, H.Con.Res. 34, On Agreeing to the Amendment, https://clerk.house.gov/evs/2011/roll275.xml, April 15, 2011.
19. Committee for a Responsible Federal Budget, "Republican Study Committee FY2012 Budget Released," http://www.crfb.org/blogs/republican-study-committee-fy2012-budget-released, April 7, 2011.

20. Rep. Ben McAdams, H.J.Res. 55 (116th), "Proposing a balanced budget amendment to the Constitution of the United States," https://www.congress.gov/bill/116th-congress/house-joint-resolution/55/text, introduced April 9, 2019.
21. Sen. Jon Tester, S.J.Res. 18 (116th), "Proposing a balanced budget amendment to the Constitution of the United States," https://www.congress.gov/bill/116th-congress/senate-joint-resolution/18/text, introduced April 4, 2019.
22. CRFB, "Analysis of the 2025 Social Security Trustees' Report," https://www.crfb.org/papers/analysis-2025-social-security-trustees-report, June 18, 2025. CRFB, "Analysis of the 2024 Medicare Trustees' Report," https://www.crfb.org/papers/analysis-2025-medicare-trustees-report, June 18, 2025.
23. Kurt Couchman, "Is Social Security in Trouble? Yes, and We Need Automatic Fiscal Stabilizers to Help," Americans for Prosperity, https://americansforprosperity.org/why-social-security-is-in-trouble/, July 20, 2022.
24. U.S. Constitution, Article III, Sec. 2, clause 2.
25. Kurt Couchman, "We should offset emergencies—just not right away," *The Hill*, https://thehill.com/opinion/white-house/425384-we-should-offset-emergencies-just-not-right-away, January 15, 2019.
26. Sen. Cindy Hyde-Smith, S.J.Res. 13 (118th), "Proposing an amendment to the Constitution of the United States relative to balancing the budget," https://www.congress.gov/bill/118th-congress/senate-joint-resolution/13, introduced February 9, 2023.
27. Sen. Mike Lee, S.J.Res. 5 (117th), "Proposing a balanced budget amendment to the Constitution of the United States," https://www.congress.gov/bill/117th-congress/senate-joint-resolution/5, introduced January 22, 2021.
28. CBO, "10-Year Economic Projections," https://www.cbo.gov/system/files/2023-02/51135-2023-02-Economic-Projections.xlsx, February 2023.
29. Mark Green, H.J.Res. 68 (116th), "Proposing a balanced budget amendment to the Constitution of the United States," https://www.congress.gov/bill/116th-congress/house-joint-resolution/68/text, introduced June 20, 2019.

30. John Ratcliffe, H.J.Res. 51 (116th), "Proposing a balanced budget amendment to the Constitution of the United States," https://www.congress.gov/bill/116th-congress/house-joint-resolution/51/text, introduced March 14, 2019.
31. Scott Perry, H.J.Res. 19 (118th), "Proposing a balanced budget amendment to the Constitution of the United States," https://www.congress.gov/bill/118th-congress/house-joint-resolution/19/text, introduced January 12, 2023.
32. Compact for America, https://www.compactforamerica.oacrg/legislation, accessed January 11, 2021.
33. National Conference of State Legislatures, "Full- and Part-Time Legislatures," https://www.ncsl.org/research/about-state-legislatures/full-and-part-time-legislatures.aspx, June 14, 2017, accessed January 23, 2021.
34. Milton Friedman and Rose Friedman, "Appendix B: A Proposed Constitutional Amendment to Limit Federal Spending," *Free to Choose: A Personal Statement*, 1980.
35. Barbara Mikkelson, "Did Warren Buffett Suggest This Plan That Could Fix the Budget Deficit?" Snopes.com, https://www.snopes.com/fact-check/hometown-buffett/, October 23, 2011.

CHAPTER 6

Constitutions Are Primarily Collections of Principles

Now that we have looked at the pitfalls of certain provisions, let us take a step back. Here, we will explore the nature of constitutional language and how it connects to statutes (laws enacted by Congress). We will also highlight the differences. Let us start with a closer look at the process of amending the Constitution.

The U.S. Constitution Is Exceptionally Difficult to Amend

Every state constitution is far easier to change than the U.S. Constitution. The process for amending the federal charter is outlined in Article V (provisos omitted):

> The Congress, whenever two thirds of both Houses shall deem it necessary, shall propose Amendments to this Constitution, or, on the Application of the Legislatures of two thirds of the several States, shall call a Convention for proposing Amendments, which, in either Case, shall be valid to all Intents and Purposes, as Part of this Constitution, when ratified by the Legislatures of three fourths of the several States, or by Conventions in three fourths thereof, as the one or the other Mode of Ratification may be proposed by the Congress...

K. Couchman, *Fiscal Democracy in America*, https://doi.org/10.1007/978-3-031-91938-1_6

Article V sets up two stages: proposal and ratification. Congress can propose an amendment with the support of two-thirds of members of each house of Congress. Or, having been called upon the application of two-thirds of states, the delegates (formally, *commissioners*) to an amendment convention can propose one or more amendments.

Regardless of who proposes an amendment, state legislatures or conventions in the states determine whether to adopt it. Once three-fourths of state legislatures or state conventions have approved a proposed amendment, it becomes an active part of the Constitution.

The Constitution does not provide for direct democracy like the initiative for constitutional changes, unlike some states. Neither the president of the United States nor any governor plays a formal role in proposing or ratifying an amendment, although they have other ways of influencing legislators.

Table 6.1 shows the historical adoption process for amendments. Congress-initiated proposals are the sole method of constitutional amendment so far. The congressional route is also the primary focus of this book. With one exception—repealing Prohibition—Congress has referred amendment proposals to state legislatures, not to conventions in the states.

Getting two-thirds of Congress to support a constitutional amendment—changing the nature of the federal government—is no small task. As Fig. 6.1 shows, neither party has come close to having the votes to do it unilaterally in recent decades. The solid line in each panel shows the majority threshold, and the dashed lines indicate the two-thirds thresholds assuming majority party unanimity.

Table 6.1 Congressional proposals with state legislature ratification dominate

		Ratification	
		3/4 of State Legislatures	*Conventions in 3/4 of States*
Proposal	2/3 Both Houses of Congress	All except XXI	XXI
	Convention, Applied for by 2/3 of States	n/a	n/a

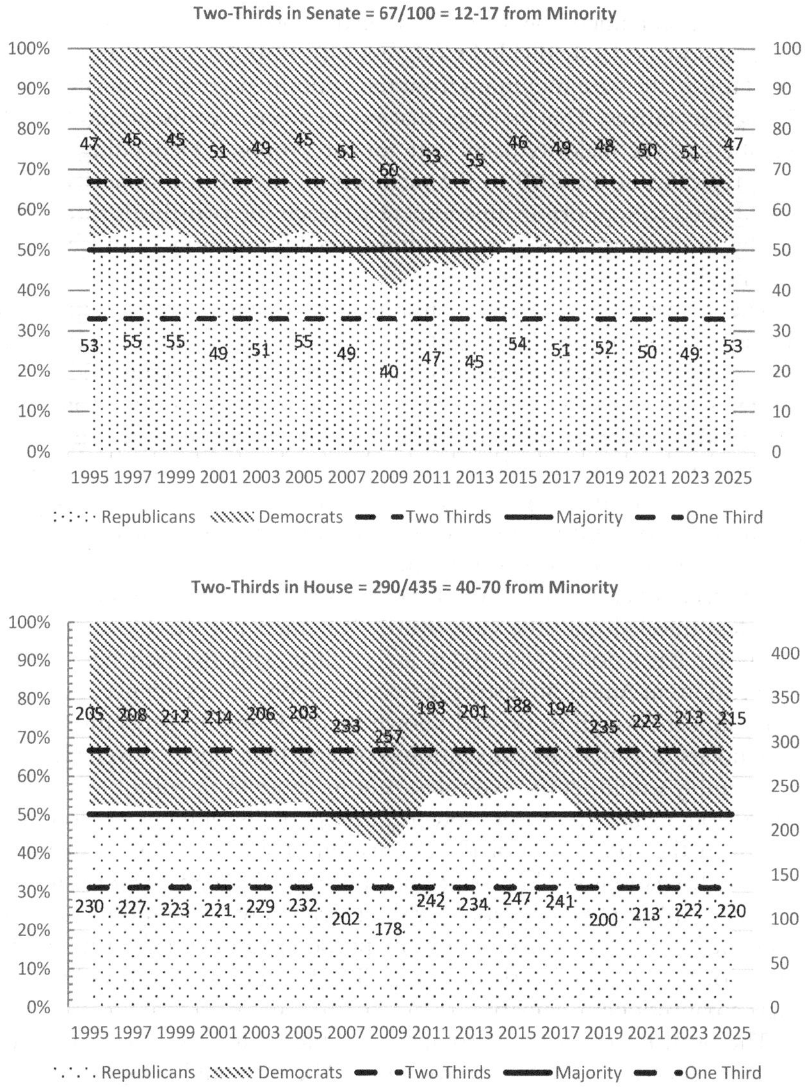

Fig. 6.1 The congressional amendment path needs many votes from both parties

A successful amendment proposal needs a broad coalition of support. In an almost-perfectly divided Congress with a 50–50 Senate and a 218–217 House, the bare minimum from the minority party is 17 senators and 72 representatives. That assumes that no members are absent and that all members of the majority party vote for the proposal. Depending on the year, typically, at least 40 to 70 members of the House minority party would need to support an amendment to reach the two-thirds threshold. Ideally, a consensus-based amendment would comfortably exceed that threshold.

The convention of states' path likewise requires broad, bipartisan support for assembling a convention to develop a proposal. As Fig. 6.2 shows, any conceivable combination of two-thirds of the states—34 of the 50 states—to apply to Congress for a convention requires some combination of Republican-leaning, competitive, and Democratic-leaning states. Ratification requires an additional four states to reach three-fourths of the total. Figure 6.2 might suggest that the coalition of support for an amendment convention would include at least all states to the left or right of the thresholds, but other groupings are possible.

Uncertainty about what could come from a convention has made this path less traveled than the Constitution's framers may have imagined. It has never been done. Few today are familiar with the rich heritage of conventions in American history, especially before independence, but they were regular enough to be well-known by the founding generation.[1]

Scholars of American conventions contend that, once convened, such an assembly would set its own rules. Among those likely rules, each state's delegation would have one vote regardless of its number of commissioners at the convention or the population of that state, and a majority of state delegations could propose one or more amendments for states to consider ratifying. The purported risk of a runaway convention would be restrained by the requirement for any proposal to obtain the support of three-fourths of state legislatures as well as by state-specific laws limiting their commissioners' activities.

The need for consensus also applies at the ratification stage, whether by state legislatures or state conventions. The threshold is higher: three-fourths of states (thirty-eight states) instead of two-thirds (thirty-four states). On the other hand, ratification is about a specific proposal rather than going to an uncertain drafting convention, and the choice is simply whether to approve it.

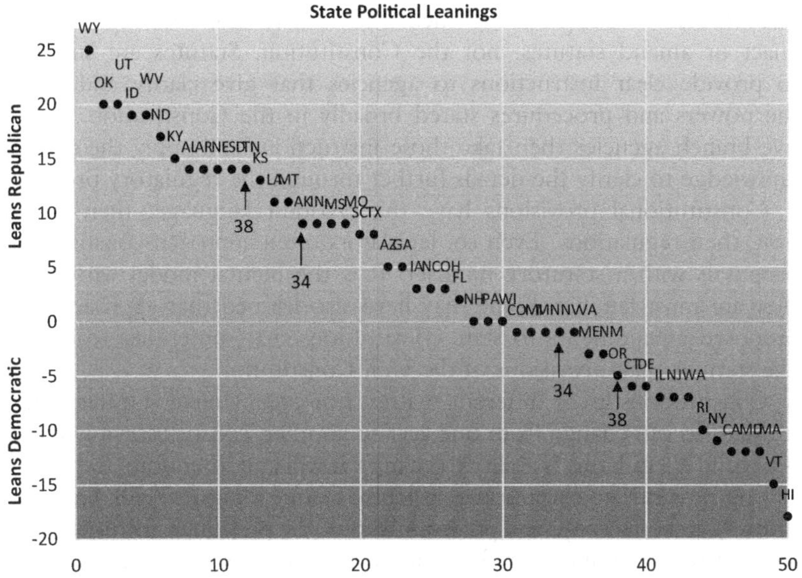

Fig. 6.2 Supermajority support requires a broad appeal (*Source* Cook Political Report)

As the adoption of prior amendments suggests, the binary choice facing state legislatures during ratification appears to be a lower hurdle than getting Congress to propose an amendment in the first place, let alone organizing a convention of states to do so. That said, Congress has proposed amendments that states did not ratify within the period stated: DC representation in Congress (proposed 1978), equal rights (1972), child labor (1924), protecting slavery (1861), stripping citizenship from any citizen who accepts a foreign title of nobility (1810), and congressional apportionment (1789).

Constitutional Language Is Little More Than a Framework

Procedures for changing the Constitution require broad support, and that has important implications for the nature of such language.

Members of Congress and their staff usually deal with legislation to enact or amend statutes, not the Constitution. Statutes are supposed to provide clear instructions to agencies that give clarity and life to the powers and procedures stated broadly in the Constitution. Executive branch agencies then take those instructions and apply their expert knowledge to clarify the details further through the regulatory process.

Constitutional provisions have the broadest language, then legislation, then regulations. Even so, legislators often approach constitutional proposals with a statutory mindset. It is the mental model with which they are most familiar. Some may have also learned that approach from proposed amendments to state constitutions that sometimes read more like statutes than provisions of the U.S. Constitution.

Constitutions are a different matter, however. Unlike statutes, which legislatures can change from one year to another, constitutional language is beyond a legislature's ability to change at will and, therefore, has greater staying power. The exceptional difficulty of amending the U.S. Constitution suggests that any new provision should be presumed to function for all time to come and therefore should not be overly prescriptive. Likewise, to the degree that a state constitution is easier to amend, legislators can relax the assumption of permanence.

Think of a constitution as the foundation of the legal architecture of a political entity with both policy and procedural features. Analogizing to physical buildings, concrete slabs and open-topped concrete basement walls do not provide much shelter. Conversely, a proper house offers comfort, but a bad foundation puts everything at risk. Neither a foundation alone nor a house without a good foundation is much of a home.

In the same way, the Constitution has largely kept its original form, though twenty-seven amendments have (mainly) improved it over the last 235 years.[2] It has been a solid basis for the relationships to evolve between the federal and state governments, between the legislative, executive, and judicial branches, and between the people and their governments. Even so, the Constitution did not build the Navy, raise revenue, establish a patent system, or do any of the many tangible things the federal government needs to do. The Constitution empowers a broadly representative Congress to fill in the gaps and tell agencies under the supervision of the president what to do and how to do it.

Meanwhile, the government's statutory, regulatory, and common-law (judge-made) legal architecture is complex and ever-changing. It includes the laws that Congress has enacted, usually with the president,[3] as well as treaties and other international agreements,[4] judicial opinions, especially from the U.S. Supreme Court, and agency regulations. All this law requires regular cultivation, but Congress has fallen further and further behind on updating the laws as the world has changed in recent decades. This mismatch between the law and existing conditions contributes to today's political malaise.[5]

Many provisions of the Constitution still lack adequate implementing legislation. Looking at these unfinished spaces with an eye toward legislation to fill them could be another worthwhile project. As we will see, thinking through implementing legislation for a principles-based BBA has been part of that story, itself primed by years of careful legislative analysis within a constitutional framework.

Perhaps nowhere is the need to clarify by statute more needed than in foreign and defense policy. Members of Congress give excessive deference to presidents on war powers and the conduct of foreign policy, much more than separation of powers would suggest. After all, the Constitution's necessary and proper clause empowers Congress to enact legislation to put reasonable terms and conditions for carrying out all "Powers vested by this Constitution in the Government of the United States or in any Department or Officer thereof."[6]

Ultimately, Congress has a duty to develop careful definitions and workable procedures. This clarification applies not only to more colorful topics like presidential removal under the 25th Amendment or treason but also to fundamentals like *legislative powers*, *executive powers*, *judicial powers*, and, perhaps, a *Republican Form of Government*.

Leaving so many questions unsettled and left to the imagination may contribute to tribal politics. Partisans can—and do—say that words and phrases mean whatever is convenient at the time. Charges of hypocrisy as circumstances change are not enough to discourage this situational framing.

A freshly enacted balanced budget amendment to the Constitution would, by definition, lack implementing legislation. Even so, anticipating that constitutional provisions are and ought to be clarified by statute reveals that statute-like language does not belong in the Constitution. Of course, a sense of what the implementing legislation could look like can affect Congress' (or a convention of states') willingness to propose one or more amendments for ratification, as later chapters will discuss.

Constitutional Language Only Gestures at What Should Be

Most constitutional provisions are principles. They set the broad strokes for federal powers and who may exercise them. Some are more detailed. In that case, however, they generally describe processes for allocating to, vesting in, and denying power to various federal and state government actors. Rarely are they self-enforcing or even refer to enforcement practices.

Consider the power of taxation. Article I, Section 8, clause 1 states, "The Congress shall have Power . . . To lay and collect Taxes, Duties, Imposts and Excises, to pay the Debts and provide for the common Defence and general Welfare of the United States; but all Duties, Imposts and Excises shall be uniform throughout the United States." The direct power of the federal government—vested in Congress—to exercise sovereign authority in raising revenue was vital to the framers after the miserable experience of trying to get the states voluntarily to fund national activities under the Articles of Confederation.

The power to both "lay and collect" taxes leaves unclear a vast set of procedures for defining, reporting, and enforcing the tax laws with proper regard for due process, privacy, and other civil liberties of taxpayers. Definitions for each term in "taxes, duties, imposts, and excises" have evolved through statute, regulation, and judicial precedent, as has the uniformity requirement.

The statutes setting forth these details are mostly in Title 26, United States Code. Printing out the official version compiled and edited by the Office of the Law Revision Counsel would come to more than 6,000 pages,[7] all derived from that handful of words.

Competing schools of constitutional interpretation disagree on what paying debts and providing for the common defense and general welfare mean. Are they independent grants of power, or are they limits on the purposes for which Congress can raise taxes? Are they merely a summation of the enumerated powers that mostly follow?

This provision gives Congress the power to raise funds for inherently governmental purposes, but it is unclear how it should occur. That is fine. It established the general principle and let the people's representatives in Congress develop the details through statutes and other processes that can adapt more readily to changing circumstances. The founders recognized that the country's needs would evolve, and much of Congress's job is to update the laws for current and anticipated conditions.

By contrast, provisions describing the qualifications of members of Congress and the procedures for selecting the president and vice president through the Electoral College are more detailed. Even they left a great deal to be clarified by statute, as, for example, the Electoral Count Act of 1887.[8] The alleged ambiguity in this statute was central to the attempt to challenge the results of the 2020 presidential election, and Congress has since revised it to prevent further misinterpretation. This highlights the importance of revisiting the laws occasionally to ensure that their text communicates the intended policy.

Moving from what is to what should be, a new proposal for constitutional amendment should generally also be a set of principles to the extent possible. Far from some ivory tower legal construct or personal preference, principles are practical when it comes to constitutional language.

In public policy, the devil is in the details. Broad principles with many options for achieving them can often attract more support than something specific. Ironically, the best supporting evidence is Congress's propensity to over-delegate legislative powers to executive branch agencies through vague statutes, which the Supreme Court has begun to rein in.[9]

The usual way of amending the U.S. Constitution requires two-thirds of both houses of Congress and three-fourths of state legislatures to agree. Big chunks of both major parties need to back something for it to have a chance. Something polarizing or partisan has no chance.

This temperance may disappoint those who push (without success) constitutional amendments that aim for something other than consensus. But that is what can work. It is much easier to adjust statutes as circumstances change. That means tinkering and tweaking can bend and mold a general principle into a sustainable and productive shape that fits the times.[10]

Take, for instance, Congress's power to raise and support armies. All reasonable people recognize at least the periodic need for competent land-based military capabilities. Most realize that a sustained and professional army is essential to our common defense. That firepower also needs careful control.

The shape of the army and its missions have changed dramatically over the last two and a half centuries. It continues to adapt to technological, geopolitical, and other circumstances. Under the Constitution's general provisions and a few related bits, Congress has molded the army through appropriations and authorizing legislation in response to perceived needs and priorities.

Still, some think that Congress will find ways around broad statements of principle. They say that a BBA must be detailed and be self-enforcing, or Congress will ignore it.

On the contrary, it is harder for the people to hold Congress accountable to complex, detailed language. People may understand constitutional principles somewhat differently, but the Constitution is concise. You and I can read the Constitution and have a relatively clear idea about what the federal government should or should not be doing. With a few exceptions, disagreements are on the margins.

Constitutions put the burden of proof on the people's representatives to show that their actions are consistent with our legal foundations. Constitutional scholar Rob Natelson has observed that the amendments have mattered immensely. Congress and agencies may follow them imperfectly, but public opinion, Supreme Court rulings, and the consciences of members of Congress have kept policy relatively faithful to most constitutional provisions.[11]

Reviewing the Amendments So Far

As noted, the Constitution already has twenty-seven amendments. Reviewing them shows that a principles-based BBA would be most consistent with successful amendments to the Constitution, while a prescriptive BBA would be out of character with that language.

The first ten are the Bill of Rights, and Congress and state legislatures adopted most of the rest in response to changing circumstances. Congress proposed what became the 27th Amendment, which bars changes to congressional compensation without an intervening election, along with the Bill of Rights, but three-fourths of states did not approve it until Michigan's legislature finally took it over the top in 1993.

Congress approved the last successful amendment proposal in 1971, setting the voting age at 18 years. That makes this the most extended period without a new proposal's ratification since the 62 years between Congress proposing the 12th Amendment in 1803 and the 13th Amendment in 1865. About 60 percent of Americans have been born since Congress last approved a successful amendment.

We can look at existing amendments to see where they fall between broadness and specificity. Quantitative perspectives can complement qualitative review, as above. Table 6.2 lists the 27 existing amendments, the number of words and sections of each, their topics, and the dates of congressional and state legislative approval. We will soon extend this approach to BBAs.

Constitutional amendments range from 16 to 435 words. The average for all 27 amendments is 113 words in 1.8 sections. The median is 52 words in a single section. Seventeen have a single section, and four others would if not for a largely extraneous second section that either duplicates the necessary and proper clause or fixes a period for ratification, which can be in an amendment proposal's preamble instead of its text.

The 8th Amendment is the shortest: sixteen words in a single section. "Excessive bail shall not be required, nor excessive fines imposed, nor cruel and unusual punishments inflicted." Note the ambiguities. *Excessive* is unclear for both bail and fines, and for that matter, what counts as fines is debatable. Is restitution a fine, or is a fine only something that goes into the general fund of the Treasury? What if it goes to a special fund, like the existing Crime Victims Fund, to provide money for restitution to victims?

Further, what is cruel or unusual? Must a prohibited punishment be both, or can it be either cruel or unusual? Who holds the power to impose bail, fines, and punishments?

At the other extreme, the post-Civil War 14th Amendment is the longest, with 435 words over five sections. It covers a lot of ground, including who is a citizen, guaranteeing privileges or immunities, due process, and equal protection under the law, barring public office to insurrectionists, guaranteeing the validity of the public debt, and more.

If the 8th Amendment raises some questions, the 14th Amendment has many more. This is not the place to attempt answers, but many have been clear from historical context and contemporary practices.

Even so, the fact that these provisions raise so many questions indicates that they are more like principles than legislation. Legislation is supposed to answer these questions as reasonably as Congress can come up with for the times when the laws apply.

The 14th Amendment is long because it is a package of principles, not (generally) because it is too much like legislation. Other lengthy amendments are about the president: revising the Electoral College in the 12th Amendment's 399 words, setting term limits for the president and the

Table 6.2 Constitutional amendments come in various sizes and shapes

#	*Subject(s)*	*Sections*	*Words*	*Proposed*	*Ratified*
1	Freedom of religion, speech, press, assembly, petition	1	45	Sept. 25, 1789	Dec. 15, 1791
2	Right to keep and bear arms	1	27	Sept. 25, 1789	Dec. 15, 1791
3	No quartering troops in homes	1	32	Sept. 25, 1789	Dec. 15, 1791
4	No unreasonable searches & seizures; warrants only with probable cause	1	54	Sept. 25, 1789	Dec. 15, 1791
5	Due process in criminal proceedings	1	108	Sept. 25, 1789	Dec. 15, 1791
6	Speedy & public trials, rights of accused	1	81	Sept. 25, 1789	Dec. 15, 1791
7	Protects trial by jury in civil suits	1	50	Sept. 25, 1789	Dec. 15, 1791
8	No excessive bail or fines, nor cruel and unusual punishment	1	16	Sept. 25, 1789	Dec. 15, 1791
9	Unenumerated rights of the people	1	21	Sept. 25, 1789	Dec. 15, 1791
10	Powers not delegated to federal government reserved to states and people	1	28	Sept. 25, 1789	Dec. 15, 1791
11	Keeps suits against states out of federal courts	1	43	March 4, 1794	Feb. 7, 1795
12	Revises Electoral College for President	1	399	Dec. 9, 1803	June 15, 1804
13	Prohibits slavery	2	47	Jan. 31, 1865	Dec. 6, 1865
14	Birthright citizenship; privileges or immunities; due process; equal protection; apportionment; bars insurrectionists from public office; validity of public debt	5	435	June 13, 1866	July 9, 1868

(continued)

Table 6.2 (continued)

#	*Subject(s)*	*Sections*	*Words*	*Proposed*	*Ratified*
15	Right to vote not denied based on race, color, or previous condition of servitude.	2	50	Feb. 26, 1869	Feb. 3, 1870
16	Authorizes income taxes	1	30	July 12, 1909	Feb. 3, 1913
17	Direct election of senators	1	134	May 13, 1912	April 8, 1913
18	Alcohol prohibition	3	112	Dec. 18, 1917	Jan. 16, 1919
19	Women's suffrage	1	39	June 4, 1919	Aug. 18, 1920
20	Presidential succession	6	353	March 2, 1932	Jan. 23, 1933
21	Repealing prohibition	3	96	Feb. 20, 1933	Dec. 5, 1933
22	Term limits for president	2	166	March 21, 1947	Feb. 27, 1951
23	Electoral College votes for District of Columbia	2	132	June 16, 1960	March 29, 1961
24	Removes poll taxes as an obstacle to voting	2	76	Aug. 27, 1962	Jan. 23, 1964
25	Presidential succession and removal	4	396	July 6, 1965	Feb. 10, 1967
26	Right to vote for those 18 years and older	2	52	March 23, 1971	July 1, 1971
27	Restriction on changing congressional pay	1	24	Sept. 25, 1789	May 7, 1992

line of succession in the 20th Amendment's 353 words, and handling a presidential vacancy or other inability to do the job in the 25th Amendment's 396 words. Many aspects of those amendments would have been difficult to enact by statute and needed a certain amount of detail. Laws do or could supplement each part, analogous to the Electoral Count Act of 1887 and proposals to clarify aspects of the 25th Amendment.

BBA Proposals by the Numbers

Let us extend this numbers-based approach to BBA proposals. Table 6.3 compares the balanced budget amendments discussed in the previous chapter with the latest versions of the two explored further in the next chapter.

Many of these BBA proposals would be the longest constitutional amendment, whether by the number of words or sections. The Barton-Istook-Goodlatte-Chabot-Nunn traditional BBA has eight sections with 313 or 325 words. The longer version mitigates a perverse incentive for military conflict.

Those with a more conservative bent are often longer, largely to counter the problems of annual balance. These include proposals from Sen. Mike Lee (R-UT), Sen. Cindy Hyde-Smith (R-MS), Rep. Scott Perry (R-PA), and Rep. John Ratcliffe (R-TX).

Proposals by moderate Democrats are long too. Former Rep. Ben McAdams' (D-UT) 8-section, 543-word BBA includes most of the faults in the traditional BBA, as well as carving Social Security and Medicare out from balance and setting aside the BBA during recessions. Sen. Jon Tester's (D-MT) 8 section, 596-word version does all that plus special treatment for disaster response funds.

The longest proposal by far comes from the Compact for America. Spanning 627 words, it includes the exceptionally bad idea of requiring states to approve federal borrowing among various others.

It is fair to ask why the length of a balanced budget amendment proposal matters and why we should care. Length is a proxy for consistency with amendments that have already demonstrated success—those that express principles and refrain from statute-like specificity for the Constitution.

The plentiful problems with provisions we have discussed support the idea of a streamlined BBA. The political reality is that a principles-based BBA can attract a broader consensus.

We still need to discuss how long a balanced budget amendment should be, why, or what specific provisions or principles they should include. That is the next chapter.

But first, two pairs of proposals are notably shorter. The Amash-Arrington-Braun Business Cycle BBA had only 270 words at the peak of its popularity, and we have trimmed it to 209 words without changing the substance. The Principles-based BBA was already concise when first

Table 6.3 Most BBA proposals are long compared to existing amendments

Sponsor	*Number*	*Description*	*Sections*	*Words*	*Cosponsors*
Rep. Bob Goodlatte (R-VA)	H.J.Res.2 (112th)	Annual balance, war incentive	8	313	226 R 16 D
Rep. Justin Amash (R-MI)	H.J.Res.81 (112th)	Business cycle balance, uniform emergency clause	5	270	45 R 14 D
Rep. Dave Brat (R-VA)	H.J.Res.55 (114th)	Balance principle, uniform emergency clause	3	113	64 R 1 D
Compact for America	Self-published	Annual balance, states approve federal borrowing	7	629	N/A
Sen. Jon Tester (D-MT)	S.J.Res.18 (116th)	Annual balance, recession allowance, entitlement/ disaster carveouts	8	596	0 R 2 D
Rep. John Ratcliffe (R-TX)	H.J.Res.51 (116th)	Annual balance, supermajorities for debt limit, withhold POTUS/ Congress' pay	11	548	5 R 0 D
Rep. Ben McAdams (D-UT)	H.J.Res.55 (116th)	Annual balance, recession allowance, entitlement carveouts	8	543	0 R 12 D
Rep. Mark Green (R-TN)	H.J.Res.68 (116th)	Annual balance, congressional veto of regulations	7	249	0 R 0 D

(continued)

Table 6.3 (continued)

Sponsor	*Number*	*Description*	*Sections*	*Words*	*Cosponsors*
Rep. Jodey Arrington (R-TX)	H.J.Res.113 (118th)	Business cycle balance, uniform emergency clause	4	209	8 R, 0 D
Sen. Cindy Hyde-Smith (R-MS)	S.J.Res.13 (118th)	Annual balance, supermajorities for debt limit and revenue	11	549	23 R 0 D
Sen. Mike Lee (R-UT)	S.J.Res.14 (118th)	Annual balance, supermajorities for debt limit and revenue, %GDP cap, no judicial involvement	9	334	1 R 0 D
Sen. Mike Braun (R-IN)	S.J.Res. 19 (118th)	Balance principle, uniform emergency clause	2	100	1 R, 0 D
Rep. Zach Nunn (R-IA)	H.J.Res.12 (118th)	Annual balance, no war incentive	8	325	19 R 0 D
Rep. Scott Perry (R-PA)	H.J.Res. 19 (118th)	Annual balance, agency justifications	9	545	4 R 0 D
Rep. Nathaniel Moran (R-TX)	H.J.Res.80 (118th)	Balance principle, uniform emergency clause	2	100	1 R, 0 D

a. Word count includes *section* and section numbers

introduced, and an updated version from Sen. Braun and Rep. Moran has an even 100 words.

Both are still longer than average. The current Business Cycle BBA with 209 words would be the fifth-longest amendment. The Principles-based BBA's 100 words would be the tenth-longest. Yet the constitutional part of the Swiss balance rule mentioned in Chapter 3 is 111 words. Perhaps that suggests a Goldilocks zone: neither too short nor too long.

Constitutional language should support timeless principles that endure over hundreds of years. When they reflect that, new constitutional proposals are most likely to succeed, persist, and benefit the American people. Many BBA proposals, however, look more like legislation or ideological principles that are not widely shared. Principles that reflect broad consensus may have the best chance for initial adoption and long-term acceptance.

Let us wrap up by looking at the Constitution's Article V amendment process and the questions that Congress would have to resolve for Article V implementing legislation. This exercise is not required to propose and ratify a BBA or any other amendment. It is simply to show that the provision setting up the amendment process is itself full of ambiguities that Congress could and probably should clarify by statute.

Clarifying the Constitution's Amendment Process

The language of Article V is reproduced at the start of this chapter, as is a summary of the proposal and ratification stages.

To recap, the traditional route for constitutional amendments is straightforward and well-understood. If two-thirds of both houses of Congress approve the same language, Congress proposes an amendment to state legislatures. It becomes part of the Constitution when ratified by legislatures in three-fourths of states.

These provisions could be more precise that two-thirds of *each* house of Congress—290 in the House and 67 in the Senate, based on current numbers and assuming no absences—must approve a proposal rather than two-thirds of the combined membership (357 total votes). Likewise, approval by state legislatures could specify separate approval by each chamber of a state's legislature. In the first case, however, each house of Congress has the power to make the rules for its proceedings. In the second, the federal government and the states separately have sovereignty in our system, so leaving it to each state to decide how and whether its legislature has approved a proposal respects each state's authority over its internal processes.

Turning to the road not traveled, Congress has never called a convention of states to propose amendments. Advocates drawing from the Article

V Library[12] claim that the requisite threshold—two-thirds of state legislatures—has been met several times, and Congress has failed to call a convention.

The Federal Fiscal Sustainability Foundation is the principal organization advancing these arguments. Led by former U.S. Comptroller General David M. Walker, former Virginia Attorney General Ken Cuccinelli, former New Hampshire state senator Jim Rubens, Admiral Bill Owens, and professors Steve H. Hanke and Barry W. Poulson, FFSF has been active in educating members of Congress, state legislators, and the public while organizing litigation in pursuit of a convention of states. They may have inspired a concurrent resolution by Rep. Jodey Arrington that would require Congress to call a convention for proposing a fiscal responsibility amendment to the Constitution. A failure to call a convention may not have been intentional, however. In politics, the simplest explanation is usually the best: ignorance. (Bewilderment may be second best: seeing the issue but having no idea what to do about it.) Neither the Clerk of the House, the Secretary of the Senate, the Library of Congress, nor the Archivist of the United States has been tasked with compiling and publishing a definitive repository of active and rescinded applications for a convention. Tracking applications would be the most important part of Article V implementing legislation.

Once Congress sets up a tracking system, another question is which applications belong together. Presumably, Congress should aggregate anything with balancing the budget or controlling the debt. It would not make sense to combine these fiscal applications with those regarding, for example, campaign finance, the Equal Rights Amendment, parental rights, term limits, and so on. But what about plenary applications, which do not specify the subject matter of amendment proposals? It could be a political decision, except the text says Congress *shall* call the convention when two-thirds of state legislatures have applied. Some guidance is appropriate.

Then again, perhaps this aggregation paradigm is mistaken. Article V says Congress "shall call" a convention "on the Application of the Legislatures of two thirds of the several States." It does not specify that the applications must be on the same subject, nor does it even imply that result with a proviso such as "for an Amendment." If any outstanding application should count toward the two-thirds threshold, the case for calling a convention several decades overdue appears to be strong.

But what does it mean to call a convention? How quickly would it have to convene, and where would it occur? It would be logical for a convention to occur in the seat of government in Washington, D.C., near the country's center of population in southern Missouri, a convenient airport hub, or perhaps the Constitution's birthplace in Philadelphia. Still, Congress could choose somewhere inconvenient like Nome, Alaska, or full of distractions like New York City or Miami. It would be reasonable for a convention to begin once delegates had time to prepare, but could Congress schedule it for several years later? Could a convention, once assembled, change the date and location of the meeting place(s)?

Can a convention, once called, be limited to the subject matter for which Congress convened it or to the limits set by state legislatures? Are the parliamentary procedures clear? Some argue that each state's delegation would collectively have one vote, because two-thirds of state legislatures must have applied for a convention, and any amendment must be ratified by three-fourths of state legislatures.[13] Others do not think that is clear at all.

It seems likely[14] that a convention of states would stick to the applicable subject matter, in part due to states' legislation requiring their commissioners to do so. Most other commissioners would likely feel duty-bound to do the same even without specific requirements. Needing three-fourths of state legislatures to approve a proposed amendment is a further bulwark. It seems clear that each state would get one vote on any question properly pending in a convention, and that states with more than one commissioner would need an intra-state-delegation majority to take a position. As a collective exercise of representatives of the sovereign states, the commission would likely choose its own officers to enforce its own rules. Even so, many members of Congress might prefer that Congress develops the proposals.

Does Congress have authority to shape the rules of a convention's proceedings, or is a convention beyond the exercise of the federal government's sovereignty? If the latter, Sen. Orrin Hatch's proposed Constitutional Convention Implementation Act (see Chapter 4) would have overreached. Perhaps, however, Congress could indicate preferences through the softer use of *should* instead of the mandatory *shall*.

Article V does, however, appear to give Congress the choice of whether a proposed amendment would be subject to ratification by state legislatures or by conventions in the states. Proposals from Congress almost always designate state legislatures as the deciders. It could be clarified, however, if Congress would say so when calling a convention applied for by state legislatures or if Congress could decide (or change its decision) after seeing what, if anything, comes out of a convention.

Moreover, some believe that the use of *may* instead of *shall* in "Mode of Ratification may be proposed by Congress" means that a convention can decide the mode of ratification, or at least Congress can leave it up to the convention. Others read the provision to say that Congress decides, but again, that question may be appropriate for Congress to settle with implementing legislation.

In addition, the failed Equal Rights Amendment suggests several other components of implementing legislation for Article V. First, if Congress (or a convention) sets a time limit for ratification, any attempts to ratify beyond that point are invalid. Second, if a ratification period ends, Congress cannot simply extend it by a majority vote—it must begin the amendment process with two-thirds approval all over again. Third, a ratification resolution can be rescinded before the thirty-eighth state legislature ratifies, but not afterward.

A BBA Is the Foundation for Further Construction

Constitutional language typically raises more questions than it answers. Principles are inherently vague and subject to interpretation. Legislation through statutes should translate enduring principles into an operating manual for a government serving the people today and for the foreseeable future.

Constitutional fiscal rules likewise cannot be ironclad, self-enforcing provisions. They should set forth broad principles and let Congress grapple with the details. Future legislators should be able to improve implementing legislation through the normal legislative process. The constitutional principle is a North Star that sets a general direction, not a detailed route for Congress.

Next, we will look at better approaches to a balanced budget amendment. After that, we will see how they measure up against concerns raised about BBAs. And then, we will consider components of the implementing legislation that would give form and function to a principles-based BBA.

Notes

1. Tom Coburn, *Smashing the DC Monopoly: Using Article V to Restore Freedom and Stop Runaway Government*, WND Books, 2017. Michael W. Kapic, *Conventions That Made America: A Brief History Of Consensus Building*, MWK Publishing, 2018.
2. The Bill of Rights and the post-Civil War amendments are strongly positive, as are the other voting rights amendments. The Prohibition Amendment (#18) takes the cake for the worst amendment on practical and legal grounds. The direct election of senators (#17) turned senators from representatives of the states to something like House members but with longer terms and full-state electorates. Both methods—selection by state legislatures and selection by general ballot—have pros and cons, so neither is obviously preferable. The income tax amendment (#16) let Congress tap a revenue geyser, paving the way for massive growth in government spending. Term limits for legislators seriously impair the power of the people's representatives, but Amendment XXII restored a norm established by George Washington for a two-term limit on presidents that President-for-life Franklin Delano Roosevelt broke. This amendment is an obstacle for would-be authoritarians at the White House.
3. U.S. Statutes at Large, https://www.govinfo.gov/app/collection/STATUTE.
4. U.S. Department of State, Treaties in Force, https://www.state.gov/treaties-in-force/.
5. U.S. CBO, "Expired and Expiring Authorizations of Appropriations for Fiscal Year 2022—Information for Legislation Enacted Through September 30, 2021," https://www.cbo.gov/publication/57739, January 14, 2022.
6. Kurt Couchman, "No presidential power is beyond Congress," https://thehill.com/opinion/white-house/369379-no-presidential-power-is-beyond-congress/, *The Hill*, January 17, 2018. Kurt Couchman, "Congress has substantial powers—if it claims them," *The Hill*, https://thehill.com/opinion/white-house/369006-congress-has-substantial-powers-if-it-claims-them/, January 15, 2018. Kurt Couchman, "The War Powers Resolution doesn't let the president start wars," *The Hill*, https://thehill.com/opinion/international/383404-the-war-powers-resolution-doesnt-let-the-president-start-wars/, April 16, 2018.

7. Title 26, United States Code, https://uscode.house.gov/view.xhtml?path=/prelim@title26&edition=prelim, accessed September 10, 2023. This includes a great deal of legislative history, reports, and other language that provides context to but is generally not directly part of existing statutes.
8. Electoral Count Act of 1887, Title 3, United States Code, Section 1-21, http://uscode.house.gov/view.xhtml?path=/prelim@title3/chapter1&edition=prelim, accessed June 6, 2022.
9. See, e.g., the Supreme Court decisions in *West Virginia v. Environmental Protection Agency*, 597 U.S. 697 (2022), restricting agencies from unilaterally deciding "major questions" of a legislative nature or in *Loper Bright Enterprises v. Raimondo*, 603 U.S. 369 (2024), clarifying that judges must not defer to agencies on the best reading of statutory text.
10. This process assumes, of course, that Congress faces healthy incentives. That is not as true as it should be, but efforts are underway to improve that.
11. Rob Natelson, "Understanding the Constitution: Constitutional Amendments Work, *The Epoch Times*, https://www.theepochtimes.com/understanding-the-constitution-constitutional-amendments-work_4027117.html, October 1, 2021.
12. Article V Library, http://article5library.org/.
13. American Legislative Exchange Council, *Article V Handbook*, https://alec.org/publication/article-v-handbook/, February 1, 2012.
14. This comes from studying documents listed in the endnotes here, as well as others, and from conversations with proponents and opponents of an Article V amendment convention. Historical precedent is not definitively binding on the present, however, particularly when historical knowledge has faded from general awareness even among those most likely to be involved in carrying out a convention. Still, recent efforts to familiarize state legislators, members of Congress, advocates, and others interested in constitutional reform with historical practice makes it more likely than not that such procedures would be followed in general form if a Convention of States were to occur.

CHAPTER 7

Next-Generation BBAs Emerge

In the mid-term election year of 2010, David Malpass was running to fill the Senate seat Hillary Clinton had vacated to join the Obama administration. Malpass had already served in the Reagan and George H.W. Bush administrations and on Capitol Hill. He had an impressive private sector background in the accounting and financial sectors and would later serve in the first Trump administration and as president of the World Bank.

Malpass scheduled a meeting with Cato Institute senior fellow Bill Niskanen. I sat in to represent government affairs. They covered a lot of ground. The Tea Party movement was in full force, and its push for a balanced budget amendment appealed to Malpass.

Bill agreed that some BBA would make sense but advised against annual balance as pro-cyclical and unpredictable. He said spending should be limited to revenue in the second prior year, maybe adjusted for inflation and population. That way, he said, policymakers would know the spending cap well before the fiscal year began, and the lag would produce a roughly countercyclical budget. An increasingly productive economy would generate small structural surpluses to help pay down the debt.

The second prior year's revenue would fit the budget timeline. The *first* prior year's revenue would come too late: final information for, say, fiscal year (FY) 2024 is available in mid-October 2024, long after long after budgeting for FY 2025 should have been completed. FY 2024 data in October 2024—as the *second* prior year's revenue for FY 2026—is

K. Couchman, *Fiscal Democracy in America*,
https://doi.org/10.1007/978-3-031-91938-1_7

perfect to inform the president's budget proposal, due to Congress the first Monday in February 2025, and the congressional budget process for FY 2026 that began in spring 2025.

I left the meeting thinking about Bill's proposal. It did not seem like he had run the numbers, but it made intuitive sense. Putting the data in a spreadsheet showed what it would look like.

The Business Cycle BBA Emerges

Niskanen's general points were all correct. No surprise there.

Yet his suggestion would create tremendous volatility to federal budgeting. True, it would be more predictable and countercyclical than annual balance. But it would require Congress to enact big changes to spending or revenue policies (or both) simply to hit fluctuating targets. This instability would create even more uncertainty for policymakers and the public.

Around that time, I had been reviewing state and local debt limits while finishing graduate school. These are typically constitutional or statutory rules that states have adopted to support fiscal responsibility and to reassure bond buyers. Many originated with the fiscal troubles of the late 1830s and early 1840s or those of the 1870s. Many are still in place. Governing outcomes reflect the interaction of formal rules like debt limits and informal institutions like bond markets and citizen expectations.

Reflecting on the Malpass-Niskanen conversation after graduating, I thought reviewing the BBAs already introduced in Congress would be a good practical use for all that book learning.

I visited Thomas.loc.gov—the predecessor of Congress.gov—and read through the BBAs from recent terms of Congress. It was not pretty. Each had similar problems: annual balance, the president's budget request in the Constitution, little time after ratification to balance, and low-and-easily-met thresholds for emergency response. The traditional BBA from the beginning of Chapter 5 had all those issues, and other versions had added new flourishes to that broken foundation.

Something better had to be possible. I returned to Niskanen's idea with the thought that averaging multiple years could smooth out revenue fluctuations. I tried various multi-year periods, all with the second prior year of revenue as the final or second-to-last year of the calculation. Averaging more years reduces the noise of economic volatility and produces a path closer to a trend, about as much as seemed possible in an uncertain world.

On the other hand, averaging more years increases the feedback period. Imagine that Congress wants to change the size of government in either direction. With annual balance, an immediate revenue increase (decrease) allows a commensurate spending increase (decrease). Capping regular spending at the revenue of the second prior year means waiting two years to increase spending in the case of a tax increase or to reduce spending in the case of a tax cut.

A revenue-based rolling average lets a revenue change phase into the spending rule. For example, a five-year rolling average would mean that FY 2024 non-emergency spending would derive from FY 2018–2023 receipts. That seemed too long. Spending would include any revenue changes in the prior year, but that year would only contribute one-fifth of the spending limit.

Ultimately, tying spending to a three-year rolling average of revenue seemed like a good balance between smoothing out fluctuations and adjusting spending for changes in revenue. Many members of Congress of both parties would later agree.

This process was all tinkering: no grand plan, just playing with a spreadsheet.

As Niskanen recommended, the final piece for the balance rule was adjusting revenue for inflation and population. Without those adjustments, a BBA based on prior tax collections would generate large structural surpluses, pay off the debt in a few decades, and then require revisiting the Constitution again.

On the other hand, adjusting for inflation and population but not productivity for those three revenue years would produce small structural surpluses. It would be roughly enough to offset emergencies. Holding total debt more-or-less constant would let economic growth drive most reductions in the debt-to-GDP ratio.

To be clear, these adjustments are not at all like Colorado's Taxpayers Bill of Rights. TABOR limits *spending growth* to the sum of inflation and population growth, leaving out productivity increases. This BBA concept adjusts prior *revenue* by inflation and population growth. Those revenue amounts include productivity increases up to the last few years of adjustments.

This rule accommodated several important features. It would tie spending and revenue together over the medium term with a small allowance to offset emergencies. Basing spending on recent revenue would give Congress advance notice and a more predictable spending cap, while the rolling average would provide stability. It would let Congress choose overall spending and revenue without putting a thumb on the scale of where those levels should be, except that they should be together.

Moving on to emergency thresholds, three-fifths was too low. Higher seemed better. James Buchanan and Gordon Tullock's *Calculus of Consent*[1] describes the tradeoff between minimizing political externalities (the costs of a majority imposing on a minority) with higher thresholds versus the lower transaction costs (easier to reach agreement) of lower thresholds. It seemed then that emergency response should require something close to unanimity.

A nine-tenths requirement seemed right at the time. But that did not consider the ability of small factions to hold an emergency package hostage to extract concessions. In addition, nine-tenths would be well above the highest threshold in the Constitution applicable to Congress—two-thirds for approving constitutional amendments, veto overrides, and, just for the Senate, convicting an impeached official and ratifying treaties.

Jumping ahead, the first version of the Business Cycle BBA had a three-fourths requirement for emergencies, but the second version introduced three months later set it at two-thirds, where it has remained ever since.

Real emergencies with good faith legislative responses have always quickly cleared a two-thirds requirement (see Table 7.1). It might have prevented Congress from approving President George W. Bush's disastrous regime change in Iraq and kept Speaker Nancy Pelosi (D-CA) from including so much nonsense in the late-2008 Wall Street bailout bill (and later, the COVID-19-related American Rescue Plan Act), however, but both outcomes would have been better for the country.

Returning to 2010, it seemed natural for the president's budget proposal to have the same requirements. Common constraints would help the president's submission be useful to Congress. The risks to the balance of powers were not clear yet. Also unknown at the time, statute already requires much from the president's budget proposal, and Congress could amend the law for the president's budget request to comply with a BBA.[2]

The two-thirds requirement for Congress to approve a constitutional amendment meant that both spending and revenue had to be on the table for reaching and sustaining balance. Even so, I tried to draft a provision to

Table 7.1 Congressional votes on emergency legislation usually exceed two-thirds

Legislation	*Year*	*House**	*Senate*
Declaration of War: World War I	1917	88.2%	93.2%
Pre-WWII Appropriations	1940	99.7%	100.0%
WWII Declaration of War: Germany	1941	100.0%	100.0%
WWII Declaration of War: Italy	1941	100.0%	100.0%
WWII Declaration of War: Japan	1941	99.7%	100.0%
Cuban Missile Crisis Resolution Authorizing Force	1962	98.2%	98.9%
Gulf of Tonkin Resolution	1965	100.0%	97.8%
Operation Desert Shield Appropriations	1990	90.3%	Unanimous Consent
Authorization for Use of Military Force against Iraq	1991	**57.7%**	Unanimous Consent
Y2K Preparation	1999	94.4%	81.8%
Defense and Emergency Appropriations, FY 2002	2001	98.6%	97.9%
9/11 Response Supplemental Appropriations	2001	100.0%	Unanimous Consent
9/11 Authorization of Military Force	2001	Unanimous Consent	100.0%
Supplemental Appropriations, FY 2002	2002	92.5%	92.9%
Authorization for Use of Military Force in Iraq	2002	69.0%	77.0%
Defense Appropriations, FY 2003	2002	96.7%	98.9%
Defense Appropriations, FY 2004	2003	96.4%	100.0%
Supplemental Appropriations, FY 2003	2003	Voice Vote	Unanimous Consent
Supplemental Appropriations, FY 2004	2003	71.1%	Voice Vote
Defense Appropriations, FY 2005	2004	97.2%	100.0%
Defense and Emergency Appropriations, FY 2006	2005	74.4%	100.0%
Hurricane Katrina Response	2005	Voice Vote	Unanimous Consent

(continued)

Table 7.1 (continued)

Legislation	*Year*	*House**	*Senate*
Hurricane Katrina Supplemental Appropriations	2005	97.4%	100.0%
Supplemental Appropriations, FY 2007	2006	86.4%	100.0%
Supplemental Appropriations, FY 2006	2006	84.0%	99.0%
Defense Appropriations, FY 2007	2006	94.7%	100.0%
Defense Appropriations, FY 2008	2007	96.4%	Voice Vote
Supplemental Appropriations, FY 2008	2007	97.2%	93.9%
Bush 2008 Stimulus Bill	2008	91.8%	83.5%
Emergency Economic Stabilization Act of 2008 (TARP)	2008	**60.6%**	74.7%
Defense Appropriations, FY 2010	2009	92.1%	89.8%
Supplemental Appropriations Act, 2009	2009	**52.8%**	94.8%
American Recovery and Reinvestment Act of 2009	2009	**57.3%**	**61.2%**

channel revenue reductions into rates instead of proliferating tax expenditures, or exemptions from taxation. It did not quite work and would eventually get dropped.

Two other aspects seemed ripe for improvement: time to balance and defining a path. A full decade to reach balance seemed more realistic than just a few years. A defined path based on declining fractions (see Table 7.2) seemed reasonable. This would gradually and predictably phase out deficits by ratcheting down spending above the limit over a decade.

This process developed three new ideas: (1) a balance-over-the-business-cycle mechanism, (2) a single supermajority for emergencies, and (3) a stepwise transition to balance. Early versions sought to cap *outlays* and had other later-addressed issues.

Also, in 2010, Cato scholar John Samples blogged about a state representative who explained his votes on Facebook.[3] John lauded this 30-year-old Michigander for transparency and real-time accountability. Soon

Table 7.2 Phasing out deficits with declining fractions

Year after ratification	*Deficit as fraction of prior year*	*Transitional deficit, starting with $1 trillion*	*Deficit reduction each year*
0 (ratification)	n/a	$1,000 billion	n/a
1	9/10	$900 billion	$100 billion
2	8/9	$800 billion	$100 billion
3	7/8	$700 billion	$100 billion
4	6/7	$600 billion	$100 billion
5	5/6	$500 billion	$100 billion
6	4/5	$400 billion	$100 billion
7	3/4	$300 billion	$100 billion
8	2/3	$200 billion	$100 billion
9	1/2	$100 billion	$100 billion
10	0	$0	$100 billion

enough, the BBA tinkering described here and Michigan representative Justin Amash would come together.

Fast-forward to Election Day 2010. It was a blowout for Republicans. Fueled by the backlash to Democratic overreach, Tea Party energy drove Republican recruitment and electoral success. True, flawed candidates limited the gains, but it was a lopsided election.

By then, I was ready to return to Capitol Hill and had gotten to know some outstanding congressional staffers in both parties. By the end of January 2011, I was on Representative Amash's team covering budget, his Budget Committee and Joint Economic Committee assignments, and many other issues.

The Business Cycle BBA Matures

Turning the BBA ideas into legislation was a team effort, and Amash was hands-on. He needed to understand every bill, every resolution, and every amendment before he took a vote or made a statement, whether on the House floor or in committee. This is rare in Congress. Ideally, he would understand legislation well before a vote so he could share his views with colleagues. Committee and party leaders did not always appreciate that.

For his own legislation, everything had to be right. We could not have unclear or unworkable language. With his commitment to an originalist understanding of the Constitution, a constitutional amendment required extra special scrutiny.

We discussed and debated everything. We consulted with the House Office of Legislative Counsel, the Congressional Budget Office, and the House Budget Committee. It was a group project, even beyond our office. Luke Kenworthy, then a legislative assistant for close ally Rep. Marlin Stutzman (R-IN), caught an issue in the deficit phase-out that we had overlooked in the pre-introduction draft. We promptly corrected that. Justin's brothers got involved.

We realized that pushing tax cuts toward rate reduction instead of tax loopholes would not work. It had to go. We agreed that the president's budget request does not belong. We settled on a single emergency threshold at three-fourths, the highest threshold in the Constitution.

Amash thought his colleagues would like a one-page summary (one-pager) and a side-by-side of the language and "plain English" descriptions (see Table 7.3). A 25-page slide deck made the extended case. We called it the Business Cycle Balanced Budget Amendment (BCBBA) to distinguish it from every other version, all based on annual balance.

We began outreach well before introducing the BCBBA. It was designated as a *spending limit* and would have required three-fourths for emergency response. It was time to build the coalition.

Amash had already stood out as an independent thinker with good relationships on both sides of the aisle. He shared materials with colleagues in committees, at member meetings, and on the floor. We sent Dear Colleague letters to other offices, talked it up at meetings, and engaged outside experts and advocates.

Some conservatives balked at the lack of a barrier to raising revenue. One staffer to a moderate Senate Republican said, "I will never let my boss support a BBA that allows tax increases." Others recognized that spending is the true cost of government that someone must pay sooner or later.

We did one-on-one meetings with House Democratic members as well. We had wonderful conversations with many Democrats, including Marcy Kaptur, Adam Smith, John Garamendi, Mike Quigley, Frank Pallone, David Cicilline, and more. Some cosponsored, some did not, but it was a great way to get to know them and to build relationships.

One future committee chair said he could not remember the last time a Republican member had come to his office to pitch him on legislation. Another said he would not cosponsor but would likely vote for it if it

Table 7.3 A "plain English" description of the BCBBA

Text of BCBBA	*Plain English*
SECTION 1. Total outlays for a year shall not exceed the average annual revenue collected in the three prior years, adjusted in proportion to changes in population and inflation. Total outlays shall include all outlays of the United States except those for payment of debt, and revenue shall include all revenue of the United States except that derived from borrowing	**Spending = rolling average of recent revenue** (average revenue of previous three, adjusted for population changes, inflation) "Outlays" include everything but debt reduction. Borrowing is not "revenue."
SECTION 2. Congress may by a roll call vote of two-thirds of each House declare an emergency and provide by law for specific outlays in excess of the limit in Section 1. The declaration shall specify reasons for the emergency designation and may authorize outlays in excess of the limit in Section 1 for up to one year	Additional emergency outlays 1) Require two-thirds support 2) Require detailed emergency declaration 3) Only last one year at a time (can be renewed)
SECTION 3. Congress shall have power to enforce this article by appropriate legislation	Reasonable implementing legislation is authorized
SECTION 4. This article shall take effect in the first year beginning at least 90 days following ratification, except that outlays may exceed the limit in Section 1 by the following portion of the prior year's outlays exceeding that limit (excepting emergency outlays provided for by Section 2): nine-tenths in the first year, eight-ninths in the second, seven-eighths in the third, six-sevenths in the fourth, five-sixths in the fifth, four-fifths in the sixth, three-fourths in the seventh, two-thirds in the eighth, and one-half in the ninth	Gradual ten-year transition, beginning the year (fiscal or calendar) starting 90 days after ratification to allow time to write implementing legislation & change policies Ratification-year deficit reduced at least 1/10th each subsequent year. Faster deficit reduction locks in that progress Emergencies don't affect baseline

went to the House floor. Another cosponsored. We were struck by the differences between members' often-angry-and-cutting-when-on-camera personas and their warmth in private.

We finally introduced the BCBBA as H.J.Res.73 (Appendix, Exhibit 16) on July 21, 2011, with 19 Republicans and Democrat Dan Lipinski (D-IL) cosponsoring. By the time we added the last cosponsor—Mike Quigley, D-IL, now a senior appropriator and a hockey fan whose crack about former Rep. Anthony Weiner's "fifth hole problem" went over our heads—on October 12, 2011, the resolution had 39 Republican and 4 Democratic cosponsors: Quigley, Lipinski, Jared Polis (D-CO), and Heath Shuler (D-NC).[4]

We took all feedback seriously. Rep. Jim Moran (D-VA) said three-fourths for emergencies was too high. He preferred three-fifths, but he could live with two-thirds. We took a closer look at constitutional supermajority requirements and realized that two-thirds is more appropriate and more appealing. That is the level for Congress to override presidents' vetoes as well as for other congressional actions.

We realized that the long title calling it a spending limit amendment was incorrect and an obstacle to broader support. Many further conversations later, BCBBA 2.0 was ready.

We re-introduced the Business Cycle BBA as H.J.Res.81 (Appendix, Exhibit 17) on October 14, 2011, with a two-thirds emergency requirement and an accurate long title for a *balanced budget amendment*.[5] Cosponsors included 22 Republicans and 8 Democrats, including Mr. Moran and future governors Jared Polis (D-CO) and Mike Michaud (D-ME), as well as future Senator Cory Gardner (R-CO), future Secretary of State Mike Pompeo (R-KS), and future White House Chief of Staff Mick Mulvaney (R-SC). By the end of the 112th Congress, 45 Republicans and 14 Democrats were cosponsors.

This all happened at the peak of Tea Party influence. Republicans had taken the House, but Harry Reid (D-NV) remained Senate Majority Leader, and Barack Obama still presided over the executive branch. House Republicans insisted that year's debt limit deal must avoid default that year while reducing the risk of future default. Congress and the president headed for a showdown.

The week before we introduced the first version of the BCBBA, Rep. Jason Chaffetz (R-UT) proposed the Cut, Cap, and Balance Act of 2011.[6] It would have raised the debt limit by $2.4 trillion when Congress proposed a particular kind of BBA to the states and would have set caps on various categories of spending. Conservatives liked it, and many outside organizations included votes on their scorecards.[7] In reality, it was flawed and lacked bipartisan support.[8]

The debt limit impasse brought frantic activity. No one wanted a default, but many Republicans believed that failing to control the debt would only defer default—via fiscal crisis—for a few years. Fighting to reduce excessive spending was existential.

The unsatisfying resolution was the Budget Control Act of 2011, enacted on August 3, 2011.[9] It raised the debt limit, set caps on annually appropriated spending, established a *super committee* of members to strike a deal on deficit reduction, and set up a vote on a balanced budget amendment later that year.

Rep. Bob Goodlatte's (R-VA) conventional BBA was the incumbent proposal and had broad support: 226 Republicans and 16 Democrats by the time Rep. Amash introduced the BCBBA.[10] Yet those 16 Democrats were predominantly moderate Democrats in the Blue Dog Coalition. By contrast, the BCBBA counted moderate, mainstream, and progressive Democrats—such as Polis, Yarmuth, and Moran—as cosponsors.

Amash and I met with House Majority Leader Eric Cantor (R-VA) and his staff. We explained the BCBBA's features, the conversations we were having, and the shortcomings of the traditional BBA. Cantor liked new ideas, good policy, building bridges, and fresh energy.

By then, Amash was known as a maverick, not a reliable vote for leadership. Even so, we could see Cantor's increasing interest, maybe even excitement. He encouraged us to keep at it, and especially to keep working to add Democratic cosponsors.

We did. Amash requested a few minutes at the regular meeting of the Blue Dog Democrats. They let him share the BCBBA and asked great questions. I pitched as many House and Senate Democratic staff as seemed possibly open to it and were willing to talk. In the process, we met great people and developed some lasting relationships.

A staffer to a senior Democratic House member said it is the kind of thing you could build a career on. A senior advisor to a Democratic senator humored me with a meeting. As we talked, he realized we were serious about developing something workable, not just another messaging BBA.

Meanwhile, Republican members most interested in a BBA convened throughout 2011 in Rep. Goodlatte's office. Attendees included Goodlatte, Amash, Mick Mulvaney (R-SC), Todd Rokita (R-IN), Steve Chabot (R-OH), and several other members and their staff.

That is where we heard that another member had copied the BCBBA with only cosmetic changes and introduced it as his own. A local Tea Party group had spliced pieces they liked from all the different BBAs. We engaged them on it and explained the problems with the non-BCBBA provisions. Surprisingly, they dropped them and pushed their representative to introduce the BCBBA with a seven-year transition to balance instead of ten.

During those meetings, Republican members also talked about "jamming the Democrats" and forcing them to be "accountable" for the Pelosi-Obama deficit surge instead of building bridges, seeking common ground, and developing shared visions and partnerships for fixing our country's problems. It was an echo chamber. Those of us in Amash's office thought it was a bad strategy.

Amash resolved to approach House Minority Whip Steny Hoyer (D-MD). Hoyer was a former Blue Dog Democrat—the most centrist faction of the Democratic party—who had voted for the traditional BBA when it passed the House in 1995.[11] Hoyer cares about fiscal responsibility. Amash hoped to persuade him that the BCBBA was the best approach.

Amash pitched Hoyer on the floor one day. Hoyer said Amash was the first Republican to raise the subject with him, and he appreciated it. But Hoyer realized that the BCBBA could pass, so he told Democratic members not to cosponsor if they had not already. We knew it was a gamble, and it did not break our way.

We did plenty of outreach to Republicans as well, but Republicans are generally on board with BBAs, even one without provisions that especially appeal to conservatives. The point is that relationships matter. A good proposal with broad appeal is the start of the process. Establishing common ground, trust, and good feelings toward each other is necessary too. Ideally, that would be common in a legislature, but there is enormous room for improvement in today's Congress.

Rep. Goodlatte's traditional BBA would ultimately get the House vote on November 18, 2011.[12] Amash did not like the idea of supporting a constitutional amendment with so many problems. I pushed him to vote for it harder than I should have. I thought it would earn him political capital to stay at the table and keep advancing the BCBBA. He did not and does not think that way. And he was the member, after all.

Sometime later, we were all back in the staff office, and he looked at me and said loudly so all could hear, "Kurt, you have the most limited government principles of anyone on my staff. You see things almost exactly the way I do. But you're also the first one willing to sell out." He was being funny, but the kernel of truth is that I am pragmatic. Moving the ball forward sometimes requires compromise.

Amash's mission was to build a coherent, constitutional, principles-based vision for federal policy, and maybe his approach will matter more in the long run. Then again, maybe we need both challengers and bargainers to create change. In any case, we mostly agreed on where to end up but differed on how to get there.

The Goodlatte BBA, H.J.Res.2, got 261 of 426 votes cast, only 61.3 percent of the House, not the two-thirds needed for a constitutional amendment. The four Republicans who voted no were Rules Chair David Dreier (CA), Budget Chair Paul Ryan (WI), former judge Louie Gohmert (TX), and Justin Amash (MI). Ryan and Gohmert feared an annual balance ratchet where spending restraint would be temporary, but revenue increases would persist. Dreier seemed disenchanted with BBAs generally.

The 161 Democrats who opposed it included BCBBA cosponsors Braley (IA), Langevin (RI), Michaud (ME), Moran (VA), Polis (CO), Quigley (IL), Schrader (OR), and Yarmuth (KY). Simply shifting those eight Democrats and four Republicans from nay to yea would have brought support up to 64 percent. We believed then, however, that if the BCBBA had come to a vote, between 70 and 75 percent of House members would have supported it.

That failed vote dissipated the energy for a BBA. As the Budget Control Act required, the Senate soon followed with its BBA votes. 67 Senators voted for BBAs then, but 47 Republicans voted for the conservative S.J.Res.10[13] by Sen. Orrin Hatch (R-UT), and 20 Democrats and 1 Republican voted for the also problematic S.J.Res.24[14] by Sen. Mark Udall (D-CO). Broad support exists for a BBA, but Congress has never voted on a well-written version.

We kept working on the BCBBA, but Congress' focus shifted. Congress has not seriously considered a BBA since then. Even so, as we prepared to re-introduce for the 114th Congress (2015–2016), we made a small but important change: replacing *outlays* with *expenditures* (Appendix, Exhibit 18). To refresh, *outlays* happen when agencies transfer money to non-federal entities, and Congress does not control them directly. *Expenditures* is a general term that is already in the Constitution and that implementing legislation can clarify.

The Principles-Based BBA Emerged from the BCBBA Lessons

Sometime during the 113th Congress (2013–2014), I found myself explaining the BCBBA to another dad at the playground. At one point, he said something like, "It sounds complicated. Can't you just say that the budget should be balanced?" I had an explanation, but his question nagged at me.

Could a BBA be principles-based instead of well-engineered and prescriptive? Eventually, the idea of a principles-based BBA seemed viable, although it would require more from implementing legislation (see Chapter 9).

Amash was already closely associated with and invested in the BCBBA, so this new approach would come along to my next adventure.

In a June 10, 2014, Republican primary election in Virginia, previously little-known Randolph-Macon College economics professor Dr. Dave Brat defeated House Majority Leader Eric Cantor. Cantor resigned soon after, setting up a simultaneous special election for the remainder of the term and the general election for the 114th Congress. Brat won both and took office in December 2014.

Brat has a Ph.D. in economics from American University and a master's degree in divinity from Princeton Theological Seminary. His campaign against Cantor had a populist tinge. He did not expect to win when he started running and only realized he might a few weeks before the primary.

Brat hired Heritage Action for America's top lobbyist, Erin Siefring, as chief of staff. She and I had been attending—and sometimes clashing at—a regular, off-the-record meeting of staff to Tea Party members and aligned organizations convened by Paul Teller, then chief of staff to Senator Ted Cruz. One attendee called it the "Mushroom Caucus" because leaders "feed us shit and keep us in the dark."

In any case, Erin interviewed me for legislative director in Brat's office. Rep. Brat was unusually casual and friendly compared to other members with whom I'd interviewed. His priorities were budget and immigration, and I had covered both, so it was a match. What became the Principles-based BBA was taking shape by then. Despite what had been learned from BCBBA discussions, we had to work through refinements before pitching other offices.

We let Amash know we would introduce the resolution soon. He hurried up and re-introduced the BCBBA as H.J.Res.54[15] two days before Brat introduced the Principles-based BBA as H.J.Res.55[16] on May 20, 2015. They cosponsored each other's BBA and were allies on much else too.

H.J.Res.55 ended up with 64 Republicans and one Democrat (Dan Lipinski of IL) as cosponsors that Congress. Here is the original language, also in Appendix, Exhibit 20, and the current, tighter version is in the introduction.

> Section 1. Expenditures and receipts shall be balanced, which may occur over more than one year to accommodate economic conditions. Expenditures shall include all expenditures of the United States except those for payment of debt, and receipts shall include all receipts of the United States except those derived from borrowing.
> Section 2. For emergency situations, two-thirds of the House of Representatives and the Senate may for limited times authorize expenditures exceeding those pursuant to rules established under Section 1. Debts incurred from such expenditures shall be paid as soon as practicable.
> Section 3. Congress shall have power to enforce this article by appropriate legislation, which shall allow not more than ten years after ratification to comply with Section 1.

The Principles-based BBA has common themes with the Business Cycle BBA. They include a single, two-thirds emergency threshold. They would give Congress a decade to reach balance after ratification. They would avoid requiring annual balance, they would not include the president's budget request, and they would steer clear of ideological provisions that alienate members. They would let Congress choose through implementing legislation whether to pursue full or primary balance, which excludes interest on the debt, due to ambiguity in the term *payment of debt* in Section 1.

Where the BCBBA is specific, however, the Principles-based BBA is general. It requires balance, but it leaves the particulars to implementing legislation. Congress could choose annual balance, although the (technically unnecessary) allowance to do it over more than one year signals that a multi-year period is better. Rather than a formulaic phase-out of deficits, it lets Congress craft a statutory path.

The Principles-based BBA would even let Congress set up a capital budget with a different multi-year balance than the operating budget. That may not be the right choice for the federal government, but many members want to treat investments differently, and this BBA would give them the option.

The Principles-based BBA should have attracted even more bipartisan support than the BCBBA, but it faced headwinds. First, the Tea Party energy around a BBA and other budget reforms had dissipated by then. Second, House Democratic leadership had strongly discouraged House Democrats from supporting BBAs. And third, Brat was less interested in building bridges with Democrats. He is a friendly guy who got along well with almost everyone, but building policy coalitions was not a priority.

Lastly, principles are appealing but raise many questions. Members of Congress know that the details matter. Without a reasonable sense of implementing legislation, the uncertainty of a principles-based approach is a leap of faith.

Shortly before the 2016 election, I left Brat's office to join Defense Priorities, a new realist foreign policy organization. Hillary Clinton's imminent presidency would be a great opportunity to help Republicans reorient from global hegemony to a foreign policy more appropriate for a republic. Oops. To everyone's surprise, including his, Donald Trump would be the next president of the United States.

My successor in Rep. Brat's office, a lawyer, wanted to closely examine the Principles-based BBA before re-introducing it. After months of delay, we met. She disclosed that she had consulted with alleged BBA experts, who told her the proposal was "really bad." I asked what they did not like, and it came down to the lack of specifics and enforcement measures.

I explained that constitutional language should be principles-based, both inherently and strategically, to reach the requisite level of consensus. She soon realized why we wrote it way, and Brat re-introduced the PBBA as H.J.Res.119 (115th Congress) soon after.

The need to design implementing legislation for a principles-based BBA became clear and urgent. We had to figure it out before the next window of opportunity opened, or we could miss another once-in-a-decade chance. We needed some kind of balance-over-the-business-cycle statutory targets.

In mid-2016, Barry Poulson and John Merrifield published *Can the Debt Growth Be Stopped?* Borrowing it from the Library of Congress, I was pleasantly surprised that it analyzed the Business Cycle BBA and the

Swiss Debt Brake and sought to synthesize them into a new fiscal rule. I reached out, and they later invited me to write a chapter about my ideal fiscal rules for an edited volume. My contribution was an essay called "Effective Fiscal Rules Build on Consensus," where I began to outline the concepts and model legislation for the statutory complements of a principles-based BBA.

Retrenchment and Resurgence for BBAs in Congress

Rep. Brat lost reelection in 2018 to charismatic, if elusive, Democratic challenger Abigail Spanberger. No one introduced the Principles-based BBA in the 116th Congress (2019–2020).

Rep. Amash led the BCBBA in each of his five terms in office, the 112th through the 116th Congresses (2011–2021). After he read the Mueller report and declared that President Trump had committed impeachable offenses, namely obstructing justice, he decided not to run again in 2020. The Business Cycle BBA also lapsed in 2021.

During the COVID-19 pandemic, Congress focused on emergency response, relief, and mitigation. By then, I had moved to the Committee for a Responsible Federal Budget, where Adam Shifriss and I were co-directors of legislative strategy specializing in our respective parties. We wrote some on budget system reforms, but our primary responsibility was congressional relations.

When the pandemic hit in March 2020, and everyone went remote, we helped Reps. Jodey Arrington (R-TX) and Scott Peters (D-CA) organize and manage a bipartisan budget group, now the Bipartisan Fiscal Forum (BFF). We hoped to lay the groundwork for pivoting back to fiscal responsibility when the crisis had passed. The group met virtually for the rest of 2020 and beyond and coalesced around a few ideas. One was to pursue "a process of establishing overall budgetary goals—such as debt-to-GDP targets—that would reduce debt limit brinkmanship as long as the budget remains on a responsible path."[17]

The 2020 elections, including the Senate runoffs in Georgia, brought razor-thin Democratic control of Congress and the White House in the 117th Congress (2021–2022). Those two years were mostly Democrats trying to enact their priorities and Republicans pushing back. Halfway through 2021, I changed jobs again, this time to Americans for Prosperity as a fiscal policy fellow. It was a chance to develop politically viable solutions to fix dysfunctional federal budgeting and drive them alongside incredible colleagues.

In the 117th Congress, Democrats managed to pass an almost entirely wasteful $1.9 trillion American Rescue Plan Act (inflation jumped immediately), a boondoggle-filled $550 billion increase in spending for "infrastructure," $80 billion in corporate welfare subsidies for domestic microchip production supposedly to compete with China, and the so-called Inflation Reduction Act, a sprawling tax-and-borrow-and-spend subsidy scheme for green energy to address climate change. Democrats abused the budget reconciliation process to enact the American Rescue Plan Act and the Inflation Reduction Act. No Republican voted for them.

These giveaways drove up the debt burden and triggered the highest inflation in 40 years.[18] Attitudes about borrowing shifted, starting with Republicans. In March 2022, Senator Mike Braun (R-IN) and Representative Jodey Arrington introduced an updated version of the Business Cycle BBA (Appendix, Exhibit 19).

The same year, then-ranking member of the Senate Budget Committee Lindsay Graham (R-SC) called for state legislatures to petition Congress for a convention of states.[19] This still-to-be-tried amendment proposing process in Article V of the Constitution has a devoted following, but time will tell if it goes anywhere.

In 2023, Senators Braun and Cynthia Lummis (R-WY) and Representative Nathaniel Moran (R-TX) proposed an updated Principles-based BBA.[20] The new, tighter version has only 100 words in two sections (here and Appendix, Exhibit 21) and is featured in the introduction.

> SECTION 1. Expenditures and receipts shall be balanced, which may occur over more than one year. Expenditures shall include all expenditures of the United States except those for payment of debt, and receipts shall include all receipts of the United States except those derived from borrowing. Congress shall achieve balance within ten years following the ratification of this article.
>
> SECTION 2. For emergency situations, two-thirds of the House of Representatives and the Senate may for limited times authorize expenditures exceeding those pursuant to rules established under Section 1. Debts incurred from such expenditures shall be paid as soon as practicable.

Representatives Nancy Mace (R-SC) and Arrington introduced variations on the Business Cycle BBA in 2023 and 2024. The difference was for the emergency spending threshold: Arrington proposed two-thirds, while Mace proposed three-fourths.[21]

The 118th Congress (2023–2024) was not going to be the window for a BBA to get two-thirds in both houses. Only a dramatic crisis could have changed that calculation. Yet it is crucial for committed champions to keep well-crafted BBAs warm and in the mix so members are ready enough to vote for them next time opportunity knocks.

Developing better BBA language has taken a lot of time and a lot of thought. Even so, repairing federal budgeting goes beyond a well-crafted BBA.

We also need a good start to implementing legislation, other complementary institutional reforms, and related supports. In addition to better policy proposals, the effort must bring many people together, regardless of their differences on other topics.

But we have one more thing to do first. We have explored problematic BBA provisions, how to think about constitutional language, and the emergence of new models. Now let us use the best arguments against BBAs to stress-test the principles-based BBA.

Notes

1. James Buchanan and Gordon Tullock, *The Calculus of Consent: Logical Foundations of Constitutional Democracy*, Michigan UP: 1962.
2. Section 1105, Title 31, United States Code.
3. John Samples, "More on Justin Amash," Cato at Liberty, https://www.cato.org/blog/more-justin-amash, July 15, 2010.
4. Rep. Justin Amash, H.J.Res.73, "Proposing a spending limit amendment to the Constitution of the United States," https://www.congress.gov/bill/112th-congress/house-joint-resolution/73, introduced July 21, 2011.
5. Rep. Justin Amash, H.J.Res.81, "Proposing a balanced budget amendment to the Constitution of the United States," https://www.congress.gov/bill/112th-congress/house-joint-resolution/81, introduced October 14, 2011.

6. Rep. Jason Chaffetz, H.R.2560, "Cut, Cap, and Balance Act of 2011, https://www.congress.gov/bill/112th-congress/house-bill/2560, introduced July 15, 2011.
7. Heritage Action for America, "Cut, Cap, and Balance Debt Reduction Plan," https://heritageaction.com/scorecard/votes/h606-2011, accessed July 15, 2022.
8. David Weina, "House To Vote On GOP's 'Cut, Cap, Balance' Plan," https://www.npr.org/2011/07/19/138498121/house-to-vote-on-doomed-gop-backed-debt-plan, July 19, 2011.
9. Sen. Tom Harkin, S. 365, "Budget Control Act of 2011," P.L.112–25, https://www.congress.gov/112/plaws/publ25/PLAW-112publ25.pdf, enacted August 2, 2011.
10. Rep. Bob Goodlatte, H.J.Res.2, "Proposing a balanced budget amendment to the Constitution of the United States," https://www.congress.gov/bill/112th-congress/house-joint-resolution/2, introduced January 5, 2011.
11. U.S. House, "Final Vote Results for Roll Call 51," https://clerk.house.gov/evs/1995/roll051.xml, January 26, 1995.
12. U.S. House, "On Motion to Suspend the Rules and Pass, as Amended," https://clerk.house.gov/Votes/2011858, November 18, 2011.
13. Sen. Orrin Hatch, S.J.Res.10, "Joint resolution proposing a balanced budget amendment to the Constitution of the United States," https://www.congress.gov/bill/112th-congress/senate-joint-resolution/10, introduced March 31, 2011.
14. Sen. Mark Udall, S.J.Res.24, "Joint resolution proposing a balanced budget amendment to the Constitution of the United States," https://www.congress.gov/bill/112th-congress/senate-joint-resolution/24, introduced August 2, 2011.
15. Rep. Justin Amash, H.J.Res.54, "Proposing a balanced budget amendment to the Constitution of the United States," https://www.congress.gov/bill/114th-congress/house-joint-resolution/54, introduced May 18, 2015.
16. Rep. Dave Brat, H.J.Res.55, "Proposing a balanced budget amendment to the Constitution of the United States," https://www.congress.gov/bill/114th-congress/house-joint-resolution/55, introduced May 20, 2015.

17. Rep. Jodey Arrington, "Arrington, Peters Pen Bipartisan Letter on Need for Budget Reform, Debt Reduction," https://arrington.house.gov/news/documentsingle.aspx?DocumentID=326, June 1, 2020. Also https://web.archive.org/web/20230531041101/https://scottpeters.house.gov/_cache/files/c/0/c00ecea6-b24c-4380-8cc3-a2aa3fc6aff0/856BD6893A80C94E183C10ABA45C9716.6.1.20-leadership-budget-reforms.pdf.
18. Kurt Couchman and Ilana Blumsack, "Bidenflation Blame Game: How Big-Spending Politicians Scapegoat Business," Americans for Prosperity, https://americansforprosperity.org/featured/afp-report-shows-that-bidenomics-not-business-creates-inflation/, June 27, 2024.
19. Sen. Lindsey Graham, "Graham: We Need a Balanced Budget Amendment To The Constitution More Than Ever," https://www.lgraham.senate.gov/public/index.cfm/2022/1/graham-we-need-a-balanced-budget-amendment-to-the-constitution-more-than-ever, January 25, 2022.
20. Sen. Mike Braun, S.J.Res. 19, "A joint resolution proposing a balanced budget amendment to the Constitution of the United States," https://www.congress.gov/bill/118th-congress/senate-joint-resolution/19/text, introduced March 15, 2023. Rep. Nathaniel Moran, H.J.Res. 80, "Proposing a balanced budget amendment to the Constitution of the United States," https://www.congress.gov/bill/118th-congress/house-joint-resolution/80, introduced July 6, 2023.
21. Rep. Jodey Arrington, H.J.Res.113, "Proposing a balanced budget amendment to the Constitution of the United States," https://www.congress.gov/bill/118th-congress/house-joint-resolution/113, introduced February 7, 2024. Rep. Nancy Mace, H.J.Res.90, "Proposing a balanced budget amendment to the Constitution of the United States," https://www.congress.gov/bill/118th-congress/house-joint-resolution/90, introduced September 18, 2023.

CHAPTER 8

A Well-Crafted BBA Stands Up to Criticism

If you're already sold on the principles-based BBA, you may be tempted to skip this chapter. But then you would miss all the fun. This is where anti-BBA arguments slide right off a well-crafted version.

As we have seen, variations on the traditional BBA include not-so-good ideas: annual balance, references to statutes, multiple emergency provisions, and more. If not for the critics, the 28th Amendment to the U.S. Constitution could have been a flawed BBA that would have frustrated policymakers and the public.

Without those efforts, the solutions discussed here probably would not have existed. No Business Cycle BBA, Principles-based BBA, various other budget upgrades, this book, and more.

In a way, they did a public service by undermining poor articulations of a good premise: that the federal government should budget responsibly. They have kept the field open for better options.

This chapter engages the best arguments from BBA critics. It focuses on objections Democratic senators raised in 1995 to the BBA that Congress nearly passed. After decades of BBA organizing and advocacy and the Republican takeover of Congress following the 1994 elections, the arguments on both sides were well-honed and articulate.

K. Couchman, *Fiscal Democracy in America*,
https://doi.org/10.1007/978-3-031-91938-1_8

Several Senate Democrats Objected to the Conventional BBA in 1995

Senators Ted Kennedy (D-MA), Patrick Leahy (D-VT), and Russ Feingold (D-WI) provided minority views for the Senate Judiciary Committee's report accompanying S.J.Res.1, the BBA ordered reported to the Senate floor in early 1995. In this report, the senators purported to speak for all Democratic senators on the committee despite divisions, such as Senator Biden's (D-DE) reluctant votes for the BBA.

The senators began:

> We agree with the Committee majority that the Federal Government should maintain a balanced budget. Indeed, all of us believe that the huge budget deficits run up during the 1980's unfairly and irresponsibly saddled future generations with burdensome debt; and all of us believe that Congress must take dramatic action to reduce the deficit and place the Nation on a course of sound fiscal management.[1]

The senators continued with objections to the proposed BBA and the general concept. Each heading here uses their words. The subsequent discussions expand on and respond to the senators' views.

The first five claims asserted that "the proposed amendment would undermine the separation of powers under Our Constitution."

> *Claim: The amendment would force the state and federal courts to resolve budgetary issues appropriately left to the elected branches of government.*

They argued that courts are "singularly ill-suited" to make fiscal policy. Correct! Weighing the costs and benefits of government activities and the revenue burdens to finance them is a legislative function that belongs exclusively to Congress, tempered by the presidential veto.

The senators were mistaken, however, that a BBA would force courts to make fiscal policy. Implementing legislation can set definitions and processes for Congress and the executive branch that the courts can buttress. Among other matters, the legislation could set targets to guide the overall balance goal, state what it means to miss the targets, and clarify how to get back on track.

The senators quoted Alexis de Tocqueville's 1848 classic *Democracy in America*. He wrote, in an entirely different context, "scarcely any political question arises in the United States that is not resolved, sooner or later, into a judicial question." America's hybrid common law (judge-made) and civil-law (legislature-made) legal system must have seemed alien to a Frenchman, where civil law predominated. Since those days, as American democracy has matured, courts have developed precedents that many legislative functions and legislative-executive relations are not their business. De Tocqueville's comment does, however, point to the importance of clear legislation.

The senators cited *Flast v. Cohen*,[2] in which "the Supreme Court found that taxpayers had standing to challenge government spending that violated the Establishment Clause." This was alarmist. The *Flast* ruling narrowly prohibits the government from spending on a specific activity: taxpayer support of religious schools, in this case. It did not address the breadth of congressionally established spending and tax choices.

The senators quoted Harvard University Law School Professor Lawrence Tribe, a progressive who helped chill state legislatures' pursuit of an amendment convention since the 1970s, and conservative solicitor general and federal judge Robert Bork that a BBA would create an explosion of litigation. Yet both were trained and served as lawyers and judges, steeped in case law about controversies before courts. They had no legislative background and did not think like legislators who cultivate statutory authorities.

They asserted that the lack of a provision to limit court authority in enforcing a BBA proves that courts would be unconstrained. In fact, it simply means that the Constitution is not the best venue to shape the judiciary's role in supporting a BBA. The necessary and proper clause gives Congress broad authority to guide court jurisdiction by statute.

The senators eventually admitted that implementing legislation could address these points before trying to wave it away with testimony by Charles Fried, a claimed centrist who had served as solicitor general for President Ronald Reagan. Well-designed implementing legislation should indeed address the role of the courts, and it could adapt to the lessons of experience more easily than constitutional language could.

Claim: The amendment would give the president broad powers to impound appropriated funds.

The senators said the BBA and the president's oath of office to uphold and defend the Constitution would interact to force the president to refrain from spending funds approved by Congress. At first glance, this may seem compelling.

Yet constitutional provisions do not exist in isolation. And, as discussed, a BBA need not require annual balance, rely on outlays, or otherwise bind so tightly and recklessly. Statutes can fill the gaps.

In any case, *impound* means the president refrains from spending funds that Congress has appropriated to pursue activities established by law. Congress enacted the Congressional Budget and Impoundment Control Act (CBA/ICA) of 1974 partly in reaction to President Richard Nixon's expansive cuts over Congress' objections and partly due to growing pressure from the states for a BBA convention. Nixon's attempted cuts were deeply problematic: they deprived agencies of funds needed to carry out statutory duties. By aggressively impounding funds, Nixon failed his constitutional duty to "take Care that the Laws be faithfully executed."[3]

The ICA may have been an overreaction, however. It requires agencies to spend all funds Congress gives them with narrow exceptions, even if agencies can accomplish their missions with less spending. The ICA is based on Congress' power to appropriate, which means approving specified funds for specified ends, but it still may go too far.

Many U.S. states and other countries do not require spending everything. North Carolina's budget, for example, is explicit: "Savings shall be effected where the total amounts appropriated are not required to perform these services and accomplish these purposes."[4] Switzerland's debt-to-GDP ratio declined rapidly for a while[5] in part because agencies often do not need to spend everything they are allowed.

The ICA and the Antideficiency Act (ADA) put boundaries around presidential spending discretion. The ADA bars the executive branch from spending without congressional appropriations. It is based on the constitutional provision that "No Money shall be drawn from the Treasury, but in Consequence of Appropriations made by Law."[6] As we will see, the Carter administration's unilateral revision of the ADA went beyond Congress' intent and created shutdowns after 1980.

Senator Kennedy offered an amendment to the BBA to bar the president from impounding funds or ordering revenue generation. Those powers properly belong to Congress under existing constitutional language. They do not need to be in a BBA. Restating them could make sense for implementing legislation, of course. The ICA already provides a path for the president to submit proposed recessions (cancelation of appropriated funds) to Congress, and Congress can handle adjustments through ordinary statutes.

Stepping back, it is curious to claim that budget changes can ONLY come from judicial overreach, presidential impoundment, or new congressional action. Each is an ad hoc, reactive strategy. Only the last is constitutionally and institutionally appropriate, but it would be naïve to expect Congress to take proper, affirmative steps to get the job done consistently.

The alternative is automatic changes outlined in law with triggered actions in response to clearly defined situations. These already exist in federal law through the Statutory Pay-as-You-Go Act of 2010 and the Fiscal Responsibility Act of 2023,[7] both revivals of earlier laws. For a state example, Arkansas' Revenue Stabilization Act imposes automatic cuts on pre-selected spending areas when overall spending would otherwise exceed revenue.[8] The next chapter describes even better options.

Claim: The proposed amendment may also confer upon the president the authority to impose taxes, duties, and fees.

Congress' first enumerated power in Article I, Sec. 8, is "To lay and collect Taxes, Duties, Imposts and Excises."[9] True, the legal conventions hold that newer provisions of law take precedence over older provisions. Yet a BBA that does not explicitly *grant* the president new powers over revenue policy would leave intact the current paradigm that Congress alone exercises tax policy powers. Insofar as Congress has (perhaps improperly) delegated revenue raising to the president, such as through certain tariff authorities, they are statutory grants that Congress could revisit by new statute.

Claim: No amendment should be proposed before the enforcement legislation called for by Sec. 6 is considered.

The senators saw that a BBA would not be self-enforcing. They rightly noted that "the balanced budget constitutional amendment itself contains no answer to any of these questions." They called for enacting legislation to be adopted before Congress would propose a BBA to the states.

The senators may have meant to use implementing legislation details to derail a BBA, but let us take it in good faith.

Members of Congress and those who advise them certainly should think through possible changes needed to carry out a BBA.

That is different from insisting on implementing legislation drafted as a single bill, let alone enacted. Instead, it is sufficient to have one or a few options for each major component.

The House and Senate Judiciary Committees have jurisdiction over constitutional amendments, but committee responsibility for implementing legislation varies by subject matter. The Budget, Rules, Senate Finance/House Ways and Means, Judiciary, and Senate HSGAC/House Oversight committees could have jurisdiction over the budget process, the congressional process generally, tax policy, the role of the courts, and inter-jurisdictional matters, respectively. Amending the Constitution is serious business, and many stakeholders have expertise to contribute.

Two other reasons advise against putting the cart before the horse. First, ratification debates may provide essential insights for implementing legislation based on state government and private sector best practices, missteps, and other insights from their experiences.

Second, the nature of deliberation over statutory details could differ quite a bit between the advocacy phase and when BBA ratification is imminent or complete. Posturing is a greater share of the former, while sobriety has greater weight in the latter. The different context during the advocacy period risks polarizing good ideas that could otherwise strengthen implementing legislation.

Claim: Proposing a balanced budget constitutional amendment that was enforceable only by Congress would be a serious mistake.

Here, the senators claim, having objected to executive and judicial ad hoc decisions to enforce a BBA, that congressional ad hockery would not guarantee compliance with a BBA. This, in turn, would have dire consequences for the public's trust in the federal government.

Fair enough, but relying entirely on ad hoc decisions from any branch is not necessary. Congress can set up clear, statutory consequences for budget breaches for the executive branch to carry out. Courts could order the executive branch to follow the law if it would otherwise fail to carry out its duties faithfully. All three branches could check and balance each other to support automatic enforcement of the Congress-passed legislation to carry out the principles of a BBA.

A BBA is intended, in part, to address time-inconsistent preferences by legislators. That is, without the public's expectation for balance, members of Congress may be tempted to depart—"just this once"—from the balance rule to give benefits to some or avoid pain to others. A feature of budget targets is tying policymakers to the mast of fiscal responsibility to protect the ship of state from the siren song of short-term expediency absent extraordinary causes.[10]

Certainly, a BBA alone is not likely to be sufficient, and complementary reforms can push congressional incentives in healthier directions. Norms in some U.S. states and other countries help produce fiscal responsibility with few additional safeguards. The political culture of Congress, however, provides little assurance that legislators would simply do their job.

On the other hand, constitutional scholar Rob Natelson has observed that specifically listing powers and duties in the Constitution has held Congress within reasonable guardrails.[11]

Finally, the public's low opinion of Congress is a mystifying reason to refrain from making it work better. Doing better imperfectly is more likely to build trust than to erode it further.

Claim: Congress should pass a concurrent resolution spelling out how to get to a balanced budget before any amendment is sent to the states.

This assertion seems like the claim about implementing legislation. That was about enforcement, however: staying in balance or staying on the path to balance. This is about the *policy changes* needed to reach balance: spending cuts, revenue increases, economic growth, or some combination.

This concurrent resolution would be a non-binding measure that does not become law. Concurrent resolutions are merely agreements between the Senate and the House. The senators proposed that members of Congress put their cards on the table for specific policy changes to eliminate deficits before a BBA vote.

Legislators act differently when an exercise is aspirational (fake) compared to when it is for real. Putting forward a good faith effort too early could provoke special interests to organize against the BBA, fiscal responsibility generally, and the specified policy changes.

That said, numerous options already exist for deficit reduction. The CBO and many other policy organizations have produced estimates for deficit reduction options or even for balancing the budget entirely.[12]

Moving toward balance will be tough, but it is necessary. Congress will need the space to make many mini-deals and some mega-deals in the years and decades to come. They can get there a little at a time and in response to the emergent politics of each moment. Trying to anticipate the full path of deficit reduction in advance would be an impetuous attempt to preempt the process of democratic deliberation.

A well-crafted budget rule can proceed without specifying all the changes needed to bring policy in line with the rule. When the American people ratified the original Constitution, the Bill of Rights, and the other seventeen amendments, Congress did not set forth the statutory details in advance. Americans agreed on the principles, and then their representatives in Congress deliberated to give them form via statute.

The next claims were that a BBA would shift burdens to state and local governments.

> *Claim: Ratification of the proposed amendment would result in the imposition of greater financial burdens on state and local governments.*

The senators said, "Cost shifting to State and local governments will be an irresistible impulse—the easy way out of our Federal deficit." It would then burden "the pocketbooks of State and local taxpayers" to "catch those who fall through a shredded Federal 'safety net' of nutrition, housing, education and medical care programs." Further, they said state and local governments should not have "to pay for the profligate budgetary practices of the Federal Government."

Without question, balancing the federal budget would affect state and local governments. Fiscal consolidation done quickly and clumsily could dent economic growth in the short term, and that could reduce state and local revenue collections. Done well, however, reducing the debt burden would increase economic growth and give states more options. Controlling the debt in the longer term is a win–win, but we—and especially politicians facing regular reelection—live very much in the short term.

The senators were likely more concerned about the spending side from reductions in federal transfers to state and local governments. That is an opportunity as well as a challenge, however. It could stimulate policy innovations that make most people better off.

Federal, state, and local regulations and subsidies impose barriers to better practices on the supply side while pumping up the demand side with funds to help targeted populations get by. Depending on the details, these supply- and demand-side factors may lead to more, less, or about the same amount of a particular good or service, but supply restrictions plus demand subsidies always drive up prices, often by a lot. This affects food, housing, health care, education, transportation, energy, and much more. BBA-related fiscal changes could benefit most people by upending cozy protectionism for suppliers and making their earnings more accountable to the consuming public and less to the political class.

This claim also assumes that transfers are always worth doing. Federal funds come with extensive strings that reduce their value to recipients. Federal money for construction projects includes mandates to benefit organized labor. Recreational lands improved through the Land and Wildlife Conservation Fund become generally unavailable for other uses forever. Roads developed or enhanced with Highway Trust Fund money can never be tolled or otherwise managed differently. Education funds require testing and other mandates. In some cases, more freedom from federal restrictions would let states do better with less money. Balancing these factors is, after all, precisely the point of a legislature.

Besides, the distinction between federal taxpayers and state and local taxpayers is artificial. They are the same people! It may be convenient for politicians at all levels to obscure the sources of revenue for government activities while shifting money around, but government spending requires revenue or borrowing.

Finally, transfers to state and local governments are a substantial part of the federal budget, but the federal government spends a lot on many other things. Members of Congress represent districts or states with numerous state and local officials, many of whom they know personally. State and local government officials already provide outsized input into Congress' decisions.

Claim: No statutory ban on unfunded mandates can bind Congress.

The senators argued that Congress would want state and local governments to do things even without being bribed with federal funds, so Congress could not stop itself from simply ordering them to do so. They said the then-proposed, and soon-after-enacted, Unfunded Mandates Reform Act "cannot prevent Congress from waiving or ignoring that legislation in order to comply with a constitutional mandate for a balanced Federal budget."

The Unfunded Mandates Reform Act has been on the books for thirty years.[13] As the senators anticipated, it has not done enough to keep Congress from bossing the states around. The House waives its rules for most legislation. The Senate can waive them with 60 votes (that is, overcome points of order), the same threshold for approving most legislation. If the votes are there on the substance, they are there for waiving the rules.

Congress cannot (or will not) discipline itself on unfunded mandates, but the Supreme Court just might. It took a big step in *NFIB v. Sebelius*.[14] Obamacare, officially the combination of the Patient Protection and Affordable Care Act of 2010 and the Health Care and Education Reconciliation Act of 2010, required the states to expand Medicaid to additional populations, or the states would lose *all* federal funding for Medicaid.

The Supreme Court held that the provision would impermissibly commandeer the states. The Court ruled that the federal government could only withhold the new Medicaid funds, not all of them. The majority opinion explained the importance of ensuring that "Spending Clause legislation does not undermine the status of the States as independent sovereigns in our federal system." Quoting an earlier case, the Court observed "the Constitution has never been understood to confer upon Congress the ability to require the States to govern according to Congress' instructions." And further, "That insight has led this Court to strike down federal legislation that commandeers a State's legislative or administrative apparatus for federal purposes."

In other words, the Constitution's supremacy clause does not give Congress the power to boss around the states. The spending clause has limits. The stage is set for the Court to liberate states further from congressional commandeering. And if Congress were to pursue balance by reducing spending to the states, its ability to push them around would be even weaker.

The following claims are that a BBA would be an unsound economic policy. The specific BBA about which they wrote would indeed have these problems, although not to the degree claimed. Those issues do not apply to better-written versions.

Claim: The proposed amendment would hamper the government's ability to deal with recessions and natural disasters.

"Because the proposed constitutional amendment requires a balanced budget each fiscal year (rather than over the course of the business cycle), it would prohibit the government from engaging in this form of 'counter-cyclical' spending; in fact, it would require the government to raise taxes and/or cut spending during economic downturns." (p. 33).

The senators argued that annual balance would worsen recessions and interfere with the government's ability to respond to other emergencies like natural disasters. Yes, a strict annual balance requirement would indeed be bad economic policy, and requiring annual balance with no exceptions would in fact hamper emergency response and make recessions more painful. Fortunately, yearly balance is not the only option, and every proposed BBA has a safety valve for emergencies.

The smart alternative to annual balance is structural balance: balance over the business cycle or the medium term. During the good years, the government would run surpluses, which would build up in a reserve fund or pay down debt. The government would draw from reserves or borrow during recessions and emergencies.

A structural balance rule would avoid significant spending cuts or tax hikes during recessions when the economy is weakest and people are hurting. Policy could be stable while the economy bounces around. A statutory balance rule could even adjust for *automatic stabilizers* like the nutrition, health, housing, and unemployment programs that get used more when times are tough. More on that in the next chapter.

BBAs include one or more safety valves for emergency spending. The Business Cycle BBA and Principles-based BBA would set the congressional threshold at two-thirds: high enough to limit abuse but low enough for emergency response. The conventional BBA would set a three-fifths threshold for whatever Congress wants to call an emergency, a simple majority for military conflict, and automatic suspension in case of war.

The Budget Control Act of 2011 set up another approach that would work for many emergencies. It requires Congress to appropriate funds to the Federal Emergency Management Agency's Disaster Relief Fund (DRF) based on the rolling average of declared-disaster DRF spending over the last decade, excluding the single highest and the single lowest years of that decade.[15] If a BBA's definition of spending is more of a principle—that is, it does not say *outlays*—then Congress could easily let budget authority build up in DRF-like accounts and become outlays as needed to address emergencies.

Alternatively, the statutory complement to a principles-based BBA could have layers. Structural balance could balance the regular budget over the medium term as spending moves along a trend. Emergency spending could go out immediately and be balanced through offsets in subsequent years. Spending on investments could be a third layer (see below).

Claim: The proposed constitutional amendment would undermine the value of Treasury bonds and drive up interest costs paid by the federal government.

This concern addresses S.J.Res.1's section requiring a three-fifths vote to raise the debt limit. Most discussion quotes a Treasury official at length about the practical difficulties for federal cash management under such a requirement, even under a balanced budget.

The senators were mostly correct. The statutory debt limit does not belong in the Constitution. It can stay in statute if we need one, just like the president's budget request. But maybe we do not need the debt limit in any form.

True, the debt limit has been a useful tool to advance legislation promoting budgetary responsibility.[16] But this conversation is about a constitutional fiscal rule buttressed by implementing legislation. In that case, the point of a debt limit would be to push Congress to follow the BBA. That is to say, the debt limit should not be in the Constitution, and it would be fine for a statutory debt limit to increase automatically if the budget meets BBA-consistent targets or for Congress to repeal the debt limit and rely on other enforcement strategies.

A well-written BBA would support the value of Treasury bonds and reduce federal interest costs. Too much federal debt reduces its value, and lenders need higher interest rates to be willing to tie up funds in government debt instead of private sector opportunities. A constitutional rule making debt scarcer would make it more valuable and push down interest rates. Reducing risks of default from either a debt limit fight or a debt crisis would likewise reduce federal borrowing costs.

Claim: The experience of the states does not support passage of the proposed constitutional amendment.

They said, "the States do not have the critical role in forming national economic policy and in stabilizing our economy that the Federal government has, nor are they responsible for overseeing a foreign policy or our national defense. Moreover, the States are hardly the model of responsible budgeting."

Yes, this is all true. The federal role is different than the states' roles. In fact, states now expect federal bailouts to fill budget holes when times are tough, and that adds to federal borrowing.

Fortunately, a principles-based BBA with balance-over-the-business-cycle implementing legislation that adjusts automatically for safety net programs, has an appropriate safety valve for other emergencies, and includes a mechanism for offsetting emergency spending subsequently can help the federal government meet macroeconomic and emergency response goals.

The state-level trickery around annual balance rules is shameful and ubiquitous. But that is a problem with annual balance. Recall from Chapter 3 that states started to get annual balance rules in the 1840s after rough patches involving bad investments in canals, railroads, and banks.[17] Annual balance is economically and politically problematic. But it got entrenched before policymakers understood business cycles, and legislators in states that have not updated their rules have had to muddle through.

That is changing. In December 2021, the American Legislative Exchange Council approved a Statement of Principles on Balancing Budgets Over the Business Cycle,[18] followed by model policy in December 2022.[19] Several states, including South Carolina, Connecticut, Indiana, Hawaii, Texas, and Washington, have rules that gesture in this direction, and efforts to improve them are underway. A February 2023 paper[20] explained, state legislators can build broad, consensus-based, bipartisan coalitions for structural balance to upgrade from outdated annual balance rules.

The senators were right that state annual balance rules are not a model for the federal government. Yet balancing over the medium term with an appropriate safety valve would be a significant improvement for the federal government, which has no comparable fiscal rules, and for the states that are not already doing so.

Next, the senators said that the BBA would forbid placing Social Security off budget and would prohibit establishing a separate capital budget. Neither claim is correct. But in any case, as we will see in Chapter 10, all federal fiscal policies belong in a single, comprehensive budget bill that Congress considers each year.

Claim: The proposed constitutional amendment would imperil Social Security.

After narrowly averting trust fund depletion in 1983, Social Security's dedicated revenue exceeded spending, and trust fund assets increased leading up to the BBA debate in 1995.[21] Today, however, Social Security surpluses are gone. Trust fund assets are declining and will be exhausted in the early 2030s.[22] Social Security surpluses cannot be misused to paper over deficits in the rest of the budget anymore. In fact, debt from imbalances in Social Security, health programs, and the interest on the debt they will produce will drive the federal government's coming debt spiral.[23]

Yet protecting Social Security from insolvency requires changing the program. That is difficult to do in one-off legislation that is easy for interest groups to polarize. As we will see soon, Congress can only properly manage federal programs by including everything in a balance requirement and in a comprehensive budget with all spending and all revenue.

Nothing the government does is so special that it should not be in the budget. Many things are, of course, higher priorities that can be treated differently in implementing legislation's automatic enforcement and by members of Congress as they decide how to make everything add up.

Social Security should be on budget, in the budget, and within a balanced budget. Precisely how it fits does not need to be resolved in advance for a BBA to make sense.

Claim: The proposed constitutional amendment would prohibit exempting capital expenditures from the balanced-budget calculation.

After just saying that the states should not be a model for a federal BBA, here they said state-like capital budgeting belongs in a federal BBA and lamented the rejection of an amendment to exclude capital expenditures from the balance calculation.

Direct federal spending on infrastructure is relatively small: 5.8% of $6.14 trillion in federal outlays for FY 2023. Federal outlays for major public physical capital investment were $356 billion. Of that, 54% was for defense direct investment, 14% was for non-defense direct investment, and 31% was for grants to state and local governments.[24] Gross private fixed investment in calendar year 2022 was nearly 13 times larger at $4.6 trillion.[25]

That said, capital spending is manageable within a balanced budget framework. Implementing legislation can distinguish between different kinds of federal activities. Federal accounting practices already do, using accrual concepts for credit programs in addition to the standard cash-based accounting elsewhere. Similarly, accounting for federal investments could track both costs and asset values.

A BBA that avoids limiting spending based on outlays could provide even more flexibility. For example, Congress could provide investment budget authority on a predictable basis. Outlays flowing from that budget authority could occur as contracts are fulfilled, just as they currently are. Grants could even be outlaid to state and local governments at higher rates during recessions for cost savings, reduced unemployment, and other macroeconomic benefits.

Or, comparable to structural balance and emergency spending, each balancing in a different way over the medium term, capital budgeting under a principles-based BBA could exist. Up-front expenditures on investments could be offset through user fees or otherwise over an asset's useful life. Pay-as-you-go spending for investments is probably fine for the federal government, but other kinds of capital budgeting are entirely plausible within the right kind of BBA, and if members of Congress wanted to do it, they could.

Finally, the senators came to their last objection to the BBA:

Claim: The balanced budget amendment would promote gridlock and undermine majority rule.

The senators observed that the proposed BBA would require supermajorities to run deficits and to increase the debt limit. They claimed it would create gridlock and enshrine minority rule.

A BBA—like many existing constitutional provisions—would indeed limit the scope of majority rule decisions in Congress. That is the goal. Majority rule has produced one decision after another to increase spending without increasing revenue or to reduce revenue without reducing spending. The point of a BBA is to keep Congress from letting spending and revenue diverge.

Yet the senators were onto something. As already discussed, supermajorities to increase the debt limit or to increase revenue, but not to reduce spending, introduce asymmetries. The senators were right that fiscal choices—spending cuts, tax increases, or vice versa—within a BBA's framework should be by majorities, whether simple in the House or qualified in the Senate.

Emergencies are different. They require setting aside the normal balance rule to deal with some new threat to life, liberty, or property. Yet emergency designations regularly get much greater congressional support than two-thirds (see Table 7–1).

The main exception has been when congressional leaders crafted emergency response legislation to meet lower thresholds to maximize benefits for their constituencies instead of focusing on a reasonable response to the crisis, such as the American Rescue and Recovery Act of 2009 and the American Rescue Plan Act of 2021. In both cases, Democrats had unified control of Congress and the White House, so they leveraged the needs of the moment to shower benefits on core constituencies.

Intuitively, simple majority rule is not necessarily ideal in every case. In *The Calculus of Consent: Logical Foundations of Constitutional Democracy,* James M. Buchanan and Gordon Tullock characterized the choice of decision thresholds as a tradeoff between transaction costs and externalities.[26] A simple majority is easier to obtain than a supermajority, but it may leave more decision-makers and those they represent outside of the coalition of support. Supermajorities increase the transaction costs but reduce the share of the public who do not support the outcome.

In other words, it usually is not right to exclude the minority party from deliberations or from being able to support emergency response. After all, Congress should develop partnerships and seek consensus on matters of major national significance, like dealing with crises. Rebalancing the allocation of powers between leaders, committees, and members in caucus rules would be a far more useful strategy for promoting deliberation and avoiding gridlock than just opposing a BBA.

In addition to signing onto the above objections with Senators Kennedy and Feingold, Senator Leahy provided separate supplemental views, likely because his staff had already written them. They largely duplicated the claims they made jointly: *S.J.Res.1 does not reduce the debt or the deficit. S.J.Res.1 will shift burdens to state and local governments. S.J.Res.1 will encourage budget gimmickry. S.J.Res.1 is loaded with loopholes. S.J.Res.1 may harm the economy. S.J.Res.1 invites constitutional clashes with the executive. S.J.Res.1 will shift power to unelected judges. S.J.Res.1 erodes the fundamental principle of majority rule. S.J.Res.1 will result in distressing surprises. S.J.Res.1 is not constitutionally necessary.*

Then-Senator Joe Biden (D-DE) submitted additional views. He began:

> I have long supported the concept of a balanced budget amendment. Amending the Constitution of the United States is an extraordinary step, but I believe an extraordinary response is necessary to address the continuing deficit problems facing the country. Notwithstanding my support for the concept of a balanced budget amendment, I remain concerned about the form such an amendment takes. The stakes are never higher, as we all recognize, than when we consider amending our basic document of governance.

He raised concerns about a president leveraging a BBA to impound funds or impose taxes. He worried about the lack of an explicit capital budget, saying, "This balanced budget amendment will pit major investments with long-term payoffs against programs with more attractive short-term economic and political returns." He lamented that the BBA would not carve out Social Security to keep its surpluses from papering over deficits elsewhere. He noted the lack of a glide path to balance and feared an economic shock from the possibility of balancing the budget suddenly. And then, Biden voted for a similar BBA after the House approved it.[27]

A well-crafted BBA and its implementing legislation would not have these issues.

We have worked through the concerns from a thirty-year-old Senate report, but we cannot quite call it a day. After all, both houses of Congress voted on BBAs in 2011, and the House did so again in 2018. Surely, opponents of a BBA had developed new arguments by then.

Well, not really. Dissenting views from House Judiciary Committee Democrats in 2011 covered the same ground as the Senate Democratic views in 1995.[28] House Judiciary Democrats launched broadsides against the conservative provisions we discussed in Chapter 5 and recycled the concerns noted above.

In June 2011, as noted, House Republicans had marked up a conservative BBA in the form of H.J.Res. 1 with supermajorities to raise the debt limit, increase revenue, or spend more than a set percentage of GDP. On August 2, 2011, President Obama signed the Budget Control Act of 2011 into law,[29] which required a BBA vote by the end of the year. In November, House leaders instead bought up H.J.Res. 2, the traditional BBA with more Democratic support than the version marked up in committee. H.J.Res.2 came up under suspension of the rules, which does not allow amendments and requires two-thirds of votes to pass. House Democrats did not confront a BBA with realistic prospects when they wrote their views on the legislation, and they did not break new rhetorical ground.

Criticisms Made in Bad Faith

Like House Democratic Leader Hoyer, Richard Kogan at the Center on Budget and Policy Priorities (CBPP) was sufficiently spooked by the apparent feasibility of Rep. Amash's Business Cycle Balanced Budget Amendment (BCBBA) to publish a deeply flawed analysis of the proposal.[30] The piece was so full of errors that it would take several additional pages to list and correct them. The most charitable interpretation is that he grossly misunderstood the proposal.

The BCBBA's basic rule is that spending would equal the rolling revenue average in the last three years, adjusted for inflation and population. Kogan claimed it would drive spending down as a percentage of GDP forever, like TABOR's spending rule in Colorado, but that is wrong. Yes, it would not adjust for the productivity component of GDP growth, but only in adjusting revenue over those three years. That would produce small structural surpluses, roughly enough to offset emergency spending. It would not force Congress to gut programs, especially as it would let Congress raise revenue with only a slight lag before adjusting the spending limit.

Similarly, Kogan's claims for year-over-year spending volatility were absurd. He said it would require federal spending cuts of "36 percent in 2012, 34 percent in 2011, and 27 percent in 2010." The actual numbers would have been 3.2 percent in 2012, 5.6 percent in 2011, and 4.0 percent in 2010. The difference was Kogan's deceptive practice of switching between actual spending and spending levels assuming the BCBBA with revenue unchanged to paint a scary picture.

Finally, Kogan flatly ignored Congress' ability to provide emergency spending during downturns. The BCBBA would limit emergency spending to one year at a time, but there is no reason Congress could not have approved such expenditures in 2008, in 2009, in 2010, and so on until Congress found sufficient savings, raised enough revenue, or the economy recovered enough.

None of that misinformation would apply to a principles-based BBA, however. Despite our commitment to engaging in good faith with BBA criticisms, the unfortunate reality is that some do not engage in honest deliberation. Good faith concerns deserve thoughtful consideration, but dishonest polemics can be identified as such and shown to be noise.

As we have seen, many criticisms of S.J.Res.1 in 1995 reflected serious design flaws. Those mistakes are fixable: some by deletion and others by redesign.

Other criticisms reflect the failure to consider implementing legislation. Some imply the belief that any restrictions on Congress would reduce its ability to do good. Others seem like misleading smears. The case against a well-crafted BBA and carefully designed implementing legislation is feeble.

Finally, some friends working toward a convention of states think a BBA must include specifics and enforcement to be effective. We share many substantive goals, but those aspects belong in statute, not the Constitution.

That is because, first, the U.S. Constitution is exceptionally difficult to change, so any changes should be assumed to be for all time to come. It is better to manage the details where management is possible: statute.

Second, constitutional provisions set strong norms for Congress. Third, reaching consensus is more likely on general principles than on specifics, to which we now turn.

Notes

1. Senate Committee on the Judiciary, Report to Accompany S.J.Res.1 (104th Congress), S. Rept. 104–5, https://www.congress.gov/104/crpt/srpt5/CRPT-104srpt5.pdf, January 24, 1995.
2. *Flast v. Cohen*, 392 U.S. 83 (1968).
3. U.S. Constitution, Article 2, Sec. 3.
4. General Assembly of North Carolina, "Current Operations Appropriations Act of 2022," Session Law 2022–74, House Bill 103, https://www.ncleg.gov/Sessions/2021/Bills/House/PDF/H103v5.pdf, accessed 10/2/22.
5. Federal Finance Administration of the Swiss Confederation, "Development of Net Debt," https://www.efv.admin.ch/efv/en/home/finanzberichterstattung/bundeshaushalt_ueb/schulden.html, August 22, 2022, accessed October 2, 2022.
6. U.S. Constitution, Article 1, Sec. 9, clause 7.
7. Chapter 20A of Title 2, United States Code, and Sen. Tom Harkin, S. 365, Budget Control Act of 2011, P.L. 112–25, enacted August 2, 2011.
8. State of Arkansas, "Revenue Stabilization Act," Act 311 of 1945, Arkansas Code Annotated, Title 19, Chapter 5.
9. U.S. Constitution, Article 1, Sec. 8, clause 1.
10. Homer, *The Odyssey*, referenced in "Tied to the Mast: Fiscal Rules and Their Uses," Peterson-Pew Budget Commission, http://budgetreform.org/document/tied-mast-fiscal-rules-and-their-uses.html, December 13, 2011.
11. Rob Natelson, "Understanding the Constitution: Constitutional Amendments Work, *The Epoch Times*, https://www.theepochtimes.com/understanding-the-constitution-constitutional-amendments-work_4027117.html, October 1, 2021.
12. CBO, "Options for Reducing the Deficit," https://www.cbo.gov/publication/58981, March 6, 2023. Heritage Foundation,

"Budget Blueprint for Fiscal Year 2023, https://www.heritage.org/budget/. Republican Study Committee, "Protecting America's Economic Security," https://rsc-hern.house.gov/news/press-releases/rsc-unveils-fy-24-budget-protecting-america-s-economic-security, June 14, 2023.
13. Unfunded Mandates Reform Act of 1995, Public Law 104–4, Chapter 25 of Title 2, United States Code, enacted March 22, 1995.
14. Supreme Court of the United States, *NFIB v. Sebelius*, https://www.supremecourt.gov/opinions/11pdf/11-393c3a2.pdf, decided June 28, 2012.
15. Sec. 101 of the Budget Control Act of 2011, Pub. L. 112–25, enacted August 2, 2011, classified to Sec. 901(b)(2)(D) of Title 2, United States Code.
16. Committee for a Responsible Federal Budget, Appendix to "Q&A: Everything You Should Know About the Debt Ceiling," https://www.crfb.org/papers/qa-everything-you-should-know-about-debt-ceiling#_Hlk431978821, accessed October 10, 2022, July 28, 2021.
17. John Joseph Wallis, Richard E. Sylla, and Arthur Grinath III, "Land, Debt, and Taxes: Origins of the U.S. State Default Crisis, 1839 to 1842," Working Paper, Federal Reserve Bank of Atlanta, https://www.atlantafed.org/-/media/documents/news/conferences/2011/sovereign-debt/papers/Wallis.pdf, 2011.
18. American Legislative Exchange Council, "Statement of Principles on Balancing Budgets Over the Business Cycle," https://alec.org/model-policy/statement-of-principles-on-balancing-budgets-over-the-business-cycle/, December 2021.
19. American Legislative Exchange Council, "A Next-Generation Tax and Expenditure Limitation Act, https://alec.org/model-policy/a-next-generation-tax-and-expenditure-limitation-act/, December 2022.
20. Kurt Couchman, "States Can Unleash Freedom and Reclaim Sovereignty With Structural Balance," Americans for Prosperity, https://americansforprosperity.org/wp-content/uploads/2023/02/2023-AFP-States-can-unleash-freedom-and-reclaim-sovereignty-with-structural-balance.pdf, February 2023. Also, see the two-page summary: https://americansforprosperity.org/wp-content/uploads/2023/02/AFP-1P-State-Structural-Balance.pdf.

21. Social Security Office of the Chief Actuary, "Old-Age, Survivors, and Disability Insurance Trust Funds, 1957–2021," https://www.ssa.gov/oact/STATS/table4a3.html, accessed October 11, 2022.
22. CBO, "10-Year Trust Fund Projections," https://www.cbo.gov/system/files/2022-05/51136-2022-05-Trust-Fund-Projections.xlsx, May 2022.
23. Brian Riedl, "Fix Social Security and Medicare to Protect Other Priorities," Peter G. Peterson Foundation, https://www.pgpf.org/expert-views/americas-fiscal-and-economic-outlook/fix-social-security-and-medicare-to-protect-other-priorities, November 8, 2021.
24. President's Budget for Fiscal Year 2025, Table 9.2—Major Public Physical Capital Investment Outlays in Current and Constant (FY 2017) Dollars: 1940–2025, *Historical Tables*, https://www.whitehouse.gov/wp-content/uploads/2024/03/hist09z2_fy2025.xlsx, March 9, 2024.
25. Bureau of Economic Analysis, National Income and Product Accounts, Table 5.2.5. Gross and Net Domestic Investment by Major Type, accessed June 26, 2024.
26. James M. Buchanan and Gordon Tullock, *The Calculus of Consent: Logical Foundations of Constitutional Democracy*, Liberty Fund, 1962.
27. Senate Roll Call Vote 98, On the Joint Resolution H.J.Res. 1, as amended, https://www.senate.gov/legislative/LIS/roll_call_votes/vote1041/vote_104_1_00098.htm, March 2, 1995.
28. House Committee on the Judiciary, Report to Accompany H.J.Res.1 (112th Congress), H. Rept. 112–117, https://www.congress.gov/112/crpt/hrpt117/CRPT-112hrpt117.pdf, June 23, 2011.
29. Sen. Tom Harkin, S. 365, the Budget Control Act of 2011, 112th Congress, https://www.congress.gov/bill/112th-congress/senate-bill/365/actions, enacted August 2, 2011.
30. Richard Kogan, "Amash Constitutional Spending Cap Would Radically Shrink Federal Budget: "Starve the Beast" on Steroids," Center on Budget and Policy Priorities, https://www.cbpp.org/research/amash-constitutional-spending-cap-would-radically-shrink-federal-budget, November 28, 2011.

CHAPTER 9

Implementing Legislation for a Principles-based BBA

The 1787 constitutional convention reached consensus on broad principles, and that is how Congress has advanced constitutional amendments ever since.

Each provision of the Constitution sets a general direction. Then it is up to Congress to fill in the details by enacting statutes. True, the president usually signs the bills Congress approves, but, if not, a two-thirds supermajority in Congress can override the veto to enact the legislation anyway.

A balanced budget amendment to the Constitution is the same. Two-thirds of members of each house of Congress and three-fourths of state legislatures are likelier to approve of a general direction than any way of turning a principle into the nuts and bolts of budget management.

Even so, implementing legislation is most likely to succeed when drafted in the same spirit of consensus-building that animates the constitutional provision.[1] Getting a majority in the House, 60 votes in the Senate, and the president's signature is no small feat, nor is two-thirds in both houses to overcome a president's veto when that becomes necessary.

K. Couchman, *Fiscal Democracy in America*,
https://doi.org/10.1007/978-3-031-91938-1_9

Ratification Is Not the End of the Road

Turning a BBA-derived fiscal goal into actionable policy goes well beyond designing the goal and associated targets. It is one thing to say we are going to sail a ship across an ocean (a principle), but selecting, outfitting, crewing, and navigating the vessel to get there is probably as complicated as designing adequate implementing legislation.

Who is responsible for hitting budget targets? How do we know if they have met them? Is there wiggle room? What happens if they miss the mark? What if they miss several targets in a row? What does it mean to get back on track? What carrots encourage compliance, and what sticks await failure? Should Congress have to vote on legislation to remedy missed targets, and if so, under what conditions? How can today's Congress reduce the risk of a future Congress switching off requirements? Can Congress create an automatic enforcement process for the executive branch to carry out that is consistent with the rule of law and politically sustainable? What role does the U.S. Supreme Court have? The states?

If that is not daunting enough, answers do not happen in a vacuum. Implementing legislation must accommodate Congress' existing committee structure, the actual balance of powers between Congress and the executive branch, Supreme Court precedent, the annual budget process, the long shadow of mostly unsuccessful budget enforcement, the expectations of the public, and members' other interests, among much else. In other words, it requires a lot of input from many people with many areas of expertise and varying amounts of assertiveness.

Statutory Details Build on Constitutional Principles

The shape of implementing legislation depends on the constitutional provision. Traditional BBA foundations would dramatically differ from the Business Cycle BBA or the Principles-based BBA. We will focus on the Principles-based BBA, which provides the most flexibility for Congress to design statutory complements.

Definitions come first. Then everything must fit together.

Expenditures: *Expenditures* is the general word in the Constitution for government spending. Clear definitions already exist in statute.[2]

Congress gives *budget authority* to agencies: "the authority provided by Federal law to incur financial obligations." Congress uses budget authority to put money in agency accounts.

Agencies pay claims as *outlays*, formally "expenditures and net lending of funds under budget authority." Outlays are when funds transfer from agency accounts to employees, contractors, states, and other non-federal entities. Other terms address other types of expenditures, such as credit authority and contract authority, but in any case, statutory definitions are covered.

Receipts: A statutory definition of *receipts* is not easy to find and seems not to exist. It would need to be added. The "Governmental Receipts" chapter of the *Analytical Perspectives* of a recent president's budget request[3] says,

> Governmental receipts are taxes and other collections from the public that result from the exercise of the Federal Government's sovereign or governmental powers.

Income from market-oriented activities does not count as receipts but is instead *offsetting collections* or *offsetting receipts* that count as negative outlays. These include insurance premiums, payment of utility bills from federal energy companies, patent application fees, and more.[4] In any case, current definitions for receipts are fine but should be codified in statute.

Balanced: The principle is that spending should not exceed revenue over some period during normal times. The traditional BBA proposal says spending should not exceed revenue within a fiscal year. The principles-based BBA allows balance over several years, in the medium term, over the business cycle, or something else. A gradual transition to structural primary balance makes a lot of sense, and we will dig into the mechanics soon.

Payment of debt: The language of the Principles-based BBA excludes *payment of debt* from the definition of expenditures. In other words, the balance is between current spending and current revenue. Balance still exists when surpluses pay down the debt. But does *payment of debt* only cover debt principal, or could it also mean debt principal AND servicing costs, that is, net interest? The Principles-based BBA is ambiguous. Implementing legislation could go either way.

If payment of debt includes both debt principal and interest, that is full or overall or total balance. If it includes only principal and not interest, that is primary balance. It is a big difference. In January 2025, CBO projected, adjusted for timing shifts, a 2035 primary deficit of $916 billion and an overall deficit of $2.7 trillion. Depending on assumptions, that means $5–$6 trillion in savings over a decade to reach primary balance or $12–$15 trillion for full balance. Compare that to projected total spending of $89 trillion and revenue of $68 trillion over the next decade.[5]

Borrowing: When the federal government borrows funds, its promise to repay carries the "full faith and credit of the United States of America." This legal obligation is more robust than expectations of payments even under, for example, Social Security or Medicare, which Congress can change at will. Politicians sometimes describe proposed changes to entitlement programs as "defaulting on sacred obligations," but that is taking poetic license.

Default carries legal ramifications that are absent when making changes to programs. The legal status of federal borrowing is well-understood, and implementing legislation must only nod to long-established precedents that borrowing means a full faith and credit pledge.

Ten years: Ten years means 3,652 days, plus or minus a few, right? Maybe not. Ratification would happen when the legislature in the 38th state approves the proposed amendment. But ratification might not come at a convenient time for Congress. Congress aspires to complete budget and appropriations legislation in the months that lead up to a fiscal year.

Congress might interpret the BBA language strictly to 3,652 days (more or less), so they would have to reach balance by the end of the ninth fiscal year after the fiscal year during which ratification occurs. Congress might instead write implementing legislation to achieve balance by the end of the tenth fiscal year beginning after ratification.

Emergencies: Existing budget law already provides definitions[6]:

> The term 'emergency' means a situation that requires new budget authority and outlays (or new budget authority and the outlays flowing therefrom) for the prevention or mitigation of, or response to, loss of life or property, or a threat to national security; and is unanticipated.

In addition,

> The term 'unanticipated' means that the underlying situation is sudden, which means quickly coming into being or not building up over time;

urgent, which means a pressing and compelling need requiring immediate action; unforeseen, which means not predicted or anticipated as an emerging need; and temporary, which means not of a permanent duration.

Those definitions allow discretion within limits. Under current law, Congress often plays fast and loose with emergency response. Under a BBA, however, emergency spending would require two-thirds support as a deviation from the general balance directive. The next section clarifies further.

Limited times: The connection to emergency spending anchors this term. Supplemental appropriations vary with circumstances, but it is common for emergency-designated funds to be available for the current fiscal year and beyond. Congress can always make changes by taking back (rescinding) funds that have not been assigned to particular uses or by adding additional funds for the same or new purposes.

As soon as practicable: Similarly, a rigid rule for emergency offsets cannot anticipate all possibilities. Hurricane damage, for instance, has random qualities, but we have enough experience to understand the likely range of exposures. The COVID-19 pandemic and the response to it were enormously more expensive and much more unpredictable.

Hurricanes and other anticipated natural disasters can be reliably offset over five or six years, but a once-in-a-generation mega-disaster may need a generation to pay off associated debt.

Constitutional language can provide a guide. It should not, however, create a straitjacket that Congress cannot change even if warranted by circumstance. After all, who knows what Americans will have to deal with in a century or two?

Definitions set the stage for more interesting parts: statutory budget targets and enforcement mechanisms.

Designing Statutory Budget Targets for a BBA

Well-crafted statutory budget targets optimize across several policy objectives. Simple is good as far as possible, but some complexity is inevitable. Consider the goals that need to be balanced against each other.

Long-term responsibility: A BBA inherently requires balance of some sort between spending and revenue. It is not the only way to lighten the debt burden, but it is what a BBA requires. This would let the economy grow faster than the debt, gradually reducing the weight of borrowing costs.

Short-term stability: Policymakers and the public do not like wild swings in policy. Individuals, businesses, and government officials value predictability and stability when making plans. Uncertainty imposes costs that increase the difficulty of planning while reducing prosperity and growth, thereby distracting from higher-value uses of resources. It also stresses people out.

Many economists think the federal government should run deficits during recessions and surpluses during booms to balance the budget over the business cycle and to stabilize overall economic output. Even for those not persuaded by such macroeconomic stabilization arguments, modest Keynesian-style stabilization is consistent with a rule for policy stability, which can include assistance programs that ramp up automatically during downturns and down during recoveries.[7]

Comprehensive: A budget goal should cover all or nearly all spending and revenue. A single metric is easier for policymakers, watchdogs, and the public to monitor. This scope is inherent to a BBA and requires bringing emergency spending into the balance rule and, if adopted, a capital budget as well.

Acknowledgements current reality: Current conditions are far from ideal, but policy has inertia. Politically viable policy changes tend to deviate incrementally from current policy. A fiscal rule must adapt to existing spending and revenue levels while being able to follow significant shifts in either or both.

Neutral: A BBA and implementing legislation are formal rules. Their adoption and faithful execution rely on other mutually reinforcing rules and on informal support from a broad set of policymakers. Rules that could accommodate more views about the proper size and scope of government activities are easier to sustain than those with a narrower vision. They are anti-fragile: they can bend without breaking.

Feasible: Budget targets must be consistent with the rest of the budget process and the congressional calendar. For example, it would not make sense to use actual outcomes for FY 2024, which concluded on September 30, 2024, and for which final data was published in October 2024, to affect the budget cycle for FY 2025, which began with a CBO report in January 2024 and was supposed to be completed (but was not) between July and September 2024. Instead, FY 2024 outcomes reported in October 2024 would inform the FY 2026 budget cycle that formally begins in early 2025 with the president's budget request.[8]

The amount of fiscal consolidation needed and the time to accomplish it are important feasibility considerations. As noted, a ten-year path to primary balance is far more viable than one to full balance.

The Responsible Budget Targets Act Is a Good Model for Primary Structural Balance

Implementing legislation for a principles-based BBA should build on structural primary balance, at least initially. It provides long-term fiscal responsibility as well as flexibility for policy and economic stability in the near term. It aims to balance the budget, excluding interest, over the medium term rather than every year.

Many see the Swiss debt brake (see Chapter 3) as the international gold standard for budget targets. It limits spending to cyclically adjusted revenue, which means revenue if the economy were growing exactly on the long-term trend.

Unfortunately, it does not transfer to the United States as well as one might hope, at least using existing CBO data for *automatic stabilizers*, the automatic changes in programs over the business cycle, and *potential GDP*, or the amount of goods and services produced if the economy is exactly at capacity. It is always possible that a new rule would push CBO to innovate and produce better inputs, but members of Congress are not likely to take that leap of faith.

Another approach would use a rolling average of GDP growth with adjustments based on federal debt changes. This model did well but did not feel politically sustainable. Admittedly, it is a subjective standard.

A more promising approach is spending caps that grow with a rolling average of GDP, adjusted through a primary-deficit-based brake. This became the Responsible Budget Targets Act that Senator Mike Braun (R-IN) and Representative Tom Emmer (R-MN) introduced in April 2022.[9] It also sets out a way to offset emergencies, generally over the six following years.

The RBTA is written to stand alone without constitutional backing, but it would carry far more weight as the manifestation of BBA principles. Adapting the language from stand-alone targets to implementing legislation requires only layering on definitions, the BBA's supermajority for emergency spending, and possibly speeding up the transition to primary balance.

Now to the mechanics. The RBTA's primary spending (excluding interest costs) cap each year would grow from the previous year's primary budget authority. The growth rate would be the rolling average of GDP growth in the prior five calendar years. If the primary budget stays in surplus, Congress could slightly exceed the five-year-rolling-average-of-GDP growth rate. After primary deficits, however, the spending growth rate would tick down by 0.2 percentage points, compared to the rolling average, after each deficit. Each additional year of primary deficits would increase the deficit brake cumulatively. Likewise, primary surpluses would gradually return to the rolling average and even go above.

The RBTA would avoid ratchet effects by letting Congress raise (or reduce) revenue and adjust the spending cap accordingly. As a statute, Congress could modify it by subsequent statute whenever revisions or rebasing might be needed. It would adjust for automatic stabilizers—benefits programs for which more people become eligible during tough times—so downturn-driven spending increases for assistance programs would not collide with rigid caps. Finally, the deficit brake would reset to zero when the budget first reaches structural primary balance.

Understandably, some in Congress might prefer spending cuts only with no revenue increases. But that is not where the median member of Congress is likely to be consistently over time. After all, a broad coalition of support will be needed to sustain budget rules, so a rule must accommodate many visions to be adopted and to endure. In the messy realm of national policymaking, it is far better to have an adaptable and politically sustainable rule than a mathematically ideal but politically brittle rule.

Figure 9.1 illustrates the hypothetical primary spending path from RBTA (dashed line) as if it had been adopted in 2000. Actual and projected revenue (dotted line) and primary spending (solid line) give context. This model takes revenue policies as given and does not show emergencies or their offsets. It shows how stable and predictable the RBTA targets would be for non-emergency policies.

Figure 9.2 shows the year-to-year percentage change in federal revenue and RBTA's structural balance spending rule. Annual balance would tie spending and revenue too tightly together. The revenue volatility from a dynamic economy would drive policy instability on both sides of the ledger. Structural balance, by contrast, smooths out economic volatility

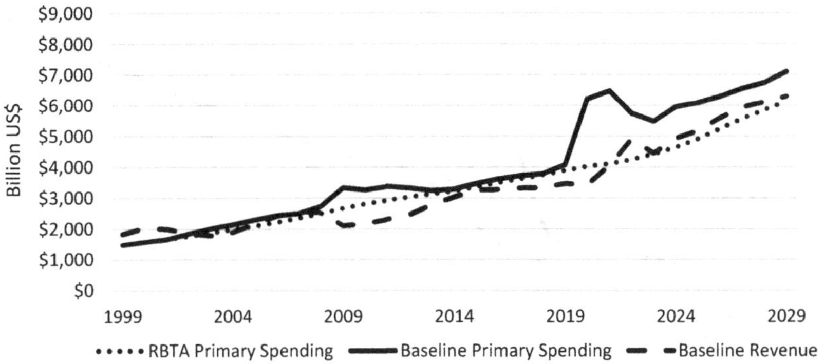

Fig. 9.1 RBTA allows stable non-emergency spending (*Sources* CBO, BEA, author's calculations)

and produces a stable and predictable path for non-emergency spending and the revenue policies needed to finance it.

Figure 9.3 shows the RBTA-as-introduced transition if Congress had adopted it in time for FY 2026, which begins on October 1, 2025. The status quo has inertia. Changing course starts small and builds over time.

The model suggests that the federal budget would reach primary balance about 11 years after enactment, although Congress could speed up that process. This timeline is the bare minimum. Congress could enact all needed savings immediately and let them build with delays when

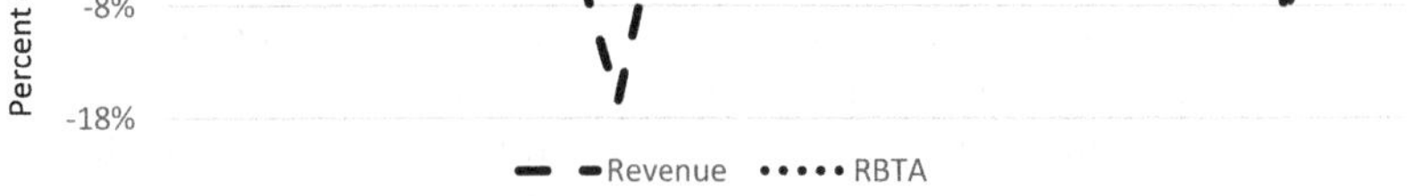

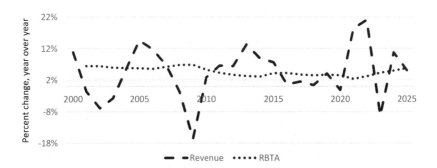

Fig. 9.2 Structural balance is far more stable than annual balance (*Sources* CBO, BEA, author's calculations)

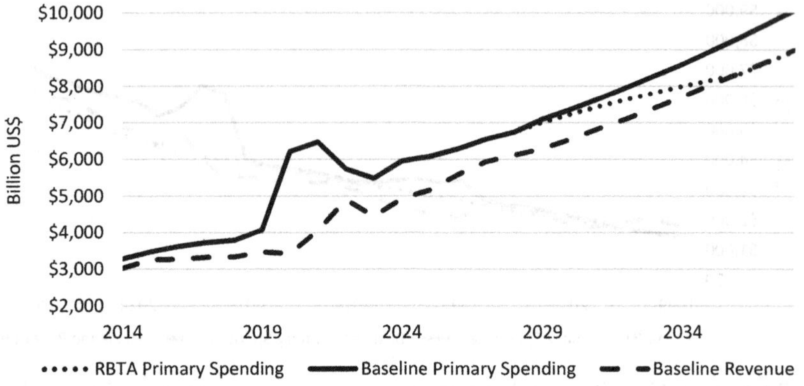

Fig. 9.3 RBTA would create a glide path to primary balance (*Sources* CBO, BEA, author's calculations)

appropriate, it could pursue a series of mini-deals each year or so, or it could combine those approaches. The debt-to-GDP ratio would peak just before reaching primary balance and decline after that if interest rates stay relatively low.

Excluding net interest makes primary balance easier to achieve. Even so, it would still slow the growth in the debt burden, as measured by the debt-to-GDP ratio. It would stabilize the debt-to-GDP ratio a year or two before reaching primary balance.

In addition to inspiring the balance rule, Switzerland's approach to emergencies is reflected in the RBTA. It is not realistic to expect immediate offsets when Congress approves funds to address crises, but a chronic failure to offset emergency response would create an easily abused budget loophole.[10] That would be mitigated with a principles-based BBA that requires a two-thirds supermajority for emergency spending. Still, the BBA's call for subsequent offsets "as soon as practicable" is a solid basis for this part of the RBTA.

The RBTA allows immediate emergency spending with no offsets, and then it reduces the caps in the subsequent six years by equal amounts. Or if Congress does not want the cuts, it can raise revenue instead. That way, Congress could address emergencies right away, but the subsequent impact on other programs or tax increases would create counterpressure to keep emergency response limited to actual needs instead of political pork.

As mentioned, the deficit brake would not kick in immediately. It skips a fiscal year to accommodate the executive and congressional budget calendars. The data needed to make the calculation becomes available early in the new fiscal year (October), which is months after Congress could have incorporated it in a last-ditch effort for the new fiscal year's planning. It is, however, perfect timing for building the following fiscal year's budget, starting with the president's budget proposal.

More information is available in the blog post "What is the Responsible Budget Targets Act?"[11] It also games out six scenarios numerically, including the basic spending growth rate, the cases of persistent primary surpluses and deficits, a transition from one to the other, emergency response, and revenue adjustments.

Under the RBTA, primary spending would continue to grow every year. Its growth *rate* would slow until primary structural deficits disappear, assuming the revenue baseline. Spending could grow faster than otherwise if the revenue projections increase. As noted, the deficit brake would reset when primary structural balance occurs. After that, the spending growth trend would again generally match the revenue growth trend with fine-tuning adjustments from the deficit brake.

Nothing would prevent Congress from enacting the RBTA (as introduced) at the same time it proposes a principles-based BBA to state legislatures. That way, core parts of implementing legislation would be a few years ahead of ratification.

Rising interest rates[12] suggest, however, that more restraint than primary balance eventually may be needed to put the budget on a sustainable, long-term path. If so, Congress could (1) adjust the RBTA to set a primary surplus target, (2) bring interest costs into the rule to target full balance, or (3) keep the rule as is and enact more savings than the rule requires.

In addition, the BBA would require two-thirds support in both houses of Congress for emergency spending. Supermajority thresholds cannot bind Congress unless they are constitutional because the Constitution otherwise gives each House free rein to set the rules for their proceedings. The combination of the constitutional supermajority and the statutory offsets would reserve emergency spending designations for actual emergencies and largely limit such spending to what is needed instead of letting the emergency designation become a budget loophole.

The Congressional Budget Office and the Department of the Treasury would play crucial roles in tracking and reporting budget information. Impartial umpires are part of the accountability and incentives that Congress needs to stay on track. It is easy to take them for granted, but their estimates and reports of budget outcome and options shape the policy conversation immensely.

Automatic Enforcement Needs an Overhaul

A clear goal is enough for some to do their duty. Others need additional incentives for their cost–benefit calculations to line up the right way. As Milton Friedman once put it, "The way you solve things is by making it politically profitable for the wrong people to do the right thing."[13] A backup plan is a good insurance policy.

Looking back to Switzerland, its national government simply follows the constitutional and statutory rules of its debt brake. The Swiss do not have additional enforcement provisions, and their political culture does fine without them.

Congress' political culture is different. For reasons we will not delve into here, Congress is not a well-oiled machine for policymaking. Fortunately, frustration by members of Congress, staff, and good government groups has stimulated solution generation and an appetite for them.

In the meantime, however, better incentives can support fiscal rules and produce better outcomes. The next chapter covers a significant improvement—Congress doing an actual budget each year—so the rest of this chapter focuses on the promise of linking targets to the debt limit and a better approach to automatic enforcement.

Trade the Debt Limit for Budget Targets

As we have discussed, the debt limit does not belong in the Constitution, whether in a balanced budget amendment or otherwise. It is a statutory construct, not a principle. It has been in statute for more than a century,[14] but it has not significantly restrained spending, revenue, or deficits in recent decades.

The debt limit is not even a useful fiscal rule. The Government Accountability Office has explained: "It does not restrict Congress's ability to pass spending and revenue legislation that affects the level of debt."[15]

Playing chicken with the debt limit risks triggering a default on federal debt. U.S. debt is the foundation for much of the global financial system, and a default would raise serious concerns about the integrity of the U.S. government and whether its debt truly is risk-free.[16] Fitch Ratings already downgraded its rating of federal debt in August 2023, and Moody's Investor Services changed the federal outlook from stable to negative in November 2023 and finally lowered its rating in May 2025.[17]

Some in Congress have proposed legislation to require the Secretary of the Treasury to prioritize payments of principal and interest on the debt to prevent default as well as certain other accounts,[18] but Congress has not enacted it. It is unclear if the Treasury Department has the systems to make it all work.

Prioritizing debt payments at least appears possible, however, according to a May 7, 2014, letter from the Treasury Department to then-Chair of the House Financial Services Committee Jeb Hensarling.[19] It said, "If the debt limit were not raised, and assuming Treasury had sufficient cash on hand, the New York Fed's systems would be technologically capable of continuing to make principal and interest payments while Treasury was not making other kinds of payments." Yet it went on to say that "this approach would be entirely experimental and create unacceptable risk to both domestic and global financial markets." In other words, even if Treasury and the Fed could pull it off, markets might lose confidence anyway.

Still, the periodic need to increase the debt limit is an opportunity to restore fiscal responsibility.[20] That is why the debt limit can play a role in implementing legislation for a BBA, not to mention teeing up votes on a principles-based BBA in the first place. Nearly all Democrats and many Republicans intensely dislike the existence of a statutory debt limit. Some have proposed eliminating or otherwise defanging it.[21]

Another option is to trade automatic debt limit suspension for the budget hitting reasonable targets. A 2020 letter to House leaders from 30 Republicans and 30 Democrats said, "We support a process for establishing overall budgetary goals—such as debt-to-GDP targets—that would reduce debt limit brinkmanship as long as the budget remains on a responsible path."[22] A BBA requires something like the Responsible Budget Targets Act instead of debt-to-GDP targets, but the outcomes could be similar.

In other words, meeting the targets, including the adjustments for emergencies and otherwise, would mean that members of Congress would not have to vote to raise the debt limit every year or two. Only if Congress exceeded the spending caps—instead of making an allowable adjustment—would members again have to vote to raise the debt limit. At the end of the prior suspension period, the debt limit would reset at the then-nominal value of debt subject to the limit, and a series of *extraordinary measures* would give Congress several more months to figure something out.

The desire to avoid voting on the debt limit would help Congress stick to budget targets. It is difficult to describe how much members of Congress dislike taking that vote, but any former or current member or staffer will swear by it.

It is reasonable to ask why a statutory debt limit may be necessary after ratification of a BBA and enactment of implementing legislation. A plausible legal reason is that the Constitution's Article 1, Section 8, clause 2, gives Congress the power to "borrow Money on the credit of the United States." The modern statutory debt limit sets a cap on how much nominal federal debt the executive branch is permitted to accrue. Congress has already delegated its power to borrow money to a large degree. Weakening Congress' control would take practice even further from that principle.

A practical reason for retaining a debt limit is that the debt would continue to increase in nominal terms, especially during the transition period from today's nearly $2 trillion deficit to primary balance. The Responsible Budget Targets Act's glide path to primary balance over ten years would allow trillions more in debt as the increase in the debt-to-GDP ratio slows, stops, and then reverses.

Even if Congress kept the budget perfectly in line with the Responsible Budget Targets Act, nominal debt would keep growing as the debt-to-GDP ratio falls. Even full balance enacted immediately—which would cause an economic shock and would therefore be a political impossibility—would not necessarily prevent the nominal debt from growing, even though the debt-to-GDP ratio would decline rapidly. That is because federal debt growth includes growth in the volume of government-provided (*direct*) loans.

Congress could keep the statutory debt limit but suspend it each year as long as the budget has been on target.[23] That would balance legal obligation with practical considerations while encouraging Congress to budget responsibly. If Congress tried to evade the BBA and its implementing legislation, having to deal with the debt limit again would exert gentle pressure on Congress to get back on track, and the statutory targets would make crystal clear what that means. This combination could avoid a debt limit default in the near term while preventing a debt crisis (and default) later.

Congress Needs a New, Incremental Approach to Automatic Enforcement

Enforcing budget targets with automatically triggered savings makes good conceptual sense. The trouble is that Congress' slapdash attempts at automatic budget enforcement have not had much success.[24]

Caps on deficits or appropriated spending under the Balanced Budget and Emergency Deficit Control Act of 1985 (and its reaffirmation in 1987), the Budget Enforcement Act of 1990, the Balanced Budget Act of 1997, the Budget Control Act of 2011, and the Fiscal Responsibility Act of 2023 were supposed to be enforced through automatic, across-the-board cuts to most annually appropriated spending accounts and a handful of direct spending accounts.

Such cuts to appropriated programs have occurred only once—in 2013—and otherwise, Congress has adjusted the caps to more tolerable levels. To be fair, deficit and spending caps helped restrain Congress in the late 1980s and 1990s. As budget official Alice Rivlin wrote about the late 1990s, "the discipline imposed by the BEA held reasonably well during the period of divided government. Each side was able to keep the other from using the surplus for its preferred purposes."[25]

The Statutory Pay-As-You-Go Act, initially adopted in the Budget Enforcement Act of 1990 and revived in 2010, tries to discourage Congress from increasing deficits by reducing revenue or increasing direct spending above current law projections. It is complicated: (1) it adds up all legislation passed in a session of Congress (January 3 at noon to the same date one year later), (2) takes the average deficit change over both the next five years and the next ten years, and, (3) if the average deficit increases over either period, it triggers commensurate spending reductions *that year* in a narrow slice of *non-exempt* (not exempt from the cuts) direct spending programs based on the larger of the five- or ten-year average.

Congress has never let the statutory PAYGO sequester occur. To do so under normal circumstances would be unpleasant. After the $1.9 trillion American Rescue Plan Act of 2021, however, statutory PAYGO would require spending cuts that would vastly exceed spending on programs from which savings are supposed to come. The PAYGO sequester would zero them out for several years in a row. Congress will not tolerate something so draconian, so it turns them off by "wiping" the PAYGO scorecards clean or shifting them to the future.

These poorly designed across-the-board sequesters have not worked and will not work. Legislators see them as "goofy meat axes," in the words of former California representative, Clinton administration budget official, and Obama administration Secretary of Defense Leon Panetta. These sequesters are easy for lobbyists to build coalitions to oppose, such as the NDD Coalition (for non-defense discretionary spending) that emerged after the Budget Control Act of 2011. They also complicate budget enforcement instead of covering everything.

A better approach would apply to the entire budget, other than principal and interest on the debt. It would target savings over the following decade so triggered savings can start small and grow, which makes them more tolerable to the public and policymakers.

It would make minor, surgical, repeatable adjustments to various direct spending programs and revenue provisions. Many such changes could be reasonable adjustments that might scale up to be part of a budget deal.

In addition, modest limits on discretionary spending could mean caps on the entire discretionary basket or separately on defense and non-defense spending. These caps could be a nominal freeze, which would be a small cut in per capita, inflation-adjusted terms, or some other fixed amount. They could also vary compared to current-law projections depending on the size of the budget breach to be offset.

We can illustrate the concept with Social Security, even though that program's finances could and maybe should be managed separately from the rest of the budget.

Given the long-term, accrual nature of Social Security, these automatic fiscal stabilizers could be in proportion to the projected imbalance in 20 years. Savings options could include a list of changes to reduce spending growth and a separate list to increase dedicated revenue. Required savings proportionate to the 20th-year imbalance could be allocated in a fixed ratio between spending growth reductions and revenue increases.

These policy decisions would be intensely political: what adjustments to make, how large each should be, when they should take effect, how much to reduce spending growth versus how much to increase revenue. CBO and Social Security Administration expertise would be invaluable for producing objective estimates of the options, but striking a deal to automatically adjust Social Security would be a political balancing act.

When savings would be triggered, the Office of Management and Budget or the Social Security Administration would make the changes required by statute without needing to exercise discretion in any significant way. After all, making policy is Congress' job, and carrying it out is the executive branch's role. Each time these adjustments would occur, the subsequent financing gap would narrow until, ideally, Social Security would eventually regain solvency. This might also expand the political space for Congress to otherwise protect and improve the program beyond what is possible with scheduled adjustments.

A similar model could enforce overall budget targets. OMB could apply savings targets based on a ratio to distinct lists of direct spending and revenue savings following a budget breach while re-establishing discretionary spending caps at tolerable levels for the following fiscal year. For automatic enforcement to be most effective, it would spread the pain. Ideally, every member of Congress would be uncomfortable without any major faction having too much motivation to take the whole thing down. Admittedly, this incremental enforcement strategy is complicated to design and negotiate, but it could work far better than the simple but ineffective sequesters tried so far.[26]

Setting the details in law for OMB to carry out is a rule-of-law approach to automatic budget enforcement. Congress would not have to do anything more for the savings to go into effect. This approach would address the concerns Senators Leahy, Kennedy, and Feingold raised in the prior chapter about ad hoc responses by any of the three branches of the federal government.

The reasonableness of this targeted, incremental strategy would increase the difficulty in Congress reaching a consensus to turn it off. That said, the point is not to trigger the savings but to encourage Congress to manage the budget proactively within reasonable budget targets.

The Courts Can Play a Role in Budget Enforcement

Robust implementing legislation probably would not give the courts much to do. Congress would set the policy, the executive branch would carry it out, and the judicial branch would make sure the executive branch does its job faithfully. The Supreme Court has become less inclined to usurp legislative powers when Congress abdicates them, but that pattern could change as the years pass.

Some court-related provisions put forward in BBAs might be acceptable in statute. The courts probably should not have the power to order a reduction in budget authority or outlays or to increase revenue beyond what is already required by statute via automatic enforcement.

The House and Senate Committees on the Judiciary are best suited to consider how implementing legislation for a BBA should involve the courts. They need not produce such provisions immediately. A feature of leaving many details to statutes is that Congress can adjust them as circumstances warrant.

That said, the risk that courts would eventually get involved is a useful stick to push Congress to enact effective implementing legislation and to be diligent in balancing the budget.

Implementing legislation for a principles-based BBA would be complex. Fortunately, several existing pieces provide a decent foundation on which to build. Definitions mostly exist already, and the Responsible Budget Targets Act's glide path to structural primary balance is achievable and reasonable. Enforcing these targets would rely partly on tying them to the debt limit and adopting a new incremental approach to automatic budget savings. The roles of the courts remain to be determined.

Perhaps the most powerful way to help Congress meet budget targets, however, is for Congress to have a decent budget process. It never has, but it should, and that is the topic of the next chapter.

Notes

1. See Kurt Couchman, "Effective Fiscal Rules Build on Consensus," in *A Fiscal Cliff: New Perspectives on the U.S. Federal Debt Crisis*, eds. Barry Poulson and John Merrifield, Cato, 2020.
2. Primarily in "Definitions," Section 3 of the Congressional Budget and Impoundment Control Act of 1974, https://uscode.house.gov/view.xhtml?req=granuleid:USC-prelim-title2-section622&num=0&edition=prelim, accessed November 6, 2022, and supplemented in "Statement of budget enforcement through sequestration; definitions," Section 250 of the Balanced Budget and Emergency Deficit Control Act of 1985, https://uscode.house.gov/view.xhtml?req=granuleid:USC-prelim-title2-section900&num=0&edition=prelim, accessed November 6, 2022.

3. "Governmental Receipts," Analytical Perspectives, *President's Budget Request for Fiscal Year 2023*, https://www.whitehouse.gov/wp-content/uploads/2022/03/ap_11_receipts_fy2023.pdf, March 28, 2022.
4. "Offsetting Collections and Offsetting Receipts," Analytical Perspectives, President's Budget Request for Fiscal Year 2023, https://www.whitehouse.gov/wp-content/uploads/2022/03/ap_12_offsetting_fy2023.pdf, March 28, 2022.
5. Congressional Budget Office, "The Budget and Economic Outlook: 2025 to 2035," https://www.cbo.gov/publication/60870, January 17, 2025.
6. Sec. 250(c)(20)/(21) of the Balanced Budget and Emergency Deficit Control Act, as added by Section 13101(a) of Title XIII of Pub. L. 101–508, classified to Section 900(c)(20)/(21) of Title 2, United States Code.
7. Congressional Budget Office, "Automatic Stabilizers in the Federal Budget: 2022 to 2032," https://www.cbo.gov/system/files/2022-10/58495-automatic-stabilizers.pdf, October 2022.
8. The FY2025 budget cycle in the executive branch takes place throughout calendar year 2024 and culminates with the president's budget request, which is due by the first Monday in February but is often late. Final 2023 data in October is perfect timing for the Office of Management and Budget in the Executive Office of the President to integrate target adjustments into the budget request in time for an early February release.
9. Rep. Tom Emmer, "Emmer, Braun Introduce Bill to Rein in Out-of-Control Government Spending," https://emmer.house.gov/2022/4/emmer-braun-introduce-bill-to-rein-in-out-of-control-government-spending, April 6, 2022.
10. Kurt Couchman, "We should offset emergencies—just not right away," The Hill, https://thehill.com/opinion/white-house/425384-we-should-offset-emergencies-just-not-right-away/, January 15, 2019.
11. Kurt Couchman, "What is the Responsible Budget Targets Act?" Americans for Prosperity, https://americansforprosperity.org/responsible-budget-targets-act/, June 21, 2023.
12. St. Louis Federal Reserve Bank, "Market Yield on U.S. Treasury Securities at 10-Year Constant Maturity," FRED Economic Data,

https://fred.stlouisfed.org/series/DGS10, accessed November 23, 2022.
13. Free to Choose Network, "Milton Friedman: Make Politically Profitable For Wrong People To Do Right Thing," https://www.youtube.com/watch?v=B_nGEj8wIP0, posted March 21, 2016.
14. "Public Debt Limit," Section 3101, Title 31, United States Code, https://uscode.house.gov/view.xhtml?req=granuleid:USC-prelim-title31-section3101&num=0&edition=prelim, accessed November 25, 2022.
15. Government Accountability Office, "The Nation's Fiscal Health: Effective Use of Fiscal Rules and Targets," https://www.gao.gov/assets/gao-20-561.pdf, September 2020.
16. Fitch Ratings, "Fitch Downgrades the United States' Long-Term Ratings to 'AA + ' from 'AAA'; Outlook Stable," https://www.fitchratings.com/research/sovereigns/fitch-downgrades-united-states-long-term-ratings-to-aa-from-aaa-outlook-stable-01-08-2023, August 1, 2023.
17. Fitch Ratings, "Fitch Downgrades the United States' Long-Term Ratings to 'AA + ' from 'AAA'; Outlook Stable," https://www.fitchratings.com/research/sovereigns/fitch-downgrades-united-states-long-term-ratings-to-aa-from-aaa-outlook-stable-01-08-2023, August 1, 2023. Davide Barbuscia and Andrea Shalal, "Moody's turns negative on US credit rating, draws Washington ire," Reuters, https://www.reuters.com/markets/us/moodys-changes-outlook-united-states-ratings-negative-2023-11-10/, November 10, 2023. Moody's Ratings, "Moody's Ratings downgrades United States ratings to Aa1 from Aaa; changes outlook to stable," https://ratings.moodys.com/ratings-news/443154, May 16, 2025.
18. Sen. Rick Scott, "Full Faith and Credit Act," S. 2809, https://www.congress.gov/bill/117th-congress/senate-bill/2809, introduced September 22, 2021.
19. Tim Reid, "Treasury says debt payments could be prioritized in default scenario," Reuters, https://www.reuters.com/article/us-usa-treasury-debt/treasury-says-debt-payments-could-be-prioritized-in-default-scenario-idUSBREA480R520140509, May 9, 2014.

20. Committee for a Responsible Federal Budget, "Q&A: Everything You Should Know About the Debt Ceiling," https://www.crfb.org/papers/qa-everything-you-should-know-about-debt-ceiling#_Hlk431978821, October 28, 2022.
21. Rep. Brendan Boyle, "Boyle reintroduces legislation to abolish the debt ceiling," https://boyle.house.gov/media-center/press-releases/boyle-reintroduces-legislation-abolish-debt-ceiling, February 15, 2021. Rep. Scott Peters, "Reps. Peters, Arrington introduce bipartisan bill to reform debt limit dance that threatens U.S. economy," https://scottpeters.house.gov/media-center/press-releases/reps-peters-arrington-introduce-bipartisan-bill-to-reform-debt-limit, December 7, 2021.
22. Rep. Scott Peters, "Reps. Peters, Arrington Lead 58 Members in Bipartisan Letter Calling on Congress to Tackle Federal Debt Post COVID Crisis," https://scottpeters.house.gov/media-center/press-releases/reps-peters-arrington-lead-58-members-in-bipartisan-letter-calling-on, June 1, 2020.
23. Kurt Couchman, "A debt limit deal with something for everyone," *The Hill*, https://thehill.com/opinion/congress-blog/3743468-a-debt-limit-deal-with-something-for-everyone/, November 20, 2022.
24. Kurt Couchman, "Better budget targets can help Congress balance near- and long-term needs," Americans for Prosperity, https://americansforprosperity.org/wp-content/uploads/2022/07/Americans-for-Prosperity-White-Paper-Better-budget-targets-can-help-Congress-balance-near-and-long-term-needs.pdf, September 12, 2022.
25. Alice Rivlin, *Divided We Fall: Why Consensus Matters*," Brookings, 2022, p. 168.
26. Kurt Couchman, "Why Social Security is in trouble and needs automatic fiscal stabilizers," Americans for Prosperity, https://americansforprosperity.org/why-social-security-is-in-trouble/, July 20, 2022. Kurt Couchman, "Why incremental adjustments are a better approach to automatic budget enforcement," Americans for Prosperity, https://americansforprosperity.org/automatic-budget-enforcement/, March 23, 2023.

CHAPTER 10

Budget Balance Requires a Functioning Federal Budget Process

We have worked through a principles-based BBA with well-crafted statutory budget goals, definitions, and politically sustainable enforcement. Even if that were all written perfectly and adopted enthusiastically, Congress's broken budget process might frustrate efforts to balance the budget.

The heart of federal budget dysfunction is that Congress only considers part of the budget each year.[1]

In addition, late budget requests from presidents keep Congress from starting its budget process on time. Brinksmanship around shutdowns means the process no longer concludes when it should, which can delay the start of the next round. Let us start with the need for a comprehensive budget.

Congress Does Not Do a Comprehensive Budget, but It Should

Congress's annual appropriations process only includes 26 percent of spending and no revenue. It covers only a minority of one side of the actual budget, as Fig. 10.1 shows.

Annually appropriated spending is subdivided into 12 bills of varying sizes (see Fig. 10.2), and members cannot shift funds across these dozen stovepipes once first established. In recent years, leaders of both parties

K. Couchman, *Fiscal Democracy in America*,
https://doi.org/10.1007/978-3-031-91938-1_10

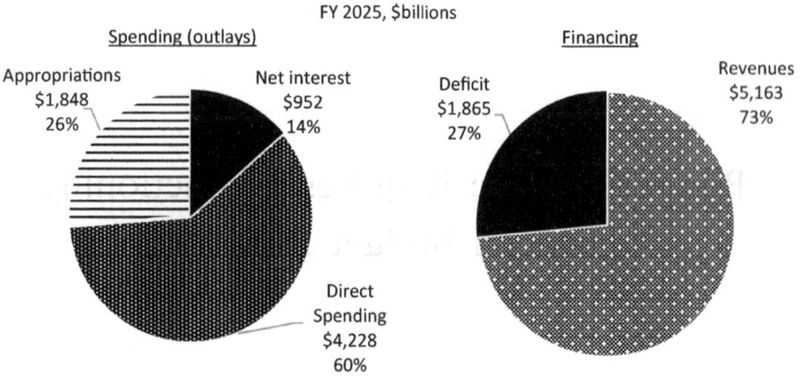

Fig. 10.1 Appropriations are an important but small share of the budget (*Source* CBO)

have tightly controlled members' ability to propose amendments within an appropriations bill, let alone across them.

Congress is supposed to manage revenue policies and direct spending other than Social Security through budget reconciliation, primarily to reduce deficits.

Unfortunately, it does not work like that anymore. Reconciliation has become an irregular tool to advance partisan priorities when the same party controls Congress and the White House.[3]

Each year, a concurrent resolution on the budget is supposed to set spending caps for the Committees on Appropriations and for the other 16 committees in each house with spending authority. It sets aggregate targets for spending, revenue, deficits, and debt and sometimes per-committee budget reconciliation targets.

In practice, the only parts of the budget resolution that matter much are reconciliation instructions during one-party control and, sometimes, appropriations caps. A budget resolution and reconciliation only require a simple majority in the Senate, while most other legislation is subject to a 60-vote threshold. As a result, the budget resolution has generally become a partisan messaging document or one-party empowerment vehicle rather than a consensus blueprint for a substantive budget process.

An actual budget could be the next step in the evolution of the congressional budget process. A real budget could upgrade today's ineffective, top-down, polarizing status quo to an annual, predictable, holistic

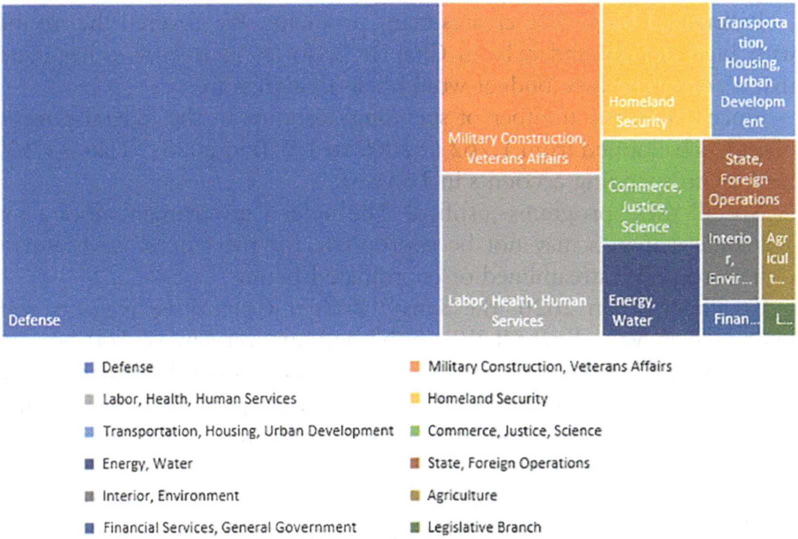

Fig. 10.2 Appropriations bills differ dramatically in size (FY 2024 initial allocations, $million) (*Source* House Committee on Appropriations[2])

budget process that includes contributions from many more members and committees.

A comprehensive budget would make backsliding more difficult and thus provide a politically sustainable way for Congress to meet budget targets and otherwise comply with a BBA. Putting all fiscal policies into consideration each year would give members many more degrees of freedom to manage budget priorities. It would also empower members of Congress and committees to build coalitions around policy changes.

A comprehensive budget would finally fulfill then-President Thomas Jefferson's 1802 vision in a letter to the Secretary of the Treasury[4]:

> We might hope to see the finances of the Union as clear and intelligible as a merchant's books, so that every member of Congress and every man of any mind in the Union should be able to comprehend them, to investigate abuses, and consequently control them.

Balkanized budgeting creates many problems. We covered the trouble with high deficits and debt in Chapter 2, so let us turn to other issues that a comprehensive budget would help Congress fix.

Since 2009, the number of spending accounts in the federal government has ballooned from 1,762 in 2009 to 1,970 in 2025.[5] That is a 12% increase in spending accounts in 16 years.

Are all these programs justified? The federal government does a lot. Yet some activities may not be appropriate for the federal government. Others could be streamlined or coordinated better.

To illustrate, in 2020, the Senate Budget Committee majority staff under Chair Mike Enzi (R-WY) published an overview of 160 housing programs administered by 20 different federal entities.[6] Chairman Enzi thought the federal government had only five proper missions in housing policy and hoped that regular portfolio budgeting reports would help Congress clean things up.[7]

Similarly, federal healthcare subsidies are about $2.5 trillion in FY 2025. CBO counts 155 health spending line items, and the Joint Committee on Taxation reports 11 health tax preferences.[8] Yet only 8.8 percent of the dollars for all those programs goes through the annual appropriations process. Done properly, a comprehensive budget would include them all.

Turning to food programs, Rep. Jim McGovern (D-MA) put it well:

> When we talk about combatting hunger on the Agriculture Committee, we talk about SNAP. But that's not the whole answer, right? If you want to talk about school feeding, you've got to go to the Education Labor. If you want to talk about food is medicine, you have to go to Ways and Means or Energy and Commerce. There needs to be a better coordinated effort to look at things more holistically. It would enable us to be better prepared for upcoming disasters whether they're climate related or pandemic related or who knows what related.[9]

Congress Funds Many Programs That Need Updates

The sprawl in budget accounts reflects a broken budget system and a breakdown of authorizations. Congressional committees are supposed to manage programs established by laws within their jurisdictions periodically. Rather than letting program overlap and duplication accumulate, committees should lead on coordinating, consolidating, and otherwise updating programs toward coherence.

Congress has not abandoned this work entirely, but many committees have fallen far behind. CBO reports that most non-defense discretionary spending lacks a current authorization for appropriations.[10] The Appropriations Committees are NOT primarily at fault; these duties belong to the authorizing committees.

Yet, as long as the Appropriations Committees keep funding these programs, authorizing committees seldom have enough reason to undertake the negotiations needed to enact new legislation. In fact, the Appropriations Committees have increasingly included authorization-like language in appropriations legislation and the reports accompanying them. That programmatic direction is supposed to come directly from the authorizing committees, but that has changed. Someone must do it. Relying on must-pass appropriations bills to carry those instructions has shifted power from authorizing to appropriations committees and has changed agency behavior accordingly.

As authorizing committees have receded, congressional leaders have stepped in as well. The special rules that structure debate for significant legislation in the House have increasingly clamped down on amendment consideration to appropriations bills.

Today's appropriations-in-isolation-focused "regular order" process does not make much sense. Moreover, this tightly controlled, incomplete approach to annual budgeting is deeply unsatisfying for most members of Congress because they do not feel like they can make a difference. Trying to hit statutory budget goals, comply with a BBA, or even complete the process on time is almost impossible this way.

It usually collapses into an omnibus appropriations package with all twelve appropriations bills and whatever else leaders, senior appropriators, and a handful of other committee leaders can agree on. Most members have little time to review the package and no opportunity to try changing it. All they can do is vote for or against it, where voting nay brings accusations of voting for a government shutdown. As we will see soon, automatic continuing appropriations would improve these dynamics, but that is not enough.

Budget Reconciliation Does Not Perform as Intended

The Congressional Budget Act of 1974 set up budget reconciliation as the fast-track process for managing revenue, direct spending programs, and the debt limit to conform to the overall budget vision. Unlike most legislation, reconciliation can pass the Senate with only a simple majority. Congress created it to reduce deficits, keep the overall budget balanced, and coordinate direct spending and revenue programs with related activities funded through appropriations. Ironically, 1974 was the low point for the debt burden, aside from the few years at the turn of the century when everything went right for balancing the budget.

Initially open-ended, reconciliation got guardrails from the multifaceted Byrd Rule in 1986 at the insistence of Senator Robert Byrd (D-WV). This rule deems extraneous any provisions that (1) would increase the deficit beyond the budget window, (2) are reported by a committee not having jurisdiction over the provision, (3) would not have a fiscal impact, (4) would have a "merely incidental" (whatever that means) fiscal impact, (5) would result in a committee failing to meet its reconciliation instructions from the budget resolution, or (6) would change Social Security.[11]

Reconciliation and the Byrd Rule complicate the budget process. It forces proponents and opponents of provisions to engage the Senate Parliamentarian—a staffer, not a member—to rule on ambiguities in the language regarding various precedents. Though the parliamentarian's decisions do not strictly bind senators, senators give them deference.[12]

Both parties have turned reconciliation into an irregular, partisan device to use during fleeting periods of unified government. It has become a tool of the majority that sidelines the minority party and usually increases deficits and debt, contrary to its original purpose.

Looking back, the incentives that shape reconciliation are clear. Without political cover from popular appropriated programs like defense and infrastructure, reconciliation could not sustain its mission of, on net, reducing spending and increasing revenue. Members of Congress do not like to disappoint people even when they know they should, and history shows that they will not unless they have enough cover.

All that said, the 1974 budget process reform improved on what came before. It created CBO, the Budget Committees, and an attempt at tools to manage the entire budget, albeit piecemeal.[13] It fell short primarily by bifurcating the budget and messing up the incentives for healthy, deliberative management.

A Comprehensive Budget Is the Next Major Upgrade

To fulfill the aims of the Congressional Budget Act, Congress might consider that a budget is inherently one plan that includes everything. As a personal finance book explains, "you need to know—not guess—how much money you have coming in, how much you're spending, and what you're spending it on."[14]

A comprehensive congressional budget would be a bill consisting of a line item for each spending program—whether annually appropriated or direct spending—and each significant revenue provision, including tax preferences.

After all, Congress expects holistic budget information in the president's budget request, in the Treasury Department's reports on the financial condition of the government, from the Government Accountability Office, and from the Congressional Budget Office. It is strange indeed that Congress does not review everything regularly itself.

Every successful business carefully reviews all costs and income in pursuit of efficiencies and profits. Some countries, for example, Germany, Switzerland, and Estonia, have constitutional mandates for the budget bill to include all spending and revenue.

Getting Congress from here to there requires careful attention to the politics and process of congressional reform.

Fortunately, many state legislatures already do something similar, and many members of Congress are former state legislators. Figure 10.3 shows that fourteen states do a single bill per budget cycle (whether annual or biennial), and another sixteen states do five or fewer bills.

Enacting a single bill is not sufficient, however: the budget must include all spending and all revenue. Colorado, for example, does a single bill that only comprises about one-third of expenditures.

A comprehensive budget would help Congress meet BBA targets because including everything provides more options to reduce or avoid deficits.

Some programs overlap or duplicate others. Some cover similar activities but work at cross purposes or have unintended interactions. Putting all in the budget would make seeing and discussing those issues easier. Congress could address some directly in the budget, while others, at

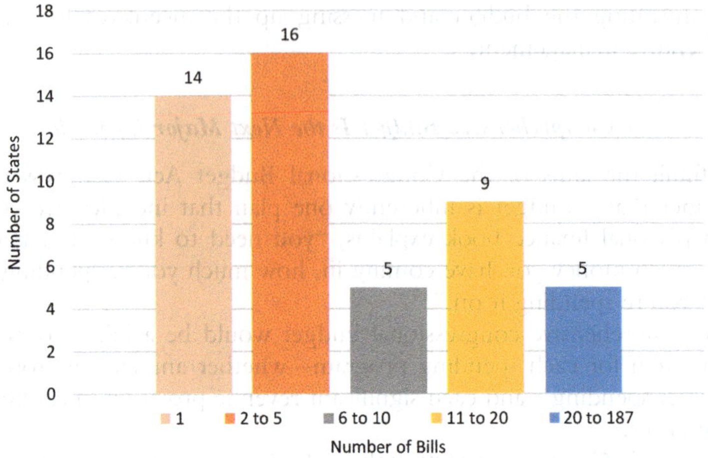

Fig. 10.3 Most states do one or a few budget bills per cycle (*Note* The sixteen states with one bill per budget cycle are Colorado, Connecticut, Florida, Georgia, Hawaii, Indiana, Maryland, Massachusetts, New Jersey, North Carolina, Rhode Island, Tennessee, and Virginia. The rest do more: Illinois (2), New Hampshire (2), New Mexico (2), South Carolina (2), California (2–3), Kansas (2–3), Washington (3), Texas (3–4), Alaska (4), Delaware (4), Ohio (4), Vermont (4), Oklahoma (1–5), Kentucky (5), Nevada (5), New York (5), Louisiana (6), Nebraska (7), Alabama (8), Minnesota (10), Arizona (10), Iowa (12), Montana (14), Utah (15), Michigan (16), Wyoming (16), Missouri (17), Pennsylvania (17), West Virginia (fewer than 20), North Dakota (46), Idaho (95), Mississippi (104), Oregon (100–150), Arkansas (187), and Maine (varies)) (*Source* National Association of State Budget Officers)

least in part, would require the authorizing committees to address them separately. These discussions would help rejuvenate the authorization process.[15]

A real budget would encourage members of Congress to root out waste. Meeting annual budget targets would encourage legislators to identify the lowest priorities.

A familiar saying in DC is that one man's waste is another man's income. Waste can mean many things. Poor program control that lets organized criminals steal from taxpayers during a pandemic is obvious. A more nuanced definition would be spending that, at the margin, provides less value than the costs of financing it, including the costs of collection and the deadweight losses imposed on society by taxation or borrowing's effects on people's incentives to work, save, and invest.[16]

In a world without clear fiscal scarcity, members care less when waste adds to the debt. When programs compete, however, reducing waste, fraud, and abuse protects what members value. In today's budget system, many legislators rationally conclude that the benefits of going after waste are not worth taking on organized interests.

BBA-based budget targets and a comprehensive budget would give members more means and motivation to confront waste. Having all spending and revenue provisions together and a hard budget constraint would empower legislators to build coalitions around proposals to add value for the people.

While shifting resources toward better uses, they would develop expertise and drive their colleagues to understand programs better. Significant numbers of members and staff usually only spend time learning about programs if they have decisions to make. Putting everything in front of members each year would be a powerful way to strengthen institutional knowledge.

An actual budget would also let Congress manage priorities. Some activities would scale back to make or to preserve room in the budget for others that provide more value. Special interests may moan about their oxen being gored, but politicians could thrive simply by explaining that giving up some things lets us have other things that we care even more about.

A comprehensive budget would change budget politics. Under reconciliation, direct spending and revenue changes are out in the open, so using it for deficit reduction is risky. Congressional Democrats discovered that in 1994, following a reconciliation bill[17] earlier that year when Republicans took control of both houses of Congress for the first time in 40 years.

Appropriated programs are among the most popular on a per-dollar basis. Putting everything into one bill would help Congress do the difficult but necessary work of protecting Social Security and federal health programs for those who need them most while updating them for modern times.

As mentioned in the introduction, at a bipartisan meeting of members of Congress a few years ago, one of the leaders told Maya MacGuineas, president of the Committee for a Responsible Federal Budget and a well-known advocate for fiscal responsibility: "We know what we need to do. We just don't know how to do it and [politically] survive."

Voting to advance national security, take care of veterans, finance infrastructure, preserve national parks, and a thousand other priorities in exchange for trimming activities about which people care less intensely is a defensible—and politically survivable—reason to vote for a budget. It would get more results from whatever amount of political will exists.

A complete budget would let Congress discard reconciliation and Byrd Rule complications. A comprehensive budget process would be straightforward: the Budget Committees' budget resolution would set toplines for all spending committees. The Appropriations Committee would still handle appropriations. The other committees would submit a line item for each direct spending program and language to effect any proposed changes.

In theory, every fiscal program could change in the annual budget, but the budget would be subject to the standard thresholds for passing legislation: a majority of the House, 60 senators, and the president's signature. In practice, each committee could review its portfolio every year, although most programs would not change regularly.

That said, if Congress does not adopt a comprehensive budget and continues to use reconciliation, significant changes are possible anyway. Congressional Democrats have shown how to use it for sweeping changes, so unified Republican control could, at least in theory, create new block grant programs to replace many existing programs and otherwise rewrite as much policy as they could agree on internally.

But that is precisely the issue with reconciliation. It is too easy to imagine major overhauls through a fast-track process even if the reality tends to disappoint. Republicans could not get significant health care reform through in 2017, and Democrats' enacted Inflation Reduction Act of 2022 was a pale shadow of the colossal House-passed Build Back Better Act. Shortly before this book went to print, unified Republicans used reconciliation to extend and expand on the Tax Cuts and Jobs Act of 2017 while driving significant savings from reducing spending but not enough to avoid increasing deficits.[18]

Reconciliation feeds polarization and animosity. Chipping away at problems yearly with bipartisan support is likely to be more productive in the long run than waiting for a once-in-a-generation tectonic shift, although reconciliation is irresistible when one party controls both houses and the White House.

A real budget would provide a known, expected, regular opportunity for members and staff to develop policy and build coalitions of support. The Senate's 60-vote threshold means the various mini-deals in a comprehensive budget must have broad support and narrow opposition. Similar efforts in the House would be more likely to become enacted policy after negotiations with the Senate.

Policy majorities for amendments could include more than moderates of both parties. They could consist of most members of one party and a smaller number of the other. Some proposals could find more support from the wings of each party than from moderates, with the bulk of votes coming from more conservative and progressive members. The shape of a policy majority for any particular proposal would be limited only by members' policy preferences, their willingness to work with others, and the organizers' skill and savvy in building coalitions both on the Hill with members and off the Hill through advocacy and other policy organizations.

This coalition building could profoundly change the culture of Congress and its effectiveness. Today's top-down process for everything drives the red-team/blue-team polarized dynamic since the only way to advance priorities is through majority party leaders. Minority party members have little choice but to tear down the majority to take power. As long-serving Rep. Tom Cole, Ph.D., (R-OK) has said, "The job of the majority is to govern. The job of the minority is to become the majority."

Stepping back, it is difficult to imagine an effective institution that systemically disenfranchises almost half its members and misses out on their potential contributions. But that is just another day in Congress.

By contrast, a real budget would make life in Congress better for everyone. It would provide far more value to build bridges and explore shared goals across the aisle. Members of the minority party would have ongoing opportunities to lead or support policy proposals. Minority party members would benefit less from poison pill, "gotcha" amendments. This shift would help the majority party manage the institution, as they could invest fewer resources into defense from partisan attacks.

A real budget would accomplish this by involving members in committees and on the floor. Giving every committee with spending authority and every member who wished to participate a stake in the annual budget would make it more likely to succeed on time each year. Members would have more skin in the game. Committees would have a recurring chance to do something meaningful.

Members would take more ownership of the overall results with a comprehensive budget. Today, Democrats insist that tax cuts and defense spending drive deficits. Republicans emphasize rapid spending growth in pension and health care programs as the overwhelming drivers of debt growth. Today's hyper-partisan environment drives each side toward separate narratives.

If everything were together, the degree to which different pieces affect outcomes would be more apparent. Partisan excuses would be weaker, and members would take more responsibility for the big picture. Chronic deficits and mounting debt are unpopular, so an actual budget would motivate members to seek out and address waste, fraud, abuse, and other low-value policies. A comprehensive budget would be inherently deficit-reducing for the foreseeable future, especially with reinforcement from a BBA and statutory targets.

A comprehensive budget would differ from an omnibus appropriations act. A comprehensive budget would include all spending and revenue, not just the 26 percent of spending covered by appropriations. A comprehensive budget would harness contributions from all committees in open markup, not just hammered out by a handful of party and committee leaders behind closed doors. Most importantly, a comprehensive budget would empower members and staff to understand and manage all federal programs and to work together toward better results.

The Mechanics of a Comprehensive Budget

In recent years, members of Congress and outside experts have developed legislation to make this possible. It began with a legal redline of the relevant statutes, and the drafting involved back-and-forth between the offices of Senator Mike Braun (R-IN), Legislative Counsel, Representative Blake Moore (R-UT), and others.

Ultimately, Sen. Braun's decision to run for governor of Indiana in 2024 meant he focused on wrapping up existing efforts instead of starting new projects that he would not get to complete. He seemed to think he could provide more value as governor than in the Senate and that Congress would have to look to the states for budget solutions.

Fortunately, this proposal still had champions in the House. In January 2024, Representatives Blake Moore (R-UT) and Marie Gluesenkamp

Perez (D-WA) introduced the Comprehensive Congressional Budget Act of 2024.[19]

CCBA is a perfecting amendment to the Congressional Budget Act of 1974 (CBA) to bring everything together. The CBA did much to strengthen Congress' power of the purse, and the CCBA would heal the rift between annually appropriated spending and everything else.

The CCBA would engage existing committees to leverage their existing jurisdictions to build a comprehensive annual budget Act. It would keep the president's budget request and other aspects of the executive budget process the same. CBO's reporting and responsibilities would not change, although a functional budget system could increase the importance of sound cost estimates.

Add Line Items to Views and Estimates

Following the president's budget request, congressional committees would continue to send views and estimates to the Budget Committees to help them build the budget resolution. Views and estimates share committees' intended legislative agendas and their estimated effects on spending and revenue.

The CCBA would require committees to include line items for their direct spending programs and a general sense of changes they anticipate including in the budget bill. Committees would not necessarily have to propose those changes later, but a preview would help stakeholders anticipate what they would need to know to engage the process productively. Even if a committee proposes no changes, the line items would provide context for other federal fiscal policies.[20]

Committees would get their initial line items from the Budget Committees. The Budget Committees already get this information from CBO, a product similar to CBO's "Spending Projections, by Budget Account"[21] but with committees of jurisdiction listed and other details.

The Budget Resolution Would Become a Framework for Governance

Better views and estimates would make the concurrent resolution on the budget matter more. It would still provide toplines for all committees with jurisdiction over spending, including the Appropriations Committee. In the context of a BBA, the sum of the spending allocations would reflect revenue-linked spending limits. The guardrails from the budget resolution's tracking, transparency, and enforcement provisions would take on new life.

CCBA would replace reconciliation with authorizing committee contributions to a complete budget. This trade would substantially strengthen the Budget Committees' coordinating, enforcement, and oversight roles.

The Budget Committee's report accompanying the budget resolution could include a comprehensive list of budget line items for the current year and the budget year. The report already provides topline spending authority broken out by committee. The CCBA would not change that, although it would give committees something useful to do with their allocations.

If both houses of Congress could not agree on a budget resolution, the budget chairs would deem budget levels for each committee a few legislative days after April 15. The levels would reflect the current law baseline that the CBO publishes in January or February each year. That way, committees would have a starting point from which to build out their pieces of the budget even with an impasse on the framework. Moderates could use this status quo backstop to keep a budget resolution from veering too far from viability.

During the initial transition to balance, however it may be defined, current law spending levels might exceed the BBA-based spending limits. Linking budget targets to the debt limit and to automatic enforcement would help Congress adopt a compliant budget resolution and ultimately the annual budget act as well.

Appropriations Committees Would Still Produce the Appropriations Bills

The Appropriations Committees would still have the discretion to subdivide the topline from the budget resolution among the twelve subcommittees (Fig. 10.2). Those subcommittees and the full committee would build out the twelve subcommittee bills as they do now, just within more holistic, overall allocations.

Instead of the Appropriations Committees reporting the twelve appropriations subcommittee bills to the floor separately, however, the twelve bills would get bundled with submissions from the authorizing committees.

Authorizing Committees Would Manage Direct Spending Programs

The authorizing committees have complete jurisdiction over direct spending programs and the authorizing statutes that establish discretionary programs. Direct spending means that authority for agencies to outlay funds is provided *directly* by an authorizing law, while appropriated spending requires appropriations separate from the statute that creates a program.

Direct spending is often called mandatory spending, but that is from the perspective of appropriators. With minor exceptions, Congress is not legally mandated to spend on anything. Describing annually appropriated and direct spending as discretionary and mandatory, respectively, is a bad habit that legislators should break.

The CCBA would require authorizing committees to manage their portfolios, produce legislative language for any direct spending policy changes, and adjust line items accordingly. Authorizing committees would settle their priorities in markups. The House Committee on Ways and Means and the Senate Committee on Finance would do likewise for revenue policies, likely in a separate title or division from their direct spending programs.

These committees could grapple with a wide variety of policy changes. Government agencies, including the Congressional Budget Office, the Government Accountability Office, the Social Security Administration, and others compile recommendations and estimates for alternative budget priorities.[22] Non-governmental organizations, including the Heritage Foundation, the Urban Institute, the American Enterprise Institute, the Committee for a Responsible Federal Budget, and many others, do likewise.[23] A comprehensive budget would give members a venue to consider these suggestions.

After markup, authorizing committees would send their line items and policy changes to get bundled with the appropriations bills. As initially introduced, the CCBA would have the Appropriations Committees put everything together and send it to the floor, but having the Budget Committees do it would empower them to enforce the guardrails. In either case, the Budget Committees would have produced current law line items to insert in case any authorizing committees do not provide a compliant submission.

These backup plans—baseline-deemed committee allocations in case of budget resolution breakdown and current-law line items if a committee gets stuck—came from a technical discussion in late 2022 with House Budget Committee staffers Jenna Spealman and Mary Popadiuk. They wondered what happens if things do not go smoothly. These changes ensure that an impasse at one stage does not derail everything like it does today.

Assembling a Complete Budget

The committees that do the bundling would not be allowed to make substantive changes to submissions from other committees. They would bundle the twelve appropriations subcommittee bills with authorizing committee submissions to assemble a comprehensive budget and report it to the floor. If the Budget Committees do the assembly, they could include budget process upgrades as well.

Floor Consideration Could Consider Amendments Across Committees

The CCBA's complete budget would harness all committees' expertise. Yet depth of knowledge can produce tunnel vision, and committees are not perfect microcosms of the overall body. Committee expertise can build the pieces, but the final say should belong to all members of Congress looking across the entire budget.

Setting the appropriations bills as the first twelve divisions followed by submissions from authorizing committees would set up the House to process amendments based on the first page proposed to be amended. That way, appropriators would always manage floor time on proposals affecting appropriations. Leaders from other committees would manage amendment debate addressing direct spending or revenue. Of course, debate managers bring in colleagues with expertise and debate skills, so plenty of non-appropriators would be involved throughout.

Opening the entire budget to amendments could be daunting, at least initially. Leaders have options to promote a productive, tolerable process, however. They could let budget deliberations play out on the floor for weeks with a reasonable schedule for debating and voting on amendments.

A bottom-up approach to filtering amendments may be possible as well. An amendment free-for-all could mean a process with higher costs than benefits. Leaders could, for example, only make in order amendments that meet thresholds for a minimum number of cosponsors, bipartisan support, a cost estimate, or other factors.[24]

Extra guardrails could help Congress adapt to a new system. As it becomes familiar and Congress' culture improves, better incentives would make some protections redundant. A genuinely open, dynamic, and deliberative budget process could emerge.

The Houses Would Iron Out Differences

Like any legislation, eventually, the House and the Senate would have to approve the same language. It is already a tradition for appropriations legislation to begin in the House, and the Constitution requires the House to initiate bills for raising revenue.

A complete budget with a revenue division would have to start in the House. Even so, the Senate could still do most of its work before receiving the House bill.

As already happens, the House and Senate could work out their differences through a conference committee with much of the work done before the conference, or they could send the bill back and forth with amendments.

A More Assertive Congress Sends a Budget to the White House

As with any legislation, an annual budget act would require either the president's signature or, in the case of a presidential veto, re-approval by each House of Congress with two-thirds support in each. It would considerably strengthen Congress, especially with the president's lack of a line-item veto.

Congressional leaders have little leverage with the White House when they try to strike four-corner deals involving the Senate majority leader, the Senate minority leader, the House Speaker, and the House minority leader. Even if something the White House does not like has broad support among legislators, it is easy for the White House to kill it under today's system, especially if members have not had a chance to vote on it recently.

With a real budget, however, all members of Congress could participate. An included proposal would come from a committee, or the majority of members of one or both houses would adopt it on the floor.

Committees have expertise and resources. Their leaders tend to have broad support, a robust staff operation, and media savvy. Successful floor amendments have a constellation of proponents. The White House would face organized and effective opposition if it tried to roll Congress. Each side would still win and lose some, but the balance would shift toward Congress.

Strictly speaking, Congress could advance a complete budget each year without changing the laws, but laws and practices should be consistent. Repealing budget reconciliation requires a change in statute, however. If reconciliation remains, the temptation to use it during one-party control would undermine a comprehensive budget's ability to drive better policy and a healthier political culture. That said, Congress could try a real budget as a pilot program for a year or two before codifying it.

A Comprehensive Budget Can Make Other Fiscal Fixes Matter

Congress has considered a wide range of other changes to federal budgeting. Many of these ideas are compatible with, or complementary to, a comprehensive budget. Several compatible ideas were in Senators Mike Enzi (R-WY) and Sheldon Whitehouse's (D-RI) bill, the Bipartisan Congressional Budget Reform Act of 2019, such as a bipartisan budget resolution, portfolio budgeting reports, and much more.[25]

Many other budget upgrades would be useful.[26] They and a comprehensive budget would be mutually reinforcing. Rather than going through them all, we will conclude with a way to get the budget process off to a good start and another to help it wrap up well.

Congress Can Push the President to Submit a Budget Request on Time

Presidents routinely submit late budget requests to Congress. They are supposed to arrive on or before the first Monday in February, but the White House has sent them as late as July. These delays hold up Congress from getting started on the new budget cycle.

In addition, Congress is supposed to receive the president's National Security Strategy every year on the same day as the budget request.[27] In practice, the White House has slipped to doing just one per four-year term and whenever they get to it. Security is a big part of the federal budget and for having a national government in the first place. Congress should receive security strategies and budget requests on time, at the same time, and every year.

But can Congress force a president's hand? Easily. Congress can withhold the invitation for the president to give the State of the Union address until Congress gets that year's budget request and national security strategy report. Presidents love delivering that speech before a joint session of Congress. Getting to do it would be a strong incentive to push staff to complete their legally required homework.

That is exactly what Senator Joni Ernst (R-IA) and Representative Buddy Carter (R-GA) proposed in the Send Us Budget Materials and International Tactics In Time Act—the SUBMIT IT Act—in February 2024 on the same day those reports were due.[28] A month later, President Biden gave his final State of the Union and submitted the budget request a few days after that, but Congress got no security strategy update.

As Fig. 10.4 shows, Congress has let recent presidents deliver the State of the Union address before getting the president's budget request, even when the budget was submitted on time! Flipping the order would push presidents to submit this information in time for Congress to move its budget process forward.

Furthermore, the State of the Union address, responses, and commentary would be more meaningful in a policy-rich context from those

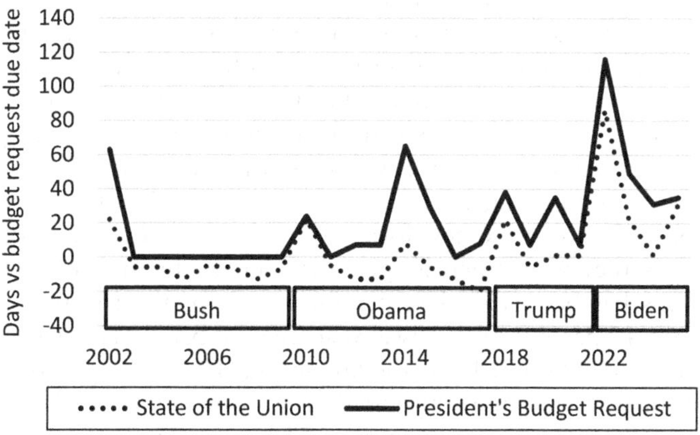

Fig. 10.4 Congress has not demanded that presidents provide key reports before the big speech (*Source* OMB, Clerk of the House)

reports. It would rebalance the federal system toward Congress by consolidating the executive branch's press opportunities while clarifying that Congress takes the lead in making policy. And, of course, a budget request that disrespects the Constitution's balanced budget requirement and related legislation would set a president up for criticism during this high-profile speech.

Congress Never Intended Government Shutdowns to Be Possible

A better start would help, but Congress has trouble completing the budget process. The threat of a government shutdown looms at least once a year, and sometimes shutdown disruptions happen. The longest shutdown so far lasted 35 days, from December 22, 2018, to January 25, 2019, when President Trump demanded more border wall funding.[29]

Shutdowns impose costs. They are not as severe as some claim, but they exist. CBO estimated that the net cost of the 35-day shutdown was a \$3 billion reduction in GDP.[30] That is not much in a then-\$21.4 trillion economy, a little less than \$10 per person, but that is little consolation for those who bore disproportionate impacts.

Much greater costs come from the poor incentives created by the possibility of shutdowns. New appropriations only need to be better than a shutdown to get the votes of most members of Congress. Leaders and senior appropriators have maximum leverage just before Christmas, when they can get colleagues to vote for massive consolidated omnibus appropriations bills without time to review and often with extra goodies for their drafters. These bills are full of bloat and other waste to avoid upsetting the many special interests with fingers in the appropriations pot and who are always ready to blanket Congress with complaints.

In the meantime, agencies are stuck in limbo for at least two and half months between the new fiscal year and the pre-Christmas omnibus. Sometimes they wait much longer: the average duration of continuing resolutions has been 152 days per fiscal year for the last two decades, more than 40 percent of the fiscal year (see the bars in Fig. 10.5).

By contrast, Rhode Island (the line in Fig. 10.5) has had comprehensive automatic continuing appropriations for generations. It almost always completes its budgets close to on time. The exception that proves the rule was when they waited to wrap up the FY 2021 budget to see if Congress would throw more pandemic relief their way. Congress did. Days later, Rhode Island's budget was law.

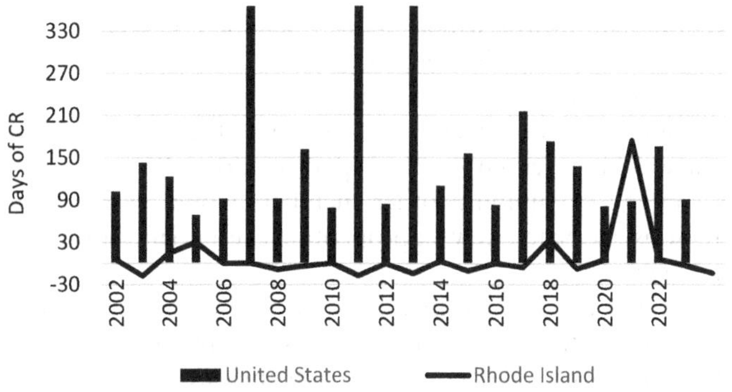

Fig. 10.5 Federal appropriations conclude far later than those in a state without shutdowns (*Source* Congressional Research Service)

If, however, even without new legislation, spending would automatically continue at the same nominal level, the new legislation would have to be better than the status quo, as Fig. 10.6 illustrates. Making sure that many more members would have a chance to shape the legislation, like with a comprehensive budget, would help it succeed and would be an essential culture change toward inclusive deliberation.

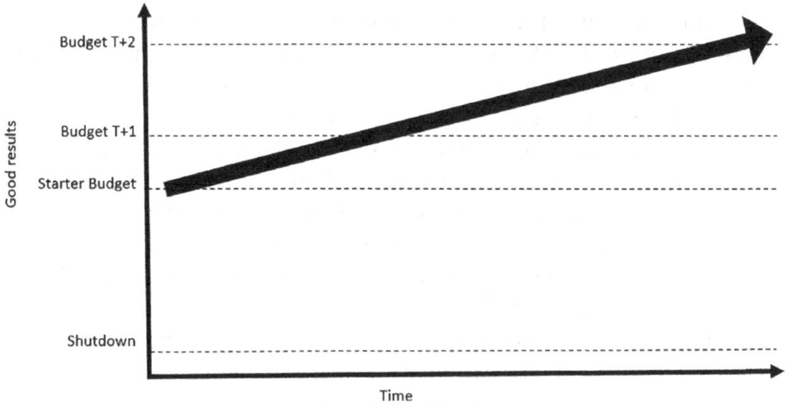

Fig. 10.6 Automatic continuing appropriations promote continual improvement

Preventing shutdowns would gently encourage Congress to clean up the budget. We know this from experience: States that have automatic continuing appropriations spend slightly less per capita.[31]

Some appropriators assert that without the risk of shutdowns, Congress would never enact new appropriations. That is wrong. Yes, today's strategy of jamming other members would end. Congress has many reasons to enact new appropriations, especially for defense and foreign affairs.

On the other hand, some members try to leverage the threat of shutdowns for policy concessions they never get. The 2013 shutdown over defunding Obamacare did not defund Obamacare. The 2015 fight was about defunding Planned Parenthood, which still gets funding. Even President Trump could not leverage the 2018–2019 shutdown to get Congress to fund the border wall. It simply does not work, but too many still fantasize that it could.[32]

The kicker is that Congress never meant for federal government shutdowns to be possible. From the 1st Congress to nearly the end of President Jimmy Carter's administration, Congress and presidents assumed that authorized and funded activities would carry on as before until Congress passed and the president signed new spending legislation. In 1980, however, the Carter administration's attorney general reinterpreted an 1884 law.[33] The first shutdown happened the next year.

Congress should return to the old approach with a new statute like the bipartisan, bicameral Prevent Government Shutdowns Act by Senators James Lankford (R-OK) and Maggie Hassan (D-NH) and by Representatives Jodey Arrington (R-TX) and Jimmy Panetta (D-CA).[34] The bill would force Congress to stay in DC and focus on enacting new appropriations bills while avoiding shutdown disruption in the meantime.

Preventing shutdowns could help implement a BBA too. Automatic continuing appropriations inherently reduce brinkmanship and help the appropriations process conclude more on time and more smoothly by removing dreams of undue leverage on all sides and focusing members on the art of the possible.[35] Since the most politically viable version of automatic continuing appropriations is flat funding in the interim, they could help nudge Congress to manage direct spending and revenue policies more actively to meet budget targets and to increase spending in the more-politically-potent-per-dollar appropriations accounts. These tendencies would be even stronger with a comprehensive budget that includes the priorities of many more members and committees.

The bifurcated congressional budget process promotes partisanship and polarization while failing to help fix fiscal imbalances and other well-known problems.

A real budget that includes all spending and all revenue while drawing on committee expertise and engaging all members would have many benefits. It would respect existing committee prerogatives and strengthen Congress as an institution. It would give Congress far more means and motive to meet BBA-based budget targets and otherwise manage federal fiscal priorities.

Getting the president to send Congress his budget request on time by threatening to withhold an invitation to deliver the State of the Union address would give Congress the information it needs to start its process on time. Ending the threat of shutdowns would help it conclude on schedule and with better results.

Notes

1. Kurt Couchman, "Unified Budgets Can Help Revive Congress," Americans for Prosperity, https://indd.adobe.com/view/ffa5b36d-118b-424d-a4a4-d16f1b849ec8, December 2021. Kurt Couchman, "What is the Comprehensive Congressional Budget Act," Americans for Prosperity, https://americansforprosperity.org/blog/what-is-the-comprehensive-congressional-budget-act/, September 5, 2024. Kurt Couchman, "Congress Can Rehabilitate the Federal Budget with a Comprehensive Budget," Submission to and 3rd place winner in the America First Policy Institute budget process reform contest, https://americansforprosperity.org/wp-content/uploads/2024/09/AFP-Couchman-Comprehensive-Congressional-Budget-AFPI.pdf, August 2024.
2. House Committee on Appropriations, "Committee Approves FY24 Subcommittee Allocations," https://appropriations.house.gov/news/press-releases/committee-approves-fy24-subcommittee-allocations, June 15, 2023.
3. Kurt Couchman, "Stand-Alone Reconciliation Must End," *The Hill*, https://thehill.com/blogs/congress-blog/economy-budget/585572-stand-alone-reconciliation-must-end/, December 13, 2021.
4. Thomas Jefferson, Letter to Secretary of the Treasury Albert Gallatin, April 1, 1802, in *The Collected Works of Thomas*

Jefferson in Twelve Volumes, collected and edited by Paul Leicester Ford, Federal Edition, https://memory.loc.gov/service/mss/mtj/mtj1/026/026_0004_0005.pdf.
5. CBO, "Spending Projections, by Budget Account," https://www.cbo.gov/data/budget-economic-data#9, accessed February 8, 2025.
6. Senate Budget Committee, "New Report Shows Need to Reform Federal Housing Programs," https://www.budget.senate.gov/chairman/newsroom/press/new-report-shows-need_to-reform-federal-housing-programs, October 22, 2020.
7. Sen. Mike Enzi, S. 2765, Bipartisan Congressional Budget Reform Act of 2019, https://www.congress.gov/bill/116th-congress/senate-bill/2765, introduced October 31, 2019.
8. CBO, "Spending Projections, by Budget Account," https://www.cbo.gov/system/files/2025-01/51142-2025-01-Spending-Projections.xlsx, January 2025. JCT, "Estimates of Federal Tax Expenditures for Fiscal Years 2024–2028," JCX-48–24, https://www.jct.gov/publications/2024/jcx-48-24/, December 11, 2024, pp. 31–32.
9. House Committee on Rules Subcommittee on Legislative and Budget Process, Hearing on "Using Budget Principles to Prepare for Future Pandemics and Other Disasters," January 19, 2022.
10. CBO, "Expired and Expiring Authorizations of Appropriations for Fiscal Year 2024—Information for Legislation Enacted Through September 30, 2023," https://www.cbo.gov/publication/59684, January 2024.
11. Extraneous matter in reconciliation legislation, Section 313 of the Congressional Budget Act of 1974 (2 U.S.C. 644), https://uscode.house.gov/view.xhtml?req=(title:2%20section:644%20edition:prelim)%20OR%20(granuleid:USC-prelim-title2-section644)&f=treesort&edition=prelim&num=0&jumpTo=true, accessed December 3, 2022.
12. James Wallner, "Senate Parliamentarian Doesn't Make the Rules" https://www.legislativeprocedure.com/blog/2022/8/6/senate-parliamentarian-doesnt-make-the-rules, August 6, 2022.
13. Paul Winfree, *A History (And Future) of the Budget Process in the United States: Budget by Fire*, Palgrave MacMillan: 2019.
14. Michele Cagan, *Budgeting 101: A Crash Course in Budgeting*," Adams Media, 2018, p. 27.

15. Kurt Couchman, “Restoring representation: 10 ways to help congressional committees get results,” Americans for Prosperity https://americansforprosperity.org/blog/restoring-representation-10-ways-to-help-congressional-committees-get-results/, December 6, 2023.
16. Christopher J. Conover, “Congress Should Account for the Excess Burden of Taxation,” Policy Analysis 669, Cato Institute, https://www.cato.org/policy-analysis/congress-should-account-excess-burden-taxation, October 13, 2010.
17. Dawn Erlandson, “The BTU Tax Experience: What Happened and Why it Happened,” Heartland Institute, https://www.heartland.org/publications-resources/publications/the-btu-tax-experience-what-happened-and-why-it-happened, September 1, 1994.
18. Rep. Jodey Arrington, H.R. 1, the One Big Beautiful Bill Act, Pub.L. 119–21, https://www.congress.gov/bill/119th-congress/house-bill/1, enacted July 4, 2025.
19. Rep. Blake Moore, H.R. 6953, “Comprehensive Congressional Budget Act of 2024,” https://www.congress.gov/bill/118th-congress/house-bill/6953, introduced January 11, 2024. Rep. Blake Moore, “U.S. Representatives Moore and Gluesenkamp Perez Introduce Legislation to Reform the Congressional Budget Process,” https://blakemoore.house.gov/media/press-releases/us-representatives-moore-and-gluesenkamp-perez-introduce-legislation-reform, January 11, 2024. Americans for Prosperity, “AFP Praises Comprehensive Budget Bill, Calls on Congress to Create a Real Budget,” https://americansforprosperity.org/press-release/afp-praises-comprehensive-budget-bill-calls-on-congress-to-create-a-real-budget/, January 11, 2024.
20. Kurt Couchman, “State-inspired line-item budgets can help Congress see the big picture,” Americans for Prosperity, https://americansforprosperity.org/state-line-item-budgets-congress/, March 29, 2023.
21. CBO, “Spending Projections, by Budget Account,” https://www.cbo.gov/data/budget-economic-data#9, accessed August 12, 2023.
22. Congressional Budget Office, “Budget Options,” https://www.cbo.gov/budget-options; Government Accountability Office, “2022 Annual Report: Additional Opportunities to Reduce Fragmentation, Overlap, and Duplication and Achieve Billions of

Dollars in Financial Benefits," https://www.gao.gov/products/gao-22-105301, May 11, 2022; Social Security Administration, "Office of the Chief Actuary's Estimates of Proposals to Change the Social Security Program or the SSI Program," https://www.ssa.gov/oact/solvency/index.html.
23. Heritage Foundation, "Budget Blueprint for Fiscal Year 2023," https://www.heritage.org/budget/index.html; Urban Institute; Paul D. Ryan and Angela Rachidi, eds, *American Renewal: A Conservative Plan to Strengthen the Social Contract and Save the Country's Finances*, American Enterprise Institute, https://www.americanrenewalbook.com/, November 2022; Committee for a Responsible Federal Budget, "The CRFB Fiscal Blueprint for Reducing Debt and Inflation," https://www.crfb.org/papers/crfb-fiscal-blueprint-reducing-debt-and-inflation, October 26, 2022.
24. Kurt Couchman, "Bottom-up filters for floor amendments in the House of Representatives," Americans for Prosperity, https://americansforprosperity.org/blog/bottom-up-filters-amendments-house-representatives/, May 10, 2024.
25. Sen. Mike Enzi, S. 2765, the Bipartisan Congressional Budget Reform Act of 2019, https://www.congress.gov/bill/116th-congress/senate-bill/2765, introduced October 31, 2019.
26. Kurt Couchman, "Six ways to overhaul the federal budget," Americans for Prosperity, https://americansforprosperity.org/six-ways-to-overhaul-the-federal-budget/, July 10, 2023. Kurt Couchman, "Six more ways to fix the federal budget," https://americansforprosperity.org/six-more-ways-to-fix-the-federal-budget/, July 17, 2023.
27. "Annual national security strategy report," Section 343 of the National Security Act of 1947, as added by Sec. 603 of Public Law 99–433, the Goldwater-Nichols Department of Defense Reorganization Act of 1986, [Section 3043, Title 50, United States Code], accessed August 20, 2023.
28. Sen. Joni Ernst, "Ernst Requires Actions, Not Just Words, from President," https://www.ernst.senate.gov/news/press-releases/ernst-requires-actions-not-just-words-from-president, February 5, 2024. Kurt Couchman, "What is the SUBMIT IT Act?" Americans for Prosperity, https://americansforprosperity.org/blog/what-is-the-submit-it-act/, March 4, 2024.

29. CRS, "Past Government Shutdowns: Key Resources," R41759, https://crsreports.congress.gov/product/pdf/R/R41759, updated June 14, 2021.
30. CBO, "The Effects of the Partial Shutdown Ending in January 2019," https://www.cbo.gov/system/files/2019-01/54937-PartialShutdownEffects.pdf, January 2019.
31. David Primo, *Rules and Restraint: Government Spending and the Design of Institutions*, Chicago UP, 2007, pp. 101–103.
32. Kurt Couchman, "What leverage? Shutdown fights don't get results," The Hill, https://thehill.com/opinion/congress-blog/4226647-what-leverage-shutdown-fights-dont-get-results/, September 27, 2023.
33. Kurt Couchman, "Government shutdowns have always been a mistake," RealClearPolicy.com, https://www.realclearpolicy.com/articles/2022/01/26/government_shutdowns_have_always_been_a_mistake_813723.html, January 26, 2022.
34. Sen. James Lankford, "Lankford, Hassan, Colleagues Want to Stop Government Shutdowns, Force Congress to Do Its Job," https://www.lankford.senate.gov/news/press-releases/lankford-hassan-colleagues-want-to-stop-government-shutdowns-force-congress-to-do-its-job, January 30, 2023, and "Lankford Continues to Push for Congress to be Held Accountable for Government Shutdowns," https://www.lankford.senate.gov/news/press-releases/lankford-continues-to-push-for-congress-to-be-held-accountable-for-government-shutdowns, January 31, 2023. Rep. Jimmy Panetta, "Rep. Panetta Introduces Bipartisan Legislation to Stop Government Shutdowns, Ensure Congress Does Its Job," https://panetta.house.gov/media/press-releases/rep-panetta-introduces-bipartisan-legislation-stop-government-shutdowns-ensure, September 26, 2023.
35. Committee for a Responsible Federal Budget, "Automatic CRs Can Improve the Appropriations Process," https://www.crfb.org/papers/better-budget-process-initiative-automatic-crs-can-improve-appropriations-process, September 17, 2020.

CHAPTER 11

Taking Federal Budgeting to the Next Level

This book lays out a bold, transformative, and entirely reasonable vision to upgrade federal budgeting. A principles-based BBA. Neutral, comprehensive, and practical statutory budget targets. Ending the risks of shutdowns and a debt ceiling default. Politically sustainable automatic enforcement. A comprehensive budget, an on-time president's budget request, and an end to an unintended 45-year experiment with shutdowns. And so on.

Legislation based on good ideas is necessary but not enough. Effective fiscal rules—indeed, any governance rules—build on and promote consensus. Broad appeal helps successive Congresses adopt and sustain them.

One Congress cannot absolutely bind a future Congress by statute. A later Congress can always revise or replace existing laws. Even so, the rules tend to stick around.

Every change to law shifts the landscape. Some alter it a lot. Laws with long-term staying power provide more benefits than disadvantages throughout shifting governance coalitions.

Consensus does not happen quickly or easily. It takes shape from people seeking better ways to move forward, asking questions, challenging assumptions, exploring alternatives, considering variations, and ultimately making choices. It is a lot of work, and it takes time.

It takes patience and hope to develop solutions between windows of opportunity. The first BBA was introduced in 1936. The Business Cycle

K. Couchman, *Fiscal Democracy in America*,
https://doi.org/10.1007/978-3-031-91938-1_11

BBA came out in 2011. The Principles-based BBA emerged in 2015. Finally, as we have discussed, Congress has a BBA appropriate for the Constitution and a clearer sense of implementing legislation and related supports.

After all, this requires members of Congress to change the systems in which they operate and with which they are familiar. A polarized, partisan environment increases the challenges as well as the opportunities.

When the window opens, those developing solutions must be ready to turn to advocacy and promotion within a multi-faceted strategy. It involves federal and state officials, Republicans and Democrats, policy experts and great communicators, challengers and bargainers, insiders and outsiders, patience, the ability to pivot quickly, and good timing. Success comes from promoting the upgrades themselves and expanding Congress's ability to adopt and use them.

Reformers cannot separate policy from politics and the congressional process. Politics is largely about enough members of Congress getting a win to advance legislation. It requires good relationships and trust. It means elevating topics on the congressional agenda to be worthy uses of relatively scarce floor time and member attention. Politics touches on what each party's base wants across many districts, factional differences between members of the same party, and ever-present fundraising considerations.

The process is more than just legislative thresholds: it includes revisions, markups, hearings, briefings, and the interplay between committees of partial or adjacent jurisdiction and more.

Expanding Congressional Capacity to Advance Better Policy

Cato Institute senior fellow Peter Van Doren used to tell congressional staff at Capitol Hill briefings that "good policy is a public good and is therefore underprovided by the political marketplace." Those backing public interest policies must shift the cost–benefit calculation for policymakers toward socially optimal levels for public goods. It is a kind of subsidy, to be crass.

Organizations across the political spectrum try to do this, or at least they pretend to try. Ultimately, the test of what Congress collectively thinks is worth doing is determined by the votes of coalitions of members of Congress.

Contrary to the image some members of Congress like to project, they and their staff are primarily generalists. Members must be able to talk about a vast range of subjects at least semi-coherently, often using notes prepared by staff. Many have varying degrees of expertise due to prior employment, personal interest, committee assignments, or other reasons. Many are former state or local government officials or legislators, and those experiences translate imperfectly to Congress.

Staff can specialize more in the Senate than the House, and House staff usually have exceptionally broad portfolios. For example, one of three or four policy staffers in a House office might cover a committee assignment as well as budget, tax, Social Security, health care, judiciary, commerce, defense, immigration, financial services, veterans, and transportation. And then one might pinch-hit on other issues when someone is swamped or out of the office.

Legislative directors often cover a similar broad scope, yet they also manage staff, review vote recommendations, coordinate with the communications team, and help build out the member's agenda.

It is intense. Member office staff meet with and absorb massive amounts of information from lobbyists, think tanks, congressional support agencies, executive branch agencies, committees, leadership, other member offices, constituents, state and local officials, and others. Most people have an agenda, and some spin the truth hard. Good congressional staff specialize in knowing where to get reliable information from the perspective of their member.

Learning whom to trust, to what degree, and on which issues takes time and experience. When many staff get good at it, they may be ready to trade a high-pressure, chaotic work environment with long hours and relatively low pay for better compensation and work-life balance than Capitol Hill can offer.

Congress has many bright and eager yet under-experienced staff who start without deep networks. It needs more seasoned and capable staff who have strong relationships. Staffers disproportionately come from upper-middle-income suburban households. Congress is far from a representative sample of the country.

In recent years, however, many public interest groups have coalesced around improving life for congressional staff. Many such groups lean left, but some centrist and right-of-center experts and organizations are also involved.

They prevailed on House Democrats to create the House Select Committee on the Modernization of Congress in the rules package at the beginning of 2019. The ModCom had an equal number of Democrats and Republicans, focused on developing recommendations with near-consensus, and experimented with small things like alternating member seating at hearings by party instead of the usual way of having all Republicans on one side and all Democrats on the other.

Over four years, the ModCom met many times and produced voluminous recommendations.[1] Their proposals addressed staff and member compensation, improving recruitment and onboarding, ongoing human resources and technology support, de-conflicting congressional scheduling, reducing polarization, and improving information and other staff resources. Most importantly, they valued strengthening relationships and trust between members across ideological, regional, and other potential divides.

Through that work and elsewhere, tangible progress is happening. House office budgets, known as the Member's Representational Allowance or MRA, have increased, potentially reducing Capitol Hill's pay disadvantages. Each staffer's compensation is still set within the office, so an increase in the office budget does not necessarily translate into higher pay. The ModCom, now reorganized as a subcommittee of the Committee on House Administration, has gotten numerous recommendations implemented and continues to push for more.

It is true that a federal government exercising only its proper constitutional powers would require less capacity. But whether the goal is to manage an expansive scope better or to move closer to a government of limited, enumerated powers, Congress needs better information and more robust capacity for the foreseeable future.

Better Incentives Can Convert Capacity into Results

Members of Congress respond to incentives. We all do. Bigger office budgets and a better working environment will not necessarily lead to better policy outcomes. If members' ability to shape policy remains limited, most will focus more on constituent services, communications, and planning their post-congressional careers.

These outcomes are what we have seen so far. American Enterprise Institute scholar Yuval Levin has lamented that members use the institution of Congress as a platform for personal branding instead of cultivating the laws that set federal policy.[2]

Rep. Amash was serious about policy and leveraged his vote explanations on his Facebook page to push colleagues to come his way. Rep. Brat quickly recognized that it would take a while before he could make a direct difference in policy, and he did not expect to be in Congress that long (he was right). He decided that messaging through opinion articles and especially television appearances was his best way to have an impact.

The proliferation of congressional communicators over the last decade reflects the pull of social media and other distributed information sources. It also shows how concentrating policymaking with congressional leaders has pushed other members into other activities. Many members and staff are dissatisfied with the situation, and the desire for change is in the air.

In January 2023, at the start of the 118th Congress, the House required 15 rounds of votes until a majority of the body elected Rep. Kevin McCarthy (R-CA) Speaker of the House. A narrow 222–213 Republican majority from the 2022 elections gave outsized leverage—"a big stick," as one member described it—to House Freedom Caucus members who wanted changes (as did many others) and were willing to fight for them (most were not).

Though messy, the results seemed promising. House GOP leaders improved their practice of the politics of inclusion. Speaker McCarthy coordinated with the House Republican Steering Committee, the organization of the House Republican Conference tasked with matching members and committee assignments, to try to get the Republican membership of each committee to reflect the conference overall.

One reporter wrote, "McCarthy said committees need to be a microcosm of the conference, with more far right Freedom Caucus members on all committees, a signal that promising committee posts have been a key part of the negotiations. Sources say McCarthy is describing this as equal representation."[3] True microcosms go beyond ideology and factor in geography, experience, temperament, and more.

Committees that reflect the conference let members sort out most of their ideological, regional, or other differences and find agreement more easily. In committees, members have relative subject matter expertise from prior knowledge and through hearings, meetings, markups, and other discussions. Committees and subcommittees foster group discussions that are small enough to work through issues. With members spread around committees, each microcosm committee can provide trusted allies for almost all other members participating in each conversation. This practice not only gives larger groups of members a way to bring information to those committees but also assures that decisions reflect their preferences when possible.

This proportional representation across multiple dimensions is crucial for budget management. It is probably necessary for reaching statutory budget targets backed up by a principles-based BBA, a comprehensive budget, effective automatic enforcement, and all the rest. A Congress in which all organs of a conference or caucus were representative samples can support the Budget Committees setting acceptable top-line levels for each committee based on the budget targets, for each committee to consider tradeoffs and make changes, and for Congress to approve a comprehensive budget that meets its goals each year.

Committees as microcosms can yield greater consensus on policy and healthier politics within the conference or caucus. This inclusivity was not the case just a few years ago, as Fig. 11.1 shows, which I built in 2016. It shows the distribution of House Republicans by their score on the Heritage Action for America scorecard, with lower-scoring moderates on the left and higher-scoring conservatives on the right.

The light and dark bars show the middle quartiles of the distribution of each House Republican entity, so the median (central member) is where they meet. The left- and right-hand whiskers show the lowest and highest quartiles. Each star shows the score of the leader of each group: the Speaker of the House, committee chairs, and the chair of the membership organizations. The distribution of the entire conference is at the top, along with the moderate Republican Main Street Partnership, the mainstream Republican Study Committee, and the conservative House Freedom Caucus. The number in parentheses is the number of members in each group at the time.

If everything had been close to a representative sample, the committee bars, whiskers, and stars would look like the House GOP Conference on the top line. They did not.

Several especially influential committees like Appropriations, Energy and Commerce, and Transportation and Infrastructure tilted toward moderates, and each had an exceptionally moderate chair. The most conservative members were overrepresented on committees with fewer legislative opportunities like Oversight, Natural Resources, and Judiciary.

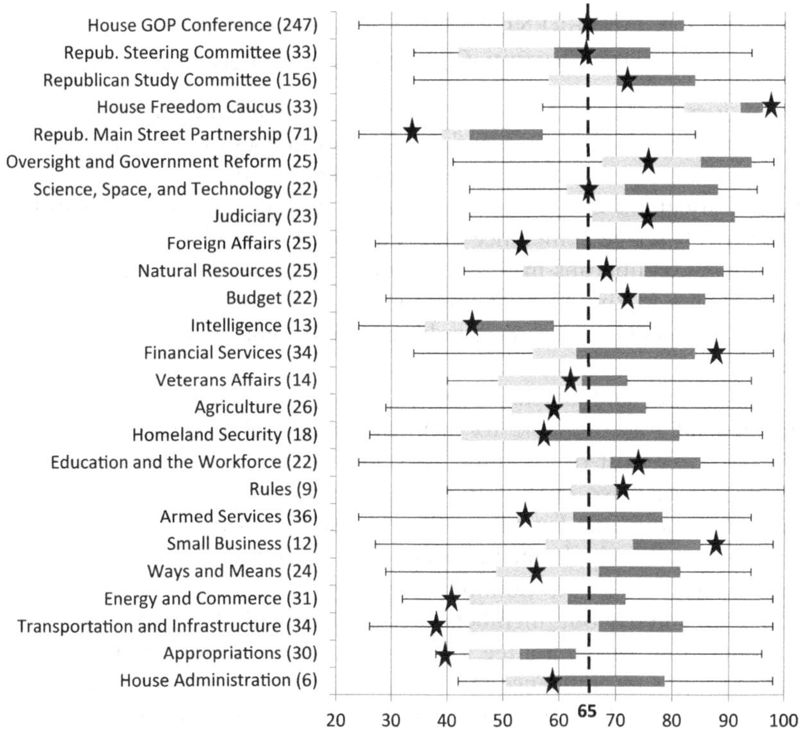

Fig. 11.1 House Republican committees were far from microcosms in 2015–2016 (*Source* Heritage Action, Clerk of the House)

These skews were not surprising, and many knew it intuitively. But this visual was powerful.

It ultimately circulated widely, to the displeasure of House Republican leaders. After a few years, it made an impact: in 2023, the Speaker of the House endorsed the concept of committees as microcosms of the conference. It would not be enough to keep a handful of Republicans and all Democrats from removing him from the speakership later in the year, but maybe, just maybe, the culture was shifting.

Conference and Caucus Rules are the Power Centers of Congress

What does any of that have to do with advancing a budget reform agenda? Committees are the once and future workhorses of Congress. Inclusive committees can do more, do it better, and do it faster. They shift more bargaining into relatively abundant committee discussions instead of relatively scarce conference meetings and floor deliberations.

House Republicans may have improved representation for committee assignments in the 118th Congress. Yet Congress would work best if House Democrats, Senate Republicans, and Senate Democrats did the same.

Conference and caucus norms matter because members of Congress are generally accountable to their conference (Republicans) or caucus (Democrats) most of the time. The citizens they represent get to weigh in twice every two years—the primary and general elections including possible runoffs in a few places—for House members and every six years for senators. Rarely do members face censure, removal from committees, expulsion, or an Ethics Committee inquiry.

Day in and day out, members affect each other in large and small ways: consideration for committee assignments, leadership positions, different paths to greater influence, the ability to get hearings, markups, and floor votes on their priorities, approval for overseas travel on co-dels (congressional delegation trips to meet with foreign officials), campaign fundraising help, and much more. In some ways, the groups for the more ideological wings, like the House Freedom Caucus and the House Republican Main Street Partnership, exist to provide strength in numbers to counter the gravitational forces from other parts of the conference.

Those dynamics will always exist, especially in a two-party system. The tensions between factions are, however, exacerbated by the rules that govern the House and Senate Republican conferences and the House and the Senate Democratic caucuses.[4] Each set of rules gives each party's leaders responsibility for a wide variety of items that could be—and perhaps should be—handled by representative samples of conference members.

We cannot dive deeply into that here, but it would be a good subject for another time. With responsibility comes power, and the current rules magnify both by concentrating them on leaders. This reinforces partisan tribalism and reduces spaces for members to form ad hoc policy coalitions.

Rebalancing responsibilities can produce healthier relationships between leaders, committees, and members. Moving everyone toward comparative advantages would give members of both parties more freedom to consider and promote different ways to balance the budget and otherwise manage fiscal priorities.

Differently distributed power can produce better results for at least two reasons. First, delegating responsibility to leaders for holding members accountable makes deciding easy. If the accountability required action by the entire conference or a decent-sized sample of it, the time and effort costs would go up, leading to less rigid enforcement of party discipline, at least by elected representatives. Members would have more freedom and responsibility for making good decisions.

Second, strength in numbers matters. Few members are such outliers that others would not stand up for them. Often, a handful or even dozens of members vote together. It is more challenging for the conference to impose sanctions on a group of similarly minded members than for a few leaders to make examples of a few. This reserves conference or caucus punishment for those who merit it, such as for a gross breach of ethics or reprehensible conduct.

It may sound like all downside from the perspective of the party mainstream and the leaders that come from it. But a party that lets members represent themselves and their districts or states more faithfully is a party that can appeal to more people. It is a party that can win more seats and secure agenda-setting power more often. It is also a party whose members solve more of their own problems and do not put as many unrealistic expectations on leaders, which can undermine leaders no matter how fair and capable they are.

The party that moves first to embrace a genuinely bottom-up model can expect persistent electoral and policy advantages. More experiments, large and small, can help members discover what works and keep building on it.

Advance Upgrades by Shifting Congress' Cost–Benefit Calculus

Members and staff constantly think about using their resources better. That includes getting reelected, increasing influence, strengthening their profiles, advancing policy priorities, and much more. It is an optimization game.[5]

Concentrated power with leaders reduces members' ability to create value from substantive policymaking. More members are less focused on policy than they used to be. Admittedly, our view of the past may be skewed by remembering the substance from Congresses past and forgetting the fluff, like how old bad music fades away while the great songs live on.

Revising the conference or caucus rules can increase the overall rewards of policy work, but it is not the only way. Outside organizations can, for example, make policy development and promotion easier—reducing costs—while boosting a member's profile or providing campaign resources, depending on the organization—increasing benefits.

Policy development and promotion have many stages. The first is identifying a problem. Members can rail about a problem for a while without saying what they want to do about it. The second stage is looking into possible fixes, ideally well-targeted, effective, and politically viable solutions. Third, someone puts the solution into legislation and manages its refinement as questions and concerns arise. Fourth is developing a coalition of support. Fifth is activating the coalition to drive members to support the solution through the process when the opportunity arises. Finally, once a solution becomes law, supporters must oversee execution and look for ways to strengthen it.

Applying that to a BBA, the peacetime run-up in debt during the Great Depression, and especially since the Great Society, has worried members of Congress. Members have proposed various BBAs and pursued deficit reduction deals. The conventional BBA seemed like a good solution, but its flaws are now clear. The Principles-based BBA stands on the shoulders of the Business Cycle BBA, and it improved from its 2015 origin to Senator Braun and Representative Moran's updates in 2023.

The BBA coalition of support includes longstanding proponents like the National Taxpayers Union, the American Legislative Exchange Council, and Americans for Prosperity, as well as the many members of Congress and state legislators who have promoted various approaches. But that is still not enough.

Reformers should be willing to engage in politics to accomplish public interest objectives. One oft-neglected strategy involves building Bootlegger and Baptist coalitions. The term comes from alcohol Prohibition and softer forms like blue laws that ban alcohol sales on Sundays. The Baptists oppose alcohol sales or consumption from a moral or other purportedly public interest perspective. The Bootleggers make money from restrictions on the legal market. They may not formally coordinate, or at least not admit to doing so, and in the eponymous case, probably do not like each other much, but both benefit from restrictions on alcohol: moral satisfaction for one and cold, hard cash for the other.

Most BBA backers and budget reformers do it out of the goodness of their hearts. They want to keep the American Dream alive for their kids and grandchildren, reduce wasteful spending, avoid a debt crisis, grow the economy, and so on. We are the Baptists. It helps that we can make a living doing it.

Who are the bootleggers? Who would profit from a fiscally responsible federal government? This does not mean the American public in general or future generations, although they obviously would. It means, in a Bootlegger-and-Baptist-style coalition, which narrow interests are already well-organized, politically influential, and would be better off with responsible budgeting instead of escalating debt burdens?

Several options come to mind. The financial sector makes money helping people hedge their bets. It could see enormous losses or bailouts with onerous strings during a financial crisis, just as the 2008 housing collapse created the conditions for the repressive Dodd-Frank Act. The financial sector could face massive turmoil and substantial tax increases during a debt crisis, so the sector might support a smart BBA and related reforms in self-defense.

Other potential winners include those who would otherwise get squeezed. As federal interest costs rise, recipients of federal funding could see declining support to preserve room in the budget for other things. The defense industry is a good example. It sells almost exclusively to governments, especially the U.S. government, and it is well-organized to share its perspectives with policymakers. The list could go on.

That does not mean the financial and defense industries are pure and good. That is precisely NOT the point. One might oppose a range of policies that put money in their pockets. (I do.) The point is this: those sectors, not necessarily the individuals within them, care about the almighty dollar at least as much as the public good. Those who want sound budgeting, however, can tolerate some nose-holding on the process to reach better outcomes.

This pragmatic approach to policymaking is challenging for those who have self-selected into public interest advocacy. It feels dirty. It is not principles-based. So what? Do we want to fix things or not?

Sound policy changes do not happen accidentally. Someone needs to plan, try, evaluate, adjust, try again, give technical assistance to legislative drafters, organize meetings, brief outside organizations and congressional audiences, testify in committee hearings, and much more.

Each step applies to the statutory upgrades as well: not only the Business Cycle BBA and the Principles-based BBA, but also the Responsible Budget Targets Act, the Comprehensive Congressional Budget Act, the Prevent Government Shutdowns Act, the SUBMIT IT Act, and more. Many have contributed to technical assistance, supporting introductions, growing cosponsors, building coalitions, and other activities.

In addition to herding cats, non-governmental organizations can increase the benefits to members of Congress for doing public interest work. Members get far more criticism than praise. Simply praising them on social media and writing opinion articles to support members' efforts goes a long way to encouraging them to keep at it. Getting others to promote them and their work is the next level up. Insofar as is possible for an organization—depending on tax status, mission, and other factors—promoting them in political campaigns, especially when contested, or for leadership or committee positions in Congress is even more appreciated.

Legislation does not just pass because it is a good idea with broad support. Congress is busy. Floor time is valuable. Policy majorities come and go. Pressing issues rise on the priority list and displace lower-tier matters, even when they cannot get signed into law. Why else would the House pass so many bills that die in the Senate or trigger a veto threat from the White House?

Good legislation often must be built and ready to go with congressional and external support for years before the moment of opportunity comes. It takes time to familiarize members of Congress, staff, advocates, committees, leadership, and the public with a concept or a specific legislative proposal. Those with technical expertise—primarily committee staff, legislative counsel, executive branch civil servants, industry, and their trusted partners—often go through multiple rounds of fixing problems and refining language.

Between opportunities, BBA proponents have kept the issue warm for decades leading up to 1982, 1995, and 2011, and now in anticipation of the next window. From time to time, the window opens, and Congress will draw from a menu of options sitting on the proverbial shelf. That takes a lot of preparation and communication, not to mention foresight or at least hope.

When the moment comes along, proponents must be quick to organize and seize it. Policy matters, as do processes for considering legislation and especially current politics.

For example, the Time to Rescue United States Trusts Act—TRUST Act—by Senators Mitt Romney (R-UT), Joe Manchin (D-WV), and Angus King (I-ME) and Representatives Mike Gallagher (R-WI) and Ed Case (D-HI) to set up separate bipartisan, bicameral commissions to extend solvency and improve Social Security, Medicare, and highway programs should have been perfect for the 2023 debt limit deal. Trust funds for those three programs will be exhausted within the next decade, and their long-term funding gaps drive the long-term debt accumulation. Fiscal commission legislation like the TRUST Act are not substitutes for fixing federal budgeting—they are complements that foster trust, give bipartisan solutions a chance, and, if they succeed, give Congress more time and breathing room to repair the system.

Romney and colleagues introduced the TRUST Act in 2019 with bipartisan congressional and external support. The Senate had voted 71–29 on a related amendment in February 2021. Senate Republicans included it in a pandemic relief counterproposal in mid-2020 without denting Democratic support.[6]

Despite their good intentions, a handful of Republican senators screwed it up. Perdue lost a runoff election in early January 2021 after failing to get majority support in the November 2020 election. Democrats pounced. Then-chair of the National Republican Senatorial (campaign) Committee Rick Scott (R-FL) released a policy agenda in 2022 calling for sunsetting all legislation every five years. Republican Leader Mitch McConnell (R-KY) tried to downplay it as not reflecting the conference, but Democrats attacked relentlessly. Sen. Ron Johnson (R-WI) said in a 2022 interview that everything should sunset each year unless Congress reaffirms it. What he meant was unclear, but Democrats claimed he was talking about Social Security and Medicare.[7]

In his 2023 State of the Union address, President Biden goaded congressional Republicans into rejecting any cuts to those programs. The taunts and reactions to them, combined with the missteps above and others created a narrative among both parties that the 2023 debt limit deal would not go there. Technically, a bipartisan commission for each would only consider changes, but even that was a bridge too far.

The TRUST Act remains an innovative and politically viable way to shore up those programs before their trust funds run. It faced strong headwinds leading up to the 2023 debt limit deal, however. They will fade, and the TRUST Act will be on the shelf for the next opportunity, possibly a debt limit deal. As the chief proponents, Romney, Manchin, and Gallagher's retirements from Congress leave a vacuum.

Finally, members need to know they have allies. For years, members of Congress and their staff would vent that they were the only ones who still cared about these issues. Advocates can relay that message, but second-hand news is not good enough. Members need to hear it from each other.

Sometimes, Congress organizes itself in response to public pressure. Yet external organizing is usually necessary on issues that are out of the spotlight. The simplest request is for members to discuss something. When members hear colleagues, donors, supporters, and regular people talk, it signals that the topic is worth considering. The more chatter an issue gets, the more members invest in it.

Members are not limited to social media or traditional media, of course. They can send each other messages called Dear Colleague letters. They can ask questions or otherwise highlight issues during committee hearings. They can bring items up at other meetings. They can offer legislation, even non-binding resolutions, send group letters to leaders or the executive branch, participate in panels and briefings, and so much more.

Creating a regular meeting of members or senior staff to discuss options is especially valuable. It also requires more work to organize and sustain. It takes serious buy-in from at least one charismatic leader, an always-compelling agenda that draws in members or staff over the dozen other things they could be doing, and a sense of purpose, the feeling that being involved will be worth it. Anticipated benefits include relationships, self-education, advancing policy priorities, building influence, getting reelected, and other factors. The cost is giving up whatever else they could be doing.

Eventually, these issues become salient enough for the relevant committees to hold hearings and markups. In the 118th Congress (2023–2024), the House Judiciary Subcommittee on the Constitution and Limited Government held a hearing on "Examining Proposed Constitutional Amendments" where BBAs were prominent.[8]

Also in the 118th Congress, House Budget Committee chair Jodey Arrington had an active budget process reform agenda, soliciting external advice, holding hearings, and approving legislation, often with bipartisan votes.[9] The committee finished the year with a hearing on "Sounding the Alarm: Pathways and Possible Solutions to the U.S. Fiscal Crisis" that included former Comptroller General and chair of the Federal Fiscal Sustainability Foundation Dave Walker promoting a convention of states for fiscal responsibility amendments, Cato Institute scholar Romina Boccia highlighting policy and process aspects of fiscal turnarounds abroad, former CBO Director Douglas Elmendorf, and me discussing design considerations for a balanced budget amendment.[10]

Advocates must intensely organize in and around Congress to get budget reforms and most other public interest legislation enacted. The better they do, the more they can accomplish. When great organizing harnesses excellent ideas for a significant window of opportunity, that is when the magic can happen.

In brief: Develop solutions as legislation. Organize. Support. Celebrate champions. Connect them. Build external and internal coalitions. Keep the fire burning for as long as it takes: usually years, sometimes decades. And then, at last, seize the moment. Or, more accurately, make use of every moment possible. And follow through.

Tough Times Elevate the Leaders Needed to Fix the Budget

Congress and Presidents Reagan, Bush, and Clinton struggled to rein in deficits. It took the better part of two decades for many rounds of spending restraint and revenue increases to achieve a balanced budget. Process changes and budget caps were crucial to preserving momentum.

That said, fortune smiled on budgeting in the 1990s. We might get lucky again. But we might not.

Better budgeting can help Congress make the tough-but-necessary decisions to put the U.S. government on a sustainable track. But what motivates members to embrace institutional changes that they know will lead to policy changes that take stuff from people, at least compared to what they are expecting?

Congress seldom acts on something until it must. Before that, something else is usually higher on the priority list. External forces, factors that politicians cannot control, often make up the secret sauce that policymakers need to truly tackle problems head on.

To hear the tales of those involved with the march toward budget balance in the 1980s and 1990s, they were responsible, they put country above party and self, and they did what had to be done. Yes, but why?

They were legitimately worried about what would happen if they failed. They had been through high inflation. They had seen a wave of bank failures.[11] They witnessed interest on the federal debt consume a huge share of federal revenue, up to 18.4 percent of revenue in 1991.[12] They saw economic mismanagement drive the Soviet Union to collapse.

Fears of nuclear Armageddon receded. At the same time, objective realities shifted the public discourse toward fears of spiraling interest, inflation, deficits, and debt driving American decline just as it became the world's only superpower.

Congress and several presidents acted to control spending and raise revenue, usually as part of debt limit deals.[13] But they never got a handle on the long-term pressures from old-age entitlement programs.[14]

Today, those chickens are coming home to roost. Over the last 30 years, Social Security went from 4.4 to 5.2 percent of GDP. Medicare went from 2.0 to 3.2 percent of GDP. Over the next 30 years, Social Security and Medicare are on track to be 5.9 and 5.4 percent of a much larger GDP and even as relatively fewer workers support each retiree.[15]

Rather than a post-Cold War peace dividend, the U.S.-led international order faces challenges from large, populous countries like Russia and China, rogue regimes like Iran and North Korea, and non-state actors like terrorists, drug cartels, and human traffickers. Many believe climate change and inequality are urgent global priorities that cannot be addressed until the federal government's finances are again on solid footing.

Net interest as a share of federal revenue is spiking again. It is already higher than the 1991 peak: 19.3 percent in fiscal year 2024 and likely to grow. We have had high inflation and interest rates. Every credible outlook for the federal budget foresees disaster. When this manuscript went to print, financial experts on Wall Street, among academia, and involved with public policy are the leading edge of a changing public conversation. It could be a roar by the time you read this.

The stage is set for tectonic shifts in federal budgeting. Moreover, the shift toward a leadership-dominated Congress has excluded many members, leaving them hungry for systemic changes that empower them to be the legislators that they want to be and that the American people need and deserve.

On their own, these forces would push members of Congress and presidents to restrain themselves. The problem is that so little of the budget is subject to regular review and opportunities for dealmaking.

Most of the budget is not only on autopilot but also has automatic deficit-growth features. Today's federal budget practices are nowhere up to this monumental task.

Harnessing the building momentum for budget correction and legislator inclusion requires new institutions. Those laid out here can support Congress as it manages the entire budget while providing loads of political cover to chip away at problems.

The history of fiscal turnarounds here and abroad suggests that policy and process will change together, probably through debt limit deals and related opportunities. The Budget Control Act of 2011 (a debt limit deal) created caps on appropriated spending, a commission to find further savings, and later votes on BBAs. Debt limit deals in coming years could include statutory changes directly while setting out a subsequent process for constitutional amendment proposals. These moments are excellent ways to advance real solutions that make better use of existing political will and have bipartisan support.

Bond market pressures could force Congress to confront budget dysfunction. Bond buyers pressured errant states to adopt budget restraints especially after broad-based turmoil in the 1840s and 1870s. They pushed the federal government to tighten up in the 1980s and 1990s. And they appear to be increasingly restless today.

Finally, President Donald J. Trump is back. He and his senior advisors have planned to make aggressive use of executive branch powers. In particular, their claims that the Impoundment Control Act is unconstitutional and therefore that the president can refuse to spend appropriated funds [16] could prompt Congress to strengthen its appropriations powers and to clarify the president's duty to take care that the laws are faithfully executed. Better budgeting could help Congress fulfill common goals with presidents, of course, and it would also give the legislature many more tools to vindicate its institutional prerogatives.

The next few years could be transformative in America, not only for responsible budgeting also for a more representative democracy. We need Congress to solve problems for the country. Our political culture and national swagger could use some rejuvenation too.

America is Ready for a BBA. Is Congress?

With that background, let us return to enacting a principles-based BBA and related legislation.

The principles-based BBA's unique qualities give it a strong chance to become the 28th Amendment to the United States Constitution. It is a flexible articulation of timeless principles with broad support: (1) balance, with the details to be specified in amendable statute, (2) a reasonable safety valve for emergencies, and (3) a realistic period for a glide slope to primary or full balance. It has broad language like existing constitutional provisions. It avoids the political and policy pitfalls that persist in other versions.

Within those principles, Congress could set up a layered approach to balance: (1) a smoothed average based on structural balance for operating expenses, (2) immediate spending for emergencies with subsequent offsets, and, perhaps, (3) some combination of pay-as-you-go and up-front spending and later revenue for investments in capital projects. And, of course, a congressional budget process that includes all spending and revenue while letting all members of Congress participate would have the most scope to meet budget targets, balance the budget, and make better use of scarce taxpayer dollars.

All that legislation would collectively support the governance needed to get the federal government to refocus on its core competencies, shedding activities that do not make sense, improving value creation for the American people, and ultimately refining the institutions that support the government's productive roles toward human flourishing: freedom, prosperity, and peace.

Members of Congress have already introduced a well-designed BBA and significant elements of implementing legislation: the Moran-Braun Principles-based BBA, the Emmer-Braun Responsible Budget Targets Act, the Ernst-Carter SUBMIT IT Act, and the Lankford-Hassan-Arrington-Panetta Prevent Government Shutdowns Act, among others.

The 118th Congress (2023–2024) was not going to be the window of opportunity. It was a good time to introduce and refine legislation, to build awareness of and support for each piece within Congress and among advocacy groups, and to plan out Bootlegger and Baptist coalitions.

Chapter 6 noted an unpredictable wrinkle: the claim that state legislatures crossed the threshold for Congress to call a convention of states for amendments in 1979. Congress got sued in 2022, but the case was dismissed without reaching the merits.[17] Further suits are expected. This litigation could lead to the United States Supreme Court finding that Congress abdicated its constitutional responsibility and ordering Congress to set a time and place for an amendment convention immediately.

If that litigation-triggered convention happens, it will turbocharge the opportunity for BBA proponents to launch a blistering pace of education, discussions, and negotiations. An imminent or actual convention of states may also prod Congress to act quickly. At that point, Congress would need to have in place a solid internal and external coalition for a well-crafted BBA. Whether Congress takes up a BBA with or without such pressure, a strong team behind well-crafted proposals can help members make more informed decisions.

Along the way, we need to keep developing and promoting the solutions. Some can advance and be enacted even without the BBA, but they all support each other. A principles-based BBA raises questions about the details, and the statutory aspects clarify enough to be credible. Likewise, a BBA on the march puts a strong wind in the sails toward figuring out effective and practical statutory approaches. Together, they are more than the sum of the parts.

A well-written BBA can provide the fire to power the budget reforms America needs. We can create a brighter future for all Americans. Perhaps we will inspire the next generation.

After all, these advancements would not be the end of the road to a more perfect union. They would be the next steps.

Future generations might take a principles-based BBA and related legislation for granted. Most of us already do so for the incredible accomplishments that came before us: the Constitution, Hamilton's creation of the Treasury Department, congressional organization, the modern budget process, and more.

The move toward better institutions will always be incomplete. As society changes, our government must adapt. In the nearer term, Congress has a robust fleet of upgrades waiting for windows of opportunity to open.

As we solve today's problems, we will refocus on tomorrow's challenges. Onward and upward!

Notes

1. Select Committee on the Modernization of Congress, "Final Report," U.S. House of Representatives, Report No. 117–646, https://www.govinfo.gov/content/pkg/GPO-CRPT-117hrpt646/pdf/GPO-CRPT-117hrpt646.pdf, December 15, 2022.

2. Yuval Levin, *A Time to Build: From Family and Community to Congress and the Campus: How Recommitting to Our Institutions Can Revive the American Dream*, Basic Books, 2020.
3. Annie Grayer, CNN, https://twitter.com/AnnieGrayerCNN/status/1611388863028625409?ref_src=twsrc%5Etfw, January 6, 2023.
4. House Republican Conference, "Conference Rules of the 118th Congress," https://www.gop.gov/conference-rules-of-the-118th-congress/, accessed September 2, 2023. House Democratic Caucus, "Rules of the Democratic Caucus, 117th Congress, https://www.dems.gov/imo/media/doc/DEM_CAUCUS_RULES_117TH_April_2021.pdf, accessed September 2, 2023. Senate Republican Conference, "History, Rules, and Precedents of the Senate Republican Conference, the 117th Congress, https://www.republican.senate.gov/wp-content/uploads/2022/09/4AD00AC45F860D42FAD37C556CB6A01F.-117th-congresss-rules-and-precedents.pdf, accessed September 2, 2023. Senate Democratic Caucus, "Rules for the Democratic Conference, United States Senate," https://www.democrats.senate.gov/rules-for-the-democratic-conference, adopted February 14, 2017, revised December 21, 2022.
5. I discussed changing members' cost–benefit calculations and congressional rules in greater depth in the lead chapter of an edited volume. Kurt Couchman, "Organizing Congress for Budget Reforms," Eds. Barry W. Poulson, John Merrifield, and Steve H. Hanke, *Public Debt Sustainability: International Perspectives*, Lexington, 2022.
6. Sen. Mitt Romney, S. 2733, "Time to Rescue United States Trusts (TRUST) Act of 2019," https://www.congress.gov/bill/116th-congress/senate-bill/2733, introduced October 29, 2019. Sen. Angus King, "King Effort to Rescue Federal Trust Funds Passes Senate in All Night Vote Session," https://www.king.senate.gov/newsroom/press-releases/king-effort-to-rescue-federal-trust-funds-passes-senate-in-all-night-vote-session, February 5, 2021. Sen. Mitt Romney, S. 4323, "Time to Rescue United States Trusts (TRUST) Act of 2020," https://www.congress.gov/bill/116th-congress/senate-bill/4323, introduced July 27, 2020. Sen. Mitt Romney, "A Common Sense Proposal": Romney TRUST Act

Included in CARES 2 Framework," https://www.romney.senate.gov/common-sense-proposal-romney-trust-act-included-cares-2-framework/, July 23, 2020. Sen. Mitt Romney, S. 1295, "Time to Rescue United States Trusts (TRUST) Act," https://www.congress.gov/bill/117th-congress/senate-bill/1295, introduced April 21, 2021.

7. Georgia Democrats, "NEW: Perdue Pledges To Gut Social Security, Medicare If Reelected," https://www.georgiademocrat.org/new-perdue-pledges-to-gut-social-security-medicare-if-reelected/, October 6, 2020. Rep. Don Beyer, "Senator Rick Scott's Plan to Raise Taxes on Working Families and Slash Essential Programs Would Cost Jobs and Reduce Economic Growth," Joint Economic Committee Democrats, https://www.jec.senate.gov/public/_cache/files/008860e7-93bd-47dd-a786-fbfdfee24868/jec---scott-plan-analysis---april-2022---final.pdf, April 2022, commenting on Rescue America, "A 12 Point Plan to Rescue America," https://rescueamerica.com/12-point-plan/, accessed September 2, 2023. Alexander Bolton, "Johnson steps on political land mine with Social Security, Medicare comments," *The Hill*, https://thehill.com/homenews/senate/3592712-johnson-steps-on-political-landmine-with-social-security-medicare-comments/, August 9, 2022.

8. House Judiciary Committee, Subcommittee on the Constitution and Limited Government, "Examining Proposed Constitutional Amendments," https://judiciary.house.gov/committee-activity/hearings/examining-proposed-constitutional-amendments, September 19, 2023.

9. Budget Process Reform Task Force, House Budget Committee, https://budget.house.gov/issues/budget-process-reform-task-force.

10. House Budget Committee, "Sounding the Alarm: Pathways and Possible Solutions to the U.S. Fiscal Crisis," https://budget.house.gov/hearing/sounding-the-alarm-pathways-and-possible-solutions-to-the-us-fiscal-crisis , December 11, 2024.

11. Federal Deposit Insurance Corporation (FDIC), *History of the Eighties: Lessons for the Future*. Vol. 1, *An Examination of the Banking Crises of the 1980s and Early 1990s*, 1997.

12. CBO, Historical Budget Data, February 2024.

13. See Appendix in Committee for a Responsible Federal Budget, "Q&A: Everything You Should Know About the Debt Ceiling," https://www.crfb.org/papers/qa-everything-you-should-know-about-debt-ceiling, May 5, 2023.
14. "For many years, it seemed like a balanced budget was an impossible dream and yet the bipartisan agreement delivered four balanced budgets in a row. However, the long-term issues affecting the fiscal solvency of Medicare and Social Security still proved to be a bridge too far." Alice Rivlin, *Divided We Fall: Why Consensus Matters*, Brookings, 2022, p. 170.
15. Office of Management and Budget, *President's Budget Request for Fiscal Year 2025*, Historical Data, "Table 8.4: Outlays by Budget Enforcement Category as Percentages of GDP: 1962–2029," March 2024. CBO, Long-Term Budget Projections: 2024–2054, March 2024.
16. Mark Paoletta and Daniel Shapiro, "The President's Constitutional Power of Impoundment," Center for Renewing America, https://americarenewing.com/the-presidents-constitutional-power-of-impoundment/, September 10, 2024.
17. *Brian Matthew McCall v. Nancy Pelosi*, 5:22-cv-00093-XR, (W.D. Tex.).

Appendix: Balanced Budget Amendment Proposals

Text presented here is the most recent version of each resolution, not necessarily the introduced version.

Exhibit 1: S.J.Res.123 (74th Congress) by Sen. Millard Tydings (D-MD).

Whereas by Section 201 of the Budget and Accounting Act, 1921, it is provided that—

The President shall transmit to Congress on the first day of each regular session the Budget, which shall set forth in summary and in detail:

(a) Estimates of the expenditures and appropriations necessary in his judgment for the support of the Government for the ensuing fiscal year; except that the estimates for such year for the legislative branch of the Government and the Supreme Court of the United States shall be transmitted to the President on or before October 15 of each year, and shall be included by him in the Budget without revision;

(b) His estimates of the receipts of the Government during the ensuing fiscal year, under (1) laws existing at the time the Budget is transmitted and also (2) under the revenue proposals, if any, contained in the Budget;

K. Couchman, *Fiscal Democracy in America*,
https://doi.org/10.1007/978-3-031-91938-1

(c) The expenditures and receipts of the Government during the last completed fiscal year;
(d) Estimates of the expenditures and receipts of the Government during the fiscal year in progress;
(e) The amount of annual, permanent, or other appropriations, including balances of appropriations for prior fiscal years, available for expenditure during the fiscal year in progress, as of November 1 of such year;
(f) Balanced statements of (1) the condition of the Treasury at the end of the last completed fiscal year, (2) the estimated condition of the Treasury at the end of the fiscal year in progress, and (3) the estimated condition of the Treasury at the end of the ensuring fiscal year if the financial proposals contained in the Budget are adopted;
(g) All essential facts regarding the bonded and other indebtedness of the Government; and
(h) Such other financial statements and data as in his opinion are necessary or desirable in order to make known in all practicable detail the financial condition of the Government.

And
Whereas by Section 202 (a) of such Act is provided that—
If the estimated receipts for the ensuing fiscal year contained in the Budget, on the basis of laws existing at the time the Budget is transmitted, plus the estimated amounts in the Treasury at the close of the fiscal year in progress, available for expenditure in the ensuing fiscal year are less than the estimated expenditures for the ensuing fiscal year contained in the Budget, the President in the Budget shall make recommendations to Congress for new taxes, loans, or other appropriate action to meet the estimated deficiency.
And
Whereas it has become necessary to supplement such Act of 1921 to strengthen the financial condition of the Government and to provide a more orderly system of balancing the Budget: Now, therefore, be it.

Resolved by the Senate and the House of Representatives of the United States of America in Congress assembled, that the President shall transmit to Congress, along with the Budget, on the first day of each regular session, a Budget bill allocating in detail to each executive department, independent commission, board, bureau, office, agency, or other establishment of the Government, including the municipal government of the

District of Columbia, the legislative branch of the Government, and the Supreme Court of the United States, such sums of money as are necessary for the support of the Government for the ensuing fiscal year.

Section 2. No legislation shall be passed by both Houses of Congress until the Budget bill shall have been passed.

Section 3. In the event Congress increases any of the allocations in the Budget bill as submitted by the President, an amount equal to such increase shall be deducted from the allocation to some other Government establishment; but in no event shall the total allocations or the total appropriations exceed the estimated revenue for the ensuing fiscal year plus the estimated amounts in the Treasury at the close of the fiscal year in progress, available for expenditure in the ensuing fiscal year, unless Congress shall provide for such excess (1) by new taxation, sufficient to liquidate such excess within the ensuing fiscal year, or (2) by authorizing the Secretary of the Treasury to borrow sums sufficient to cover such excess, in which case the legislation authorizing such borrowing shall be accompanied by new taxation which will liquidate the amount borrowed within a period of not more than fifteen years.

Section 4. In case there is an estimated deficit for the fiscal year in progress or a deficit is carried over from any prior fiscal year, such deficits shall be provided for before any other allocations are made.

Section 5. This joint resolution shall be ineffective in time of war and until the expiration of one full fiscal year after the termination thereof.

Exhibit 2: H.J.Res.579 (74th Congress) by Rep. Harold Knutson (R-MN). 145 Words

Section 1. The public debt of the United States shall be limited in peacetime on a basis of population in each decennial census to twenty billion dollars on a basis of the census of 1930.

Section 2. Whenever the public debt of the United States reaches twenty billion dollars in peacetime every measure appropriating money must be accompanied by a tax unless included in the Federal Budget, which must be covered by a tax in full whenever said debt limit has been reached.

Section 3. The Congress shall have power to enforce this article by appropriate legislation.

Section 4. This article shall be inoperative unless it shall have been ratified as an amendment to the Constitution by legislatures in the several

States, as provided in the Constitution, within seven years from the date of the submission hereof to the States by the Congress.

Exhibit 3: S.J.Res.126 (84th Congress) by Sens. Harry Byrd (D-VA) & Styles Bridges (R-NH). 243 Words

Section 1. On or before the fifteenth day after the beginning of each regular session of the Congress, the President shall transmit to the Congress a budget which shall set forth his estimates of the receipts of the Government, other than trust funds, during the ensuing fiscal year under the laws then existing and his recommendations with respect to expenditures to be made from funds other than trust funds during such ensuing fiscal year, which shall not exceed such estimate of receipts. If the Congress shall authorize expenditures to be made during such ensuing fiscal year in excess of such estimated receipts, it shall not adjourn for more than three days at a time until action has been taken necessary to balance the budget for such ensuing fiscal year. In case of war or other grave national emergency, if the President shall so recommend, the Congress by a vote of three-fourths of all the Members of each House may suspend the foregoing provisions for balancing the budget for periods, either successive or otherwise, not exceeding one year each.

Section 2. This article shall take effect on the first day of the calendar year next following the ratification of this article.

Section 3. This article shall be inoperative unless it shall have been ratified as an amendment to the Constitution by the legislatures of three-fourths of the several States within seven years from the date of its submission to the States by the Congress.

Exhibit 4: H.J.Res.1064 (93rd Congress) by Rep. Floyd Spence (R-SC) + 23 Cosponsors. 613 Words

Section 1. On or before the fifteenth day after the beginning of each regular session of the Congress, the President shall transmit to the Congress a budget which shall set forth separately—

(1) his estimate of the receipts of the Government, other than trust funds, during the ensuing fiscal year under the laws then existing;

(2) his recommendations with respect to outlays to be made from funds other than trust funds during such ensuing fiscal year; and
(3) if such recommendations exceed such estimate, a surtax rate which the President determines to be necessary to be applied with respect to the income tax of taxpayers to those portions of taxable years of taxpayers occurring during such fiscal year, so that such receipts will equal such outlays.

Such surtax shall be effective and so applied to such fiscal year except as otherwise provided in Section 2 of this article.

Section 2. During the first quarter of each fiscal year, and during the third quarter of each fiscal year, the Speaker of the House of Representatives shall—

(1) estimate the receipts of the Government, other than trust funds, during such fiscal year;
(2) estimate outlays to be made from funds other than trust funds during such fiscal year; and
(3) (A) if such estimate of outlays exceeds such estimate of receipts, determine a surtax rate which the Speaker considers necessary to be applied, with respect to the income tax of taxpayers, to those portions of taxable years of taxpayers remaining in such fiscal year, so that such receipts will equal such outlays;
(B) if such estimate of outlays equals such estimate of receipts, determine that no surtax rate is necessary to be applied.

Any such determination shall be effective, and so applied, with respect to the remainder of such fiscal year commencing on the first day of the first month commencing at least thirty days after such determination by the Speaker. The surtax rate determined by the President under Section 1 of this article shall not thereafter be applied commencing with such effective date.

Section 3. During the last month of each fiscal year, the President shall review whether the receipts of the Government, other than trust funds, for such year will be less than the outlays other than trust funds for that fiscal year. If he finds that such receipts are going to be less than such outlays, he shall determine a surtax rate which he considers necessary to be applied with respect to the income tax of taxpayers, so that taxes received by the Government from such surtax, when added to other receipts of the Government, will equal such outlays. Such surtax shall be effective, and so applied, as determined by the President only during the next succeeding fiscal year. The surtax effective and applied under this section is in addition to any other surtax that may be effective and applied under this article and may not be superseded or modified under Section 1 or 2 of this article.

Section 4. The provisions of Sections 1, 2, and 3 of this article may be suspended in the case of a grave national emergency declared by Congress (including a state of war formally declared by Congress) by a concurrent resolution, agreed to be a rollcall vote of three-fourths of all the Members of each House of Congress, with each such resolution providing the period of time (not exceeding one year) during which those provisions are to be suspended.

Section 5. This article shall take effect on the first day of the calendar year next following the ratification of this article.

Section 6. The Congress shall have power to enforce this article by appropriate legislation.

Exhibit 5: A Proposed Constitutional Amendment to Limit Federal Spending by the Federal Amendment Drafting Committee, Convened by the National Tax Limitation Committee, 1979. 493 Words

Section 1. To protect the people against excessive governmental burdens and to promote sound fiscal and monetary policies, total outlays of the Government of the United States shall be limited.

(a) Total outlays in any fiscal year shall not increase by a percentage greater than the percentage increase in nominal gross national product in the last calendar year ending prior to the beginning of said fiscal year. Total outlays shall include budget and off-budget outlays, and exclude redemptions of the public debt and emergency outlays.

(b) If inflation for the last calendar year is more than three percent, the permissible percentage increase in total outlays for that fiscal year shall be reduced by one-fourth of the excess of inflation over three percent. Inflation shall be measured by the difference between the percentage increase in nominal gross national product and the percentage increase in real gross national product.

Section 2. When, for any fiscal year, total revenues received by the Government of the United States exceed total outlays, the surplus shall be used to reduce the public debt of the United States until such debt is eliminated.

Section 3. Following declaration of an emergency by the President, Congress may authorize, by a two-thirds vote of both Houses, a specified amount of emergency outlays in excess of the limit for the current fiscal year.

Section 4. The limit on total outlays may be changed by a specified amount by a three-fourths vote of both Houses of Congress when approved by the Legislatures of a majority of the several States. The change shall become effective for the fiscal year following approval.

Section 5. For each of the first six fiscal years after ratification of this article, total grants to States and local governments shall not be a smaller fraction of total outlays than in the three fiscal years prior to the ratification of this article. Thereafter, if grants are less than that fraction of total outlays, the limit on total outlays shall be decreased by an equivalent amount.

Section 6. The Government of the United States shall not require, directly or indirectly, that States or local governments engage in additional or expanded activities without compensation equal to the necessary additional costs.

Section 7. This article may be enforced by one or more members of the Congress in an action brought in the United States District Court for the District of Columbia, and by no other persons. The action shall name as defendant the Treasurer of the United States, who shall have authority over outlays by any unit or agency of the Government of the United States when required by a court order enforcing the provisions of this article. The order of the court shall not specify the particular outlays to be made or reduced. Changes in outlays necessary to comply with the order of the court shall be made no later than the end of the third full fiscal year following the court order.

Exhibit 6: S.J.Res.58 (97th Congress) by Sen. Strom Thurmond (R-SC) + 62 Cosponsors. 345 Words

Section 1. Prior to each fiscal year, the Congress shall adopt a statement of receipts and outlays for that year in which total outlays are no greater than total receipts. The Congress may amend such statement provided revised outlays are no greater than revised receipts. Whenever three-fifths of the whole number of both Houses shall deem it necessary, Congress in such statement may provide for a specific excess of outlays over receipts by a vote directed solely to that subject. The Congress and the President shall, pursuant to legislation or through exercise of their powers under the first and second articles, ensure that actual outlays do not exceed the outlays set forth in such statement.

Section 2. Total receipts for any fiscal year set forth in the statement adopted pursuant to this article shall not increase by a rate greater than the rate of increase in national income in the year or years ending not less than six months nor more than twelve months before such fiscal year, unless a majority of the whole number of both Houses of Congress shall have passed a bill directed solely to approving specific additional receipts and such bill has become law.

Section 3. The Congress may waive the provisions of this article for any fiscal year in which a declaration of war is in effect.

Section 4. Total receipts shall include all receipts of the United States except those derived from borrowing and total outlays shall include all outlays of the United States except those for repayment of debt principal.

Section 5. The Congress shall enforce and implement this article by appropriate legislation.

Section 6. On and after the date this article takes effect, the amount of Federal public debt limit as of such date shall become permanent and there shall be no increase in such amount unless three-fifths of the whole number of both Houses of Congress shall have passed a bill approving such increase and such bill has become law.

Section 7. This article shall take effect for the second fiscal year beginning after its ratification.

Exhibit 7: H.J.Res.350 (97th Congress) by Rep. Edgar Jenkins (D-GA) and Barber Conable (R-NY) + 230 Cosponsors. 286 Words

Section 1. Prior to each fiscal year, the Congress shall adopt a statement of receipts and outlays for that year in which total outlays are not greater than total receipts. The Congress may amend such statement provided revised outlays are no greater than revised receipts. Whenever three-fifths of the whole number of both Houses shall deem it necessary, Congress in such statement may provide for a specific excess of outlays over receipts by a vote directed solely to that subject. The Congress and the President shall, pursuant to legislation or through exercise of their powers under the first and second articles, ensure that actual outlays do not exceed the outlays set forth in such statement.

Section 2. Total receipts for any fiscal year set forth in the statement adopted pursuant to this article shall not increase by a rate greater than the rate of increase in national income in the year or years ending not less than six months nor more than twelve months before such fiscal year, unless a majority of the whole number of both Houses of Congress shall have passed a bill directed solely to approving specific additional receipts and such bill has become law.

Section 3. The Congress may waive the provisions of this article for any fiscal year in which a declaration of war is in effect.

Section 4. Total receipts shall include all receipts of the United States except those derived from borrowing and total outlays shall include all outlays of the United States except those for repayment of debt principal.

Section 5. This article shall take effect for the second fiscal year beginning after its ratification.

Section 6. The Congress shall enforce and implement this article by appropriate legislation.

Exhibit 8: H.J.Res.103 (103rd Congress) by Rep. Charlie Stenholm (D-TX) + 174 Republican and 90 Democratic Cosponsors [Similar to H.J.Res.321 (100th), 268 (101st), and 290 (102nd)]. 307 Words

Section 1. Total outlays for any fiscal year shall not exceed total receipts for that fiscal year, unless three-fifths of the whole number of each House of Congress shall provide by law for a specific excess of outlays over receipts by a rollcall vote.

Section 2. The limit on the debt of the United States held by the public shall not be increased, unless three-fifths of the whole number of each House shall provide by law for an increase by a rollcall vote.

Section 3. Prior to each fiscal year, the President shall transmit to the Congress a proposed budget for the United States Government for that fiscal year, in which total outlays do not exceed total receipts.

Section 4. No bill to increase revenue shall become law unless approved by a majority of the whole number of each House by a rollcall vote.

Section 5. The Congress may waive the provisions of this article for any fiscal year in which a declaration of war is in effect. The provisions of this article may be waived for any fiscal year in which the United States is engaged in military conflict which causes an imminent and serious military threat to national security and is so declared by a joint resolution, adopted by a majority of the whole number of each House, which becomes law.

Section 6. The Congress shall enforce and implement this article by appropriate legislation, which may rely on estimates of outlays and receipts.

Section 7. Total receipts shall include all receipts of the United States Government except those derived from borrowing. Total outlays shall include all outlays of the United States Government except for those for repayment of debt principal.

Section 8. This article shall take effect beginning with fiscal year 1999 or with the second fiscal year beginning after its ratification, whichever is later.

Exhibit 9: S.J.Res.225 (99th Congress) by Sen. Strom Thurmond (R-SC). 83 Words

Section 1. Outlays of the United States for any fiscal year shall not exceed receipts to the United States for that year, unless three-fifths of the whole number of both Houses of Congress shall provide for a specific excess of outlays over receipts.

Section 2. The Congress may waive the provisions of this article for any fiscal year in which a declaration of war is in effect.

Section 3. This article shall take effect for the second fiscal year beginning after its ratification.

Exhibit 10: S.J.Res.41 (103rd Congress) by Sen. Paul Simon (D-IL) + 37 Republican + 18 Democratic Cosponsors. 308 Words

Section 1. Total outlays for any fiscal year shall not exceed total receipts for that fiscal year, unless three-fifths of the whole number of each House of Congress shall provide by law for a specific excess of outlays over receipts by a rollcall vote.

Section 2. The limit on the debt of the United States held by the public shall not be increased, unless three-fifths of the whole number of each House shall provide by law for such an increase by a rollcall vote.

Section 3. Prior to each fiscal year, the President shall transmit to the Congress a proposed budget for the United States Government for that fiscal year, in which total outlays do not exceed total receipts.

Section 4. No bill to increase revenue shall become law unless approved by a majority of the whole number of each House by a rollcall vote.

Section 5. The Congress may waive the provisions of this article for any fiscal year in which a declaration of war is in effect. The provisions of this article may be waived for any fiscal year in which the United States is engaged in military conflict which causes an imminent and serious military threat to national security and is so declared by a joint resolution, adopted by a majority of the whole number of each House, which becomes law.

Section 6. The Congress shall enforce and implement this article by appropriate legislation, which may rely on estimates of outlays and receipts.

Section 7. Total receipts shall include all receipts of the United States Government except those derived from borrowing. Total outlays shall include all outlays of the United States Government except for those for repayment of debt principal.

Section 8. This article shall take effect beginning with fiscal year 1999 or with the second fiscal year beginning after its ratification, whichever is later.

Exhibit 11: H.J.Res.1 (104th Congress) by Rep. Joe Barton (R-TX) + 171 Republican + 6 Democratic Cosponsors. 308 Words

Section 1. Total outlays for any fiscal year shall not exceed total receipts for that fiscal year, unless three-fifths of the whole number of each House of Congress shall provide by law for a specific excess of outlays over receipts by a rollcall vote.

Section 2. The limit on the debt of the United States held by the public shall not be increased, unless three-fifths of the whole number of each House shall provide by law for such an increase by a rollcall vote.

Section 3. Prior to each fiscal year, the President shall transmit to the Congress a proposed budget for the United States Government for that fiscal year in which total outlays do not exceed total receipts.

Section 4. No bill to increase revenue shall become law unless approved by a majority of the whole number of each House by a rollcall vote.

Section 5. The Congress may waive the provisions of this article for any fiscal year in which a declaration of war is in effect. The provisions of this article may be waived for any fiscal year in which the United States is engaged in military conflict which causes an imminent and serious military threat to national security and is so declared by a joint resolution, adopted by a majority of the whole number of each House, which becomes law.

Section 6. The Congress shall enforce and implement this article by appropriate legislation, which may rely on estimates of outlays and receipts.

Section 7. Total receipts shall include all receipts of the United States Government except those derived from borrowing. Total outlays shall include all outlays of the United States Government except for those for repayment of debt principal.

Section 8. This article shall take effect beginning with fiscal year 2002 or with the second fiscal year beginning after its ratification, whichever is later.

Exhibit 12: S.J.Res.1 (104th Congress) by Sen. Bob Dole (R-KS) + 38 Republican + 8 Democratic Cosponsors. 308 Words

Section 1. Total outlays for any fiscal year shall not exceed total receipts for that fiscal year, unless three-fifths of the whole number of each House of Congress shall provide by law for a specific excess of outlays over receipts by a rollcall vote.

Section 2. The limit on the debt of the United States held by the public shall not be increased, unless three-fifths of the whole number of each House shall provide by law for such an increase by a rollcall vote.

Section 3. Prior to each fiscal year, the President shall transmit to the Congress a proposed budget for the United States Government for that fiscal year, in which total outlays do not exceed total receipts.

Section 4. No bill to increase revenue shall become law unless approved by a majority of the whole number of each House by a rollcall vote.

Section 5. The Congress may waive the provisions of this article for any fiscal year in which a declaration of war is in effect. The provisions of this article may be waived for any fiscal year in which the United States is engaged in military conflict which causes an imminent and serious military threat to national security and is so declared by a joint resolution, adopted by a majority of the whole number of each House, which becomes law.

Section 6. The Congress shall enforce and implement this article by appropriate legislation, which may rely on estimates of outlays and receipts.

Section 7. Total receipts shall include all receipts of the United States Government except those derived from borrowing. Total outlays shall include all outlays of the United States Government except for those for repayment of debt principal.

Section 8. This article shall take effect beginning with fiscal year 2002 or with the second fiscal year beginning after its ratification, whichever is later.

Exhibit 13: H.J.Res.2 (112th Congress) by Rep. Bob Goodlatte (R-VA) + 226 Republican + 16 Democratic Cosponsors. 325 Words

Section 1. Total outlays for any fiscal year shall not exceed total receipts for that fiscal year, unless three-fifths of the whole number of each House of Congress shall provide by law for a specific excess of outlays over receipts by a rollcall vote.

Section 2. The limit on the debt of the United States held by the public shall not be increased, unless three-fifths of the whole number of each House shall provide by law for such an increase by a rollcall vote.

Section 3. Prior to each fiscal year, the President shall transmit to the Congress a proposed budget for the United States Government for that fiscal year in which total outlays do not exceed total receipts.

Section 4. No bill to increase revenue shall become law unless approved by a majority of the whole number of each House by a rollcall vote.

Section 5. The Congress may waive the provisions of this article for any fiscal year in which a declaration of war is in effect. The provisions of this article may be waived for any fiscal year in which the United States is engaged in military conflict which causes an imminent and serious military threat to national security and is so declared by a joint resolution, adopted by a majority of the whole number of each House, which becomes law. Any such waiver must identify and be limited to the specific excess or increase for that fiscal year made necessary by the identified military conflict.

Section 6. The Congress shall enforce and implement this article by appropriate legislation, which may rely on estimates of outlays and receipts.

Section 7. Total receipts shall include all receipts of the United States Government except those derived from borrowing. Total outlays shall include all outlays of the United States Government except for those for repayment of debt principal.

Section 8. This article shall take effect beginning with the fifth fiscal year beginning after its ratification.

Exhibit 14: S.J.Res.10 (112th Congress) by Sen. Orrin Hatch (R-UT) + 47 Republican Cosponsors. 553 Words

Section 1. Total outlays for any fiscal year shall not exceed total receipts for that fiscal year, unless two-thirds of the duly chosen and sworn Members of each House of Congress shall provide by law for a specific excess of outlays over receipts by a roll call vote.

Section 2. Total outlays for any fiscal year shall not exceed 18 percent of the gross domestic product of the United States for the calendar year ending before the beginning of such fiscal year, unless two-thirds of the duly chosen and sworn Members of each House of Congress shall provide by law for a specific amount in excess of such 18 percent by a roll call vote.

Section 3. Prior to each fiscal year, the President shall transmit to the Congress a proposed budget for the United States Government for that fiscal year in which—

(1) total outlays do not exceed total receipts; and.
(2) total outlays do not exceed 18 percent of the gross domestic product of the United States for the calendar year ending before the beginning of such fiscal year.

Section 4. Any bill that imposes a new tax or increases the statutory rate of any tax or the aggregate amount of revenue may pass only by a two-thirds majority of the duly chosen and sworn Members of each House of Congress by a roll call vote. For the purpose of determining any increase in revenue under this section, there shall be excluded any increase resulting from the lowering of the statutory rate of any tax.

Section 5. The limit on the debt of the United States shall not be increased, unless three-fifths of the duly chosen and sworn Members of each House of Congress shall provide for such an increase by a roll call vote.

Section 6. The Congress may waive the provisions of Sections 1, 2, 3, and 5 of this article for any fiscal year in which a declaration of war against a nation-state is in effect and in which a majority of the duly chosen and sworn Members of each House of Congress shall provide for a specific excess by a roll call vote.

Section 7. The Congress may waive the provisions of Sections 1, 2, 3, and 5 of this article in any fiscal year in which the United States is engaged in a military conflict that causes an imminent and serious military threat to national security and is so declared by three-fifths of the duly chosen and sworn Members of each House of Congress by a roll call vote. Such suspension must identify and be limited to the specific excess of outlays for that fiscal year made necessary by the identified military conflict.

Section 8. No court of the United States or of any State shall order any increase in revenue to enforce this article.

Section 9. Total receipts shall include all receipts of the United States Government except those derived from borrowing. Total outlays shall include all outlays of the United States Government except those for repayment of debt principal.

Section 10. The Congress shall have power to enforce and implement this article by appropriate legislation, which may rely on estimates of outlays, receipts, and gross domestic product.

Section 11. This article shall take effect beginning with the fifth fiscal year beginning after its ratification.

Exhibit 15: S.J.Res.24 (112th Congress) by Sen. Mark Udall (D-CO) + 5 Democratic Cosponsors. 390 Words

Section 1. Total outlays for any fiscal year shall not exceed total receipts for that fiscal year, unless three-fifths of the whole number of each House of Congress shall provide by law for a specific excess of outlays over receipts by a roll call vote.

Section 2. Prior to each fiscal year, the President shall transmit to the Congress a proposed budget for the United States Government for that fiscal year in which total outlays do not exceed total receipts.

Section 3. Sections 1 and 2 of this Article shall not apply during any fiscal year in which a declaration of war is in effect or in which the United States is engaged in military conflict which causes an imminent and serious military threat to national security and is so declared by a joint resolution, adopted by a majority of the whole number of each House, which becomes law.

Section 4. The Congress shall enforce and implement this article by appropriate legislation, which may rely on estimates of outlays and receipts.

Section 5. Except as provided in the second clause, total receipts shall include all receipts of the United States Government other than those derived from borrowing, and total outlays shall include all outlays of the United States Government other than those for repayment of debt principal.

The receipts (including attributable interest) and outlays of the Federal Old-Age and Survivors Insurance Trust Fund and the Federal Disability Insurance Trust Fund, or any fund that is a successor to either such fund, shall not be considered to be receipts or outlays for purposes of this article.

Section 6. Congress shall not pass any bill that provides a net reduction in individual income taxes for those with incomes over $1,000,000 (as may be adjusted by Congress to account for inflation) if, after enactment, total outlays would exceed total receipts in any fiscal year affected by the bill.

Section 7. No court of the United States or of any State shall enforce this article by ordering any reduction in the Social Security benefits authorized by law, including any benefits provided from the Federal Old-Age and Survivors Insurance Trust Fund, the Federal Disability Insurance Trust Fund, or any fund that is a successor to either such fund.

Section 8. This article shall take effect beginning with the fifth fiscal year beginning after its ratification.

Business Cycle BBA

Exhibit 16: H.J.Res.73 (112th Congress) by Rep. Justin Amash (R-MI) + 39 Republican + 4 Democratic Cosponsors. 284 Words

Section 1. Total outlays for a year shall not exceed the average annual revenue collected in the three prior years, adjusted in proportion to changes in population and inflation. Total outlays shall include all outlays of the United States except those for payment of debt, and revenue shall include all revenue of the United States except that derived from borrowing.

Section 2. Three-fourths of the whole number of each House of Congress may by roll call vote declare an emergency and provide by law for specific outlays in excess of the limit in Section 1. The declaration shall specify reasons for the emergency designation and shall limit the period in which outlays may exceed the limit in Section 1 to no longer than one year.

Section 3. All revenue in excess of outlays shall reduce the debt of the United States. Upon the retirement of such debt, revenue in excess of outlays shall be held by the Treasury to be used as specified in Section 2.

Section 4. The Congress shall have power to enforce and implement this article by appropriate legislation.

Section 5. This article shall take effect in the first year beginning at least 90 days following ratification, except that outlays shall not surpass the sum of the limit described in Section 1 and the following portion of the prior year's outlays exceeding that limit (excepting emergency outlays as provided for in Section 2): nine-tenths in the first year, eight-ninths in the second, seven-eighths in the third, six-sevenths in the fourth, five-sixths in the fifth, four-fifths in the sixth, three-fourths in the seventh, two-thirds in the eighth, one-half in the ninth, and the limit shall bind in the tenth year and thereafter.

Exhibit 17: H.J.Res.81 (112th Congress) by Rep. Justin Amash (R-MI) + 45 Republican + 14 Democratic Cosponsors. 280 Words

Section 1. Total outlays for a year shall not exceed the average annual revenue collected in the three prior years, adjusted in proportion to changes in population and inflation. Total outlays shall include all outlays of the United States except those for payment of debt, and revenue shall include all revenue of the United States except that derived from borrowing.

Section 2. Two-thirds of each House of Congress may by roll call vote declare an emergency and provide by law for specific outlays in excess of the limit in Section 1. The declaration shall specify reasons for the emergency designation and shall limit the period in which outlays may exceed the limit in Section 1 to no longer than one year.

Section 3. All revenue in excess of outlays shall reduce the debt of the United States. Upon the retirement of such debt, revenue in excess of outlays shall be held by the Treasury to be used as specified in Section 2.

Section 4. The Congress shall have power to enforce and implement this article by appropriate legislation.

Section 5. This article shall take effect in the first year beginning at least 90 days following ratification, except that outlays shall not surpass the sum of the limit described in Section 1 and the following portion of the prior year's outlays exceeding that limit (excepting emergency outlays as provided for in Section 2): nine-tenths in the first year, eight-ninths in the second, seven-eighths in the third, six-sevenths in the fourth, five-sixths in the fifth, four-fifths in the sixth, three-fourths in the seventh, two-thirds in the eighth, one-half in the ninth, and the limit shall bind in the tenth year and thereafter.

Exhibit 18: H.J.Res.54 (114th Congress by Rep. Justin Amash (R-MI) + 4 Republican + 1 Democratic Cosponsors. 217 Words

Section 1. Total expenditures for a year shall not exceed the average annual revenue collected in the three prior years, adjusted in proportion to changes in population and inflation. Total expenditures shall include all expenditures of the United States except those for payment of debt, and revenue shall include all revenue of the United States except that derived from borrowing.

Section 2. Congress may by a roll call vote of two-thirds of each House declare an emergency and provide by law for specific expenditures in excess of the limit in Section 1. The declaration shall specify reasons for the emergency designation and may authorize expenditures in excess of the limit in Section 1 for up to one year.

Section 3. Congress shall have power to enforce this article by appropriate legislation.

Section 4. This article shall take effect in the first year beginning at least 90 days following ratification, except that expenditures may exceed the limit in Section 1 by the following portion of the prior year's expenditures exceeding that limit (excepting emergency expenditures provided for by Section 2): nine-tenths in the first year, eight-ninths in the second, seven-eighths in the third, six-sevenths in the fourth, five-sixths in the fifth, four-fifths in the sixth, three-fourths in the seventh, two-thirds in the eighth, and one-half in the ninth.

Exhibit 19: S.J.Res.42 (117th Congress) by Sen. Mike Braun (R-IN) / H.J.Res.77 (117th Congress) by Rep. Jodey Arrington (R-TX) + 2 Republican Cosponsors. 217 Words

Section 1. Total expenditures for a year shall not exceed the average annual revenue collected in the three prior years, adjusted in proportion to changes in population and inflation. Total expenditures shall include all expenditures of the United States except those for payment of debt, and revenue shall include all revenue of the United States except that derived from borrowing.

Section 2. Congress may by a roll call vote of two-thirds of each House declare an emergency and provide by law for specific expenditures in excess of the limit in Section 1. The declaration shall specify reasons for the emergency designation and may authorize expenditures in excess of the limit in Section 1 for up to one year.

Section 3. Congress shall have power to enforce this article by appropriate legislation.

Section 4. This article shall take effect in the first year beginning at least 90 days following ratification, except that expenditures may exceed the limit in Section 1 by the following portion of the prior year's expenditures exceeding that limit (excepting emergency expenditures provided for by Section 2): nine-tenths in the first year, eight-ninths in the second, seven-eighths in the third, six-sevenths in the fourth, five-sixths in the fifth, four-fifths in the sixth, three-fourths in the seventh, two-thirds in the eighth, and one-half in the ninth.

Principles-based BBA

Exhibit 20: H.J.Res.55 (114th Congress) by Rep. Dave Brat (R-VA) + 64 Republican + 1 Democratic Cosponsors. 119 Words

Section 1. Expenditures and receipts shall be balanced, which may occur over more than one year to accommodate economic conditions. Expenditures shall include all expenditures of the United States except those for payment of debt, and receipts shall include all receipts of the United States except those derived from borrowing.

Section 2. For emergency situations, two-thirds of the House of Representatives and the Senate may for limited times authorize expenditures exceeding those pursuant to rules established under Section 1. Debts incurred from such expenditures shall be paid as soon as practicable.

Section 3. Congress shall have power to enforce this article by appropriate legislation, which shall allow not more than ten years after ratification to comply with Section 1.

Exhibit 21: S.J.Res.19/H.J.Res.80 (118th Congress) by Sen. Mike Braun (R-IN) + 1 Republican Cosponsor and Rep. Nathaniel Moran (R-TX). 100 Words

Section 1. Expenditures and receipts shall be balanced, which may occur over more than one year. Expenditures shall include all expenditures of the United States except those for payment of debt, and receipts shall include all receipts of the United States except those derived from borrowing. Congress shall achieve balance within ten years following the ratification of this article.

Section 2. For emergency situations, two-thirds of the House of Representatives and the Senate may for limited times authorize expenditures exceeding those pursuant to rules established under Section 1. Debts incurred from such expenditures shall be paid as soon as practicable.

Index

K. Couchman, *Fiscal Democracy in America*,
https://doi.org/10.1007/978-3-031-91938-1

9783031919374